T0178825

Metaheuristics for String Problems in Bio-informatics

Metaheuristics Set

coordinated by
Nicolas Monmarché and Patrick Siarry

Volume 6

Metaheuristics for String Problems in Bio-informatics

Christian Blum
Paola Festa

WILEY

First published 2016 in Great Britain and the United States by ISTE Ltd and John Wiley & Sons, Inc.

ISTE Ltd
27-37 St George's Road
London SW19 4EU
UK

www.iste.co.uk

John Wiley & Sons, Inc.
111 River Street
Hoboken, NJ 07030
USA

www.wiley.com

Library of Congress Control Number: 2016945029

British Library Cataloguing-in-Publication Data
A CIP record for this book is available from the British Library
ISBN 978-1-84821-812-3

Contents

Preface

DNA (deoxyribonucleic acid) acts as the information archive of most living beings. Due to the fact that a strand of DNA can be expressed as a set of four-letter character strings, so-called *string problems* have become abundant in bioinformatics and computational biology. Each year, new optimization problems dealing with DNA (or protein) sequences are being formulated that require efficient optimization techniques to arrive at solutions. From this perspective, bioinformatics is a burgeoning field for optimization experts and computer scientists in general. In this book, we will focus on a mixture of well-known and recent string optimization problems in the bioinformatics field. We will focus on problems that are combinatorial in nature.

One of the obstacles for optimization practitioners is the atypical nature of these problems, i.e. although combinatorial in nature, these problems are rather different to the classical traveling salesman problem or the quadratic assignment problem. This implies that a different type of expertise is required to efficiently solve many of these problems. Therefore, one of the main goals of this book is to pass on this kind of expertise and experience to newcomers to this field. The book provides several examples of very successful (hybrid) metaheuristics for solving specific string problems. One such example concerns the use of beam search (an incomplete branch and bound method) in solving longest common subsequence problems. The application of this algorithm in 2009 marked a breakthrough in the solution of this type of problem.

Finally, we would like to address a few words to the interested readers, especially biologists. We apologize for any imprecision in the description of biological processes, which we have tried to keep to a minimum. Keep in mind that, after all, we are only computer scientists and mathematicians.

Christian BLUM
Paola FESTA
June 2016

Acknowledgments

This work was supported by grant TIN2012-37930-C02-02 from the Spanish Government. Support from CSIC (Spanish National Research Council) and IKERBASQUE (Basque Foundation for Science) is also acknowledged. We thank RDlab[1], a BarcelonaTech facility, for allowing us to perform the experiments partly in the high-performance computing environment.

1 http://rdlab.lsi.upc.edu.

List of Acronyms

ACO   Ant Colony Optimization
B&B   Branch & Bound
CMSA   Construct, Merge, Solve & Adapt
CO   Combinatorial Optimization
DNA   Deoxyribonucleic Acid
DP   Dynamic Programming
EA   Evolutionary Algorithm
GA   Genetic Algorithm
ILP   Integer Linear Programming
ILS   Iterated Local Search
IP   Integer Programming
LNS   Large Neighborhood Search
MCSP   Minimum Common String Partition
MSFBC   Most Strings With Few Bad Columns
RNA   Ribonucleic Acid
SA   Simulated Annealing
TS   Tabu Search
TSP   Traveling Salesman Problem
UMCSP   Unbalanced Minimum Common String Partition

1

Introduction

In computer science, a string s is defined as a finite sequence of characters from a finite alphabet Σ. Apart from the alphabet, an important characteristic of a string s is its length which, in this book, will be denoted by $|s|$. A string is, generally, understood to be a data type i.e. a string is used to represent and store information. For example, words in a specific language are stored in a computer as strings. Even the entire text may be stored by means of strings. Apart from fields such as information and text processing, strings arise in the field of bioinformatics. This is because most of the genetic instructions involved in the growth, development, functioning and reproduction of living organisms are stored in a molecule which is known as *deoxyribonucleic acid* (DNA) which can be represented in the form of a string in the following way. DNA is a nucleic acid that consists of two biopolymer strands forming a double helix (see Figure 1.1). The two strands of DNA are called polynucleotides as they are composed of simpler elements called nucleotides. Each nucleotide consists of a nitrogen-containing nucleobase as well as deoxyribose and a phosphate group. The four different nucleobases of DNA are cytosine (C), guanine (G), adenine (A) and thymine (T). Each DNA strand is a sequence of nucleotides that are joined to one another by covalent bonds between the sugar of one nucleotide and the phosphate of the next. This results in an alternating sugar–phosphate backbone (see Figure 1.1). Furthermore, hydrogen bonds bind the bases of the two separate polynucleotide strands to make double-stranded DNA. As a result, A can only bind with T and C can only bind with G. Therefore, a DNA molecule can be stored as a string of symbols from $\Sigma = \{A, C, T, G\}$ that represent one of the two polynucleotide strands. Similarly, most proteins can be stored as a string of letters from an alphabet of 20 letters, representing the 20 standard amino acids that constitute most proteins.

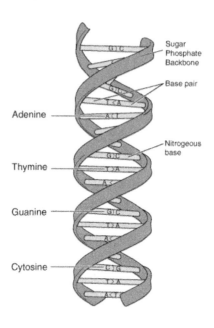

Figure 1.1. *DNA double helix (image courtesy of Wikipedia)*

As a result, many optimization problems in the field of computational biology are concerned with strings representing, for example, DNA or protein sequences. In this book we will focus particularly on recent works concerning string problems that can be expressed in terms of *combinatorial optimization* (CO). In early work by Papadimitriou and Steiglitz [PAP 82], a CO problem $\mathcal{P}$ is defined by a tuple $(\mathcal{S}, f)$, where $\mathcal{S}$ is a finite set of objects and $f : \mathcal{S} \mapsto \mathbb{R}^+$ is a function that assigns a non-negative cost value to each of the objects $s \in \mathcal{S}$. Solving a CO problem $\mathcal{P}$ requires us to find an object s^* of minimum cost value[1]. As a classic academic example, consider the well-known *traveling salesman problem* (TSP). In the case of the TSP, set $\mathcal{S}$ consists of all Hamiltonian cycles in a completely connected, undirected

---

1 Note that searching for a solution with minimum cost value with respect to f is the same as searching for a solution with maximum cost value with respect to $-f$. Therefore, generality is not limited when only referring to minimization.

graph with positive edge weights. The objective function value of such a Hamiltonian cycle is the sum of the weights of its edges.

Unfortunately, most CO problems are difficult to optimality solve in practice. In theoretical terms, this is confirmed by corresponding results about non-deterministic (NP)-hardness and non-approximability. Due to the hardness of CO problems, a large variety of algorithmic and mathematical approaches have emerged to tackle these problems in recent decades. The most intuitive classification labels these approaches as either *complete/exact* or *approximate* methods. Complete methods guarantee that, for every instance of a CO problem of finite size, there is an optimal solution in bounded time [PAP 82, NEM 88]. However, assuming that P $\neq$ NP, no algorithm that solves a CO problem classified as being NP-hard in polynomial time exists [GAR 79]. As a result, complete methods, in the worst case, may require an exponential computation time to generate an evincible optimal solution. When faced with large size, the time required for computation may be too high for practical purposes. Thus, research on approximate methods to solve CO problems, also in the bioinformatics field, has enjoyed increasing attention in recent decades. In contrast to complete methods, approximate algorithms produce, not necessarily optimal, solutions in relatively acceptable computation times. Moreover, note that in the context of a combinatorial optimization problem in bioinformatics, finding an *optimal solution* is often not as important as in other domains. This is due to the fact that often the available data are error prone.

In the following section, we will give a short introduction into some of the most important complete methods, including integer linear programming and dynamic programming. Afterward, some of the most popular approximate methods for combinatorial optimization are reviewed. Finally, the last part of this chapter outlines the string problems considered in this book.

1.1. Complete methods for combinatorial optimization

Many combinatorial optimization problems can be expressed in terms of an *integer programming* (IP) problem, in a way that involves maximizing or minimizing an *objective function* of a certain number of *decision variables*, subject to inequality and/or equality constraints and integrality restrictions on the decision variables.

Formally, we require the following ingredients:

1) a n-dimensional vector $x = (x_1, x_2, \ldots, x_n) \in \mathbb{Z}^n$, where each x_j, $j = 1, 2, \ldots, n$, is called a *decision variable* and x is called the *decision vector*;

2) m scalar functions $\{g_i(x) : \mathbb{R}^n \to \mathbb{R}, \ i = 1, 2, \ldots, m\}$ of the decision vector x;

3) a m-dimensional vector $b = (b_1, b_2, \ldots, b_m) \in \mathbb{R}^m$, called the *right-hand side* vector;

4) a scalar function $z(x) : \mathbb{R}^n \to \mathbb{R}$ of the decision vector x.

With these ingredients, an IP problem can be formulated mathematically as follows:

$$
\begin{aligned}
\text{(IP)} \min \ (\text{resp. max}) \quad & z(x) \\
\text{s.t.} \qquad\qquad\qquad & \\
g_1(x) &\approx b_1 \\
g_2(x) &\approx b_2 \\
\cdots &\approx \cdots \\
g_m(x) &\approx b_m \\
x &\in \mathbb{Z}^n,
\end{aligned}
$$

where $\approx \ \in \{\leq, =, \geq\}$. Therefore, the set

$$
X = \{x \in \mathbb{Z}^n \mid g_i(x) \approx b_i, \ i = 1, 2, \ldots, m\}
$$

is called a *feasible set* and consists of all those points $x \in \mathbb{Z}^n$ that satisfy the m constraints $g_i(x) \approx b_i$, $i = 1, 2, \ldots, m$. Function z is called the *objective function*. A feasible point $x^* \in X$, for which the objective function assumes the minimum (respectively maximum) value i.e. $z(x^*) \leq z(x)$ (respectively $z(x^*) \geq z(x)$) for all $x \in X$ is called an *optimal solution* for (IP).

In the special case where $X \subset \mathbb{Z}^n$ is a finite set, the (IP) problem is a CO problem. The optimization problems in the field of computational biology described in this book are concerned with strings and can be classified as CO problems. Most of them have a binary nature, i.e. a feasible solution to any of these problems is a n-dimensional vector $x \in \{0, 1\}^n$, where for each x_i it is necessary to choose between two possible choices. Classical binary CO problems are, for example, the 0/1 knapsack problem, assignment and matching problems, set covering, set packing and set partitioning problems [NEM 88, PAP 82].

In what follows, unless explicitly noted, we will refer to a general integer linear programming (ILP) problem in standard form:

$$\text{(ILP)} \quad \min \quad z(x) = c'x \qquad\qquad [1.1]$$

$$\text{s.t.} \quad Ax = b \qquad\qquad [1.2]$$

$$x \geq 0 \text{ and integer}, \qquad\qquad [1.3]$$

where $A \in \mathbb{R}^{m \times n}$ is the matrix of the *technological coefficients* a_{ij}, $i = 1, 2, \ldots, m$, $j = 1, 2, \ldots, n$, $b \in \mathbb{R}^m$ and $c \in \mathbb{R}^n$ are the m-dimensional array of the *constant terms* and the n-dimensional array of the objective function coefficients, respectively. Finally, $x \in \mathbb{Z}^n$ is the n-dimensional array of the decision variables, each being non-negative and integer. ILP is linear since both the objective function [1.1] and the m equality constraints [1.2] are linear in the decision variables $x_1, \ldots, x_n$.

Note that the integer constraints [1.3] define a lattice of points in $\mathbb{R}^n$, some of them belonging to the feasible set X of ILP. Formally, $X = P \cap \mathbb{Z}^n \subset P$, where $P = \{x \in \mathbb{R}^n \mid Ax = b, \ x \geq 0\}$ (Figure 1.2).

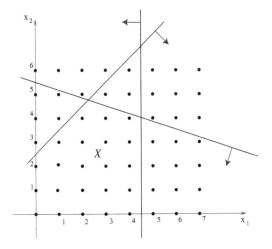

Figure 1.2. *Graphical representation of the feasible region X of a generic ILP problem: $X = P \cap \mathbb{Z}^2 \subset P$, where $P = \{x \in \mathbb{R}^2 \mid Ax = b, \ x \geq 0\}$*

Many CO problems are computationally intractable. Moreover, in contrast to linear programming problems that may be solved efficiently, for example by the *simplex method*, there is no single method capable of solving all of them efficiently. Since many of them exhibit special properties, because they are defined on networks with a special topology or because they are characterized by a special cost structure, the scientific community has historically lavished its efforts on the design and development of *ad hoc* techniques for specific problems. The remainder of this section is devoted to the description of mathematical programming methods and to dynamic programming.

1.1.1. *Linear programming relaxation*

A simple way to approximately solving an ILP using mathematical programming techniques is as follows:

a) Relax the integer constraints [1.3], obtaining the following continuous linear programming problem in the standard form:

$$\text{(ILP-c) min } z(x) = c'x$$
$$\text{s.t. } Ax = b$$
$$x \geq 0.$$

ILP-c is called the *linear programming relaxation* of ILP. It is the problem that arises by the replacement of the integer constraints [1.3] by weaker constraints that state that each variable x_j may assume any non-negative real value. As already mentioned, ILP-c can be solved by applying, for example, the simplex method [NEM 88]. Let x^* and $z^*_{(\text{ILP-c})} = z(x^*)$ be the optimal solution and the optimal objective function value for ILP-c, respectively. Similarly, let x^*_I and $z^*_{(\text{ILP})} = z(x^*_I)$ be the optimal solution and the optimal objective function value for ILP, respectively.

Note that since $X \subset P$, we have:

$$z^*_{(\text{ILP-c})} = \min\{c'x \mid x \in P\} \leq \min\{c'x \mid x \in X\} = z^*_{(\text{ILP})}.$$

therefore, $z^*_{(\text{ILP-c})}$ is a *lower bound* for $z^*_{(\text{ILP})}$.

b) If $x^* \in \mathbb{Z}^n$, then x^* is also an optimal solution for ILP, i.e.

$$z^*_{(ILP-c)} = z^*_{(ILP)}.$$

The procedure described above generally results in failure, as the optimal solution x^* to the linear programming relaxation typically does not have all integer components, except for in special cases such as problems whose formulation is characterized by a totally unimodular matrix A (see the transportation problem, the assignment problem and shortest path problems with non-negative arc lengths). Furthermore, it is wrong to try to obtain a solution x_I for ILP by rounding all non-integer components of x^*, because it may lead to infeasible solutions, as shown in Example 1.1 below.

EXAMPLE 1.1.– Let us consider the following integer linear program:

$$\max x_2$$
$$x_1 \geq \tfrac{1}{4} \ (a)$$
$$x_1 \leq \tfrac{3}{4} \ (b)$$
$$x_2 \leq 2 \ (c)$$
$$x_1, x_2 \geq 0 \text{ and integer.}$$

The corresponding feasible set X is depicted in Figure 1.3. Optimal solutions of its linear relaxation are all points $x^* = (x_1^*, x_2^*)$, with $x_1^* \in \left[\tfrac{1}{4}, \tfrac{3}{4}\right]$ and $x_2^* = 2$. Therefore, $x^* \notin \mathbb{Z}^2$. Moreover, $x_I \notin X$, since either $x_I = (0, 2)$ or $x_I = (1, 2)$.

Summarizing, the possible relations between ILP and its linear programming relaxation ILP-c are listed below and X^* and P^* denote the set of optimal solutions for ILP and ILP-c, respectively:

1) $P = \emptyset \Longrightarrow X = \emptyset$;

2) $z^*_{(ILP)} = \infty \Longrightarrow z^*_{(ILP-c)} = \infty$ (not possible in the case of combinatorial optimization problems);

3) $P^* \neq \emptyset, X^* \neq \emptyset \Longrightarrow z^*_{(ILP-c)} \leq z^*_{(ILP)}$ (lower bound);

4) $y \in P^*, y \in \mathbb{Z}^n \Longrightarrow y \in X^*$ and

$$z(y) = z^*_{(ILP-c)} = z^*_{(ILP)};$$

5) $X = \emptyset$, but $P^* \neq \emptyset$, as for the problem described in Example 1.1, whose feasible set is depicted in Figure 1.3;

6) $X = \emptyset$, but $z^*_{(\text{ILP-c})} = \infty$ (not possible in the case of combinatorial optimization problems), as for the following problem, whose feasible set is shown in Figure 1.4:

$$\max x_2$$
$$x_1 \geq \tfrac{1}{4} \text{ (a)}$$
$$x_1 \leq \tfrac{3}{4} \text{ (b)}$$
$$x_1, x_2 \geq 0 \text{ and integer.}$$

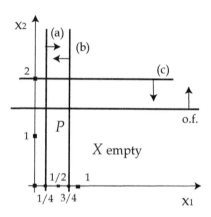

Figure 1.3. *Feasible set of the problem described in Example 1.1.*
$x^* = (x_1^*, x_2^*)$, *with* $x_1^* \in \left[\tfrac{1}{4}, \tfrac{3}{4}\right]$ *and* $x_2^* = 2$, $x^* \notin \mathbb{Z}^2$. *Furthermore,*
$x_I \notin X$, *since either* $x_I = (0, 2)$ *or* $x_I = (1, 2)$

Even if it almost always leads to failure while finding an optimal solution to ILP, linear programming relaxation is very useful in the context of many exact methods, as the lower bound that it provides avoids unnecessary explorations of portions of the feasible set X. This is the case with branch and bound (B&B) algorithms, as explained in section 1.1.2.1. Furthermore, linear programming relaxation is a standard technique for designing approximation algorithms for hard optimization problems [HOC 96, VAZ 01, WIL 11].

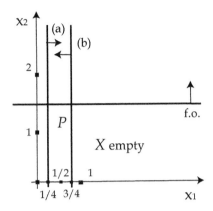

Figure 1.4. *Feasible set of the problem described in point (6) below Example 1.1:* $X = \emptyset$, *but* $z^*_{(ILP\text{-}c)} = \infty$

1.1.2. Cutting plane techniques

Historically, cutting plane techniques were the first algorithms developed for ILP that could be proved to converge in a finite number of steps. A cutting plane algorithm iteratively finds an optimal solution x^* following linear programming relaxation ILP-c. If x^* has at least one fractional component, a constraint satisfied by all integer solutions belonging to P, but not satisfied by x^*, is identified. This constraint, which is violated by x^* and is added to the mathematical formulation of ILP-c, is called a *cut*. Formally, given $x^* \in P$, $a \in \mathbb{R}^n$ and $b \in \mathbb{R}$, the constraint $a'x \leq b$ is a cut if the following two conditions hold:

1) $a'x \leq b, \forall\, x \in X$;

2) $a'x^* > b$.

Any cutting plane algorithm proceeds in iterations, as shown in Algorithm 1.1. Different cutting plane algorithms differ from each other in the method they adopt to identify the cut to be added to the current linear programming formulation ILP-c$_k$ at each iteration. Since the number of iterations performed corresponds to the number of cuts needed, it is intuitive that stronger cuts imply fewer iterations. Unfortunately, most state-of-the-art cutting plane techniques can cut only small portions of P.

Algorithm 1.1. General Cutting Plane Technique

1: **input:** an ILP problem
2: **initialization:** Set ILP-c$_0$:=ILP-c, $x_0^* := x^*$, $k := 0$
3: **while** x_k^* not integer **do**
4:     find a cut $a_k' x \leq b_k$ for x_k^*
5:     obtain ILP-c$_{k+1}$ by adding the cut $a_k' x \leq b_k$ to ILP-c$_k$
6:     find an optimal solution x_{k+1}^* for ILP-c$_{k+1}$
7:     $k := k + 1$
8: **end while**
9: **output:** optimal solution x_k^* to ILP

A feasible solution $x \in \mathbb{R}^n$ of a system $Ax = b$ of equality constraints, $A \in \mathbb{R}^{m \times n}$ and $b \in \mathbb{R}^m$, is a *basic solution* if the n components of x can be partitioned into m non-negative *basic* variables and $n - m$ *non-basic* variables in a way such that the m columns of A, corresponding to the basic variables, form a non-singular submatrix B (basis matrix), and the value of each non-basic variable is 0. In 1958, Gomory [GOM 58] proposed the most famous and well-known cutting plane method, whose basic idea is to exploit important information related to the $m \times m$ non-singular submatrix B of A corresponding to the m currently basic variables in the optimal continuous solution x^*.

Let us consider a generic iteration k of Gomory's algorithm. Suppose that the optimal continuous solution x_k^* has at least one fractional component. Let x_h be such a variable. Clearly, x_h must be a basic variable and let us suppose it is carried in the tth row of the optimal table. We can observe that the equation associated with the tth row of the optimal table can be stated as follows:

$$x_h + \sum_{j \in N} \bar{a}_{tj} x_j = \bar{b}_t,$$

where:

– N is the set of non-basic variables;

– $\bar{a}_{tj}$, $j \in N$ are the elements of the tth row of the optimal table corresponding to the columns of the non-basic variables;

– $\bar{b}_t$ is a fractional constant, by hypothesis.

Since $x_j \geq 0$, for all $j = 1, 2, \ldots, n$, we have:

$$x_h + \sum_{j \in N} \lfloor \bar{a}_{tj} \rfloor x_j \leq x_h + \sum_{j \in N} \bar{a}_{tj} x_j = \bar{b}_t.$$

Moreover, since x_j must assume an integer value, the following inequality holds:

$$x_h + \sum_{j \in N} \lfloor \bar{a}_{tj} \rfloor x_j \leq \lfloor \bar{b}_t \rfloor. \qquad [1.4]$$

The tth row of the optimal table is referred to as the *row generating the cut* and inequality [1.4] is the cut that Gomory's algorithm uses at each iteration, until it is not obtained in an optimal continuous solution $x_k^* \in \mathbb{Z}^n$. It can easily be proved that the cut [1.4] is still satisfied by all feasible integer solution, but violated by x_k^*, since the current value of the hth component of x_k^* is $\bar{b}_t$, the components of x_k^* corresponding to the non-basic variables are zero, and $\lfloor \bar{b}_t \rfloor \leq \bar{b}_t$.

1.1.2.1. *Branch and Bound*

An alternative exact approach is B&B, which is an *implicit enumeration technique* because it can prove the optimality of a solution without explicitly visiting all valid solutions when it finishes. Almost always outperforming the cutting plane approach, it is a *divide and conquer* framework that addresses ILP by dividing it into a certain number of subproblems, which are "simpler" because they are smaller in size.

Given the following ILP:

$$(ILP_0) \min z(x) = c'x$$
$$\text{s.t.}$$
$$Ax \approx b$$
$$x \geq 0 \text{ and integer,}$$

with feasible set X_0 and optimal objective function value given by:

$$z_{(ILP_0)}^* = \min\{z(x) \mid x \in X_0\},$$

we obtain ILP_0 B&B partitions in a certain number of subproblems $\text{ILP}_1, \ldots, \text{ILP}_{n_0}$, whose totality represents ILP_0. Such a partition is obtained by partitioning X_0 into the subsets $X_1, \ldots, X_{n_0}$ such that:

– for $i = 1, \ldots, n_0$, X_i is the feasible set of subproblem ILP_i;

– for $i = 1, \ldots, n_0$, $z^*_{\text{ILP}_i} = \min\{z(x) \mid x \in X_i\}$ is the optimal objective function value of subproblem ILP_i;

$$- \bigcup_{k=1}^{n_0} X_k = X_0, \quad \bigcap_{k=1}^{n_0} X_k = \emptyset.$$

Note that, since any feasible solution of ILP_0 is feasible for at least one subproblem among $\text{ILP}_1, \ldots, \text{ILP}_{n_0}$, it clearly results that:

$$z^*_{\text{ILP}_0} = \min_{i=1,\ldots,n_0} z^*_{\text{ILP}_i}.$$

Therefore, ILP_0 is solved by solving $\text{ILP}_1, \ldots, \text{ILP}_{n_0}$, i.e. for each ILP_i, $i = 1, \ldots, n_0$. One of the three options given below will hold true:

– an optimal solution to ILP_i is found; or

– it can be proved that ILP_i is unfeasible ($X_i = \emptyset$); or

– it can be proved that an optimal solution to ILP_i is not better than a known feasible solution to ILP_0 (if any).

Each ILP_i subproblem, $i = 1, \ldots, n_0$, has the same characteristics and properties as ILP_0. Hence, the procedure described above can be applied to solve it, i.e. its feasible set X_i is partitioned and so on.

The whole process is usually represented dynamically by means of a decision tree, also called a *branching tree* (see Figure 1.5), where:

– the choice of the term *branching* refers to the partitioning operation of X_i sets;

– the choice of the classical terms used in graph and tree theory include:

- root node (corresponding to the original problem ILP_0),

- father and children nodes,

- leaves, each corresponding to some ILP_i subproblem, $i > 0$, still to be investigated.

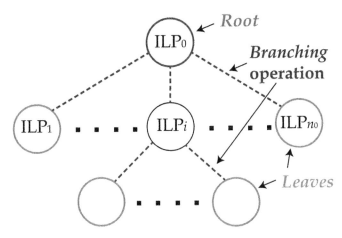

Figure 1.5. *Branch and bound branching tree*

It is easily understandable and intuitive that the criterion adopted to fragment every ILP_i (sub)problem, $i = 0, 1, \ldots, n_0$, has a huge impact on the computational performance of a B&B algorithm. In the literature, several different criteria have been proposed to perform this task, each closely connected to some specific procedure, called a *relaxation technique*. Among the well-known relaxation techniques, those that ought to be mentioned are:

– linear programming relaxation;

– relaxation by elimination;

– surrogate relaxation;

– Lagrangian relaxation;

– relaxation by decomposition.

The most frequently applied relaxation technique is linear programming relaxation. To understand the idea underlying this technique, let us consider ILP_0 with feasible set X_0 depicted in Figure 1.6. The optimal solution to its linear programming relaxation (with feasible set P_0) is $x^* = \left(\frac{3}{2}, 2\right)$, with $x_1^* = \frac{3}{2}$. Clearly, in the optimal integer solution it must be either $x_1 \leq 1$ or $x_1 \geq 2$. Therefore, one can proceed by separately adding to the original integer formulation of ILP_0 the constraints $x_1 \leq 1$ and $x_1 \geq 2$, respectively. By adding constraint $x_1 \leq 1$, the subproblem $\text{ILP}_{x_1 \leq 1}$ is generated, with the optimal solution $x^*_{x_1 \leq 1}$. Similarly, by adding constraint $x_1 \geq 2$, the subproblem $\text{ILP}_{x_1 \geq 2}$ is generated, with the optimal solution $x^*_{x_1 \geq 2}$. In this way, ILP_0 is partitioned into the two subproblems $\text{ILP}_{x_1 \leq 1}$ and $\text{ILP}_{x_1 \geq 2}$, whose feasible sets (see Figure 1.7) are X_1 and X_2 such that $X_1 \cup X_2 = X_0$ and $X_1 \cap X_2 = \emptyset$. An optimal solution to ILP_0 is obtained with the best solution between $x^*_{x_1 \leq 1}$ and $x^*_{x_1 \geq 2}$.

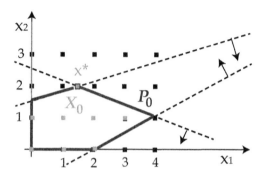

Figure 1.6. *B&B scenario*

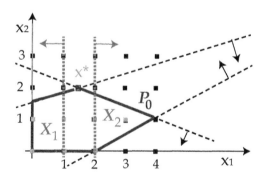

Figure 1.7. *B&B partitioning (branching)*

More generally, given ILP_0, one needs to solve its linear programming relaxation:

$$(ILP_0\text{-c}) \min z(x) = c'x$$
$$\text{s.t.}$$
$$Ax \approx b$$
$$x \geq 0,$$

with feasible set P_0. Let $x^*_{P_0}$ be an optimal solution to ILP_0-c. If all components of $x^*_{P_0}$ are integer, then $x^*_{P_0}$ is an optimal solution to ILP_0. Otherwise, (see Figure 1.8) a fractional component $[x^*_{P_0}]_h$ ($[x^*_{P_0}]_h = a \notin \mathbb{Z}$) is chosen and the following two subproblems are identified:

$$(ILP_1) \min z(x) = c'x$$
$$\text{s.t.}$$
$$Ax \approx b$$
$$x_h \leq \lfloor a \rfloor$$
$$x \geq 0 \text{ and integer,}$$

and

$$(ILP_2) \min z(x) = c'x$$
$$\text{s.t.}$$
$$Ax \approx b$$
$$x_h \geq \lceil a \rceil$$
$$x \geq 0 \text{ and integer.}$$

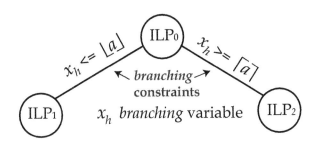

Figure 1.8. *Branching:* $[x^*_{P_0}]_h = a \notin \mathbb{Z}$

Identifying subproblems ILP_1 and ILP_2 starting from ILP_0 corresponds to performing a *branching operation*. Variable x_h is called the *branching variable*. Subproblems ILP_1 and ILP_2 are *children* of ILP_0 as they are obtained by adding the *branching constraints* $x_h \leq \lfloor a \rfloor$ and $x_h \geq \lceil a \rceil$, respectively to the formulation of ILP_0.

Since ILP_1 and ILP_2 are still integer problems, they are approached with the same procedure, i.e. for each of them its linear relaxation is optimally solved and, if necessary, further branching operations are performed. Proceeding in this way, we obtain a succession of *hierarchical subproblems* that are more constrained and hence easier to solve. As already underlined, the whole process is represented dynamically by means of a decision tree, also called a *branching tree*, whose root node corresponds to the original problem, ILP_0. Any child node corresponds to the subproblem obtained by adding a branching constraint to the formulation of the problem corresponding to its father node.

Generally speaking, the constraints of any subproblem ILP_t corresponding to node t in the branching tree are the following ones:

1) the constraints of the original problem, ILP_0;

2) the branching constraints that label the unique path in the branching tree from the root node to node t (node t "inherits" the constraints of its ancestors).

In principle, the branching tree could represent all possible branching operations and, therefore, be a complete decision tree that enumerates all feasible solutions to ILP_0. Nevertheless, as explained briefly, thanks to the *bounding criterion*, entire portions of the feasible region X_0 that do not contain the optimal solution are not explored or, in other words, a certain number of feasible solutions are not generated, since they are not optimal.

Let us suppose that the B&B algorithm is evaluating subproblem ILP_t and let x_{opt} be the best current solution (*incumbent solution*) to ILP_0 (i.e. x_{opt} is an optimal solution to at least one subproblem, ILP_k, $k > 0$ and $k \neq t$, among those subproblems already investigated). Let $z_{\text{opt}} = z(x_{\text{opt}})$, where initially $z_{\text{opt}} := +\infty$ and $x_{\text{opt}} := \emptyset$.

Recalling the possible relations existing between a linear integer program and its linear programming relaxation described in section 1.1.1, it is useless to operate a branch from ILP_t if any of the following three conditions holds:

1) The linear programming relaxation ILP_t-c is infeasible (hence, ILP_t is infeasible as well). This happens when the constraints of the original problem, ILP_0, and the branching constraints from the root of the branching tree to node t are inconsistent;

2) The optimal solution to linear programming relaxation ILP_t-c is integer. In this case, if necessary, x_{opt} and z_{opt} are updated.

3) The optimal solution to linear programming relaxation ILP_t-c is not integer, but:

$$z^*_{(ILP_t\text{-c})} \geq z_{opt}. \qquad [1.5]$$

In the latter case, it is clearly useless to keep partitioning X_t. This is because none of the feasible integer solutions are better than the incumbent solution x_{opt}, since it always holds that $z^*_{(ILP_t)} \geq z^*_{(ILP\text{-}c_t)}$. Inequality [1.5] is called the *bounding criterion*.

1.1.2.2. *Choice of branching variable*

Suppose that the B&B algorithm is investigating subproblem ILP_t and that a branching operation must be performed because none of the three conditions listed above is verified. Let $x^*_{P_t}$ be an optimal solution to ILP_t-c and suppose that it has at least two fractional components, i.e.

$$F = \{l \in \{1,\dots,n\} \mid [x^*_{P_t}]_l \notin \mathbb{Z}\}; \qquad |F| \geq 2$$

The most commonly used criteria adopted to choose the branching variable x_h are as follows:

1) h is randomly selected from set F;

2) $h = \min\{l \mid l \in F\}$ (h is the minimum index in F);

3) $h = \min\{[x^*_{P_t}]_l \mid l \in F\}$ (h is the index in F corresponding to the minimum fractional value).

1.1.2.3. *Generation/exploration of the branching tree*

A further issue that still remains to be determined is the criterion for generating/exploring the branching tree. At each iteration, a B&B algorithm maintains and updates a list Q of *live nodes* in the branching tree, i.e. a list of the current leaves that correspond to the *active* subproblems:

$$Q = \{\mathrm{ILP}_i \mid \mathrm{ILP}_i \text{ to be investigated and } z^*_{\mathrm{ILP}_i\text{-c}} < z_{\mathrm{opt}}\}.$$

Two main techniques are adopted to decide the next subproblem in Q to be investigated:

– *Depth first:* recursively, starting from the last generated node t corresponding to subproblem ILP_t whose feasible region X_t must be partitioned, its left child is generated/explored, until node k corresponding to subproblem ILP_k is generated from which no branch is needed. In the latter case, backtracking is performed to the first active node $j < k$ that has already been generated. Usually, set Q is implemented as a *stack* and the algorithm stops as soon as $Q = \emptyset$, i.e. when a backtrack to the root node must be performed.

This technique has the advantages of being relatively easier to implement and of keeping the number of active nodes low. Moreover, it produces feasible solutions rapidly, which means that good approximate solutions are obtained even when stopped rather early (e.g. in the case of the running time limit being reached). On the other hand, deep backtracks must often be performed.

– *Best bound first:* at each iteration, the next active node to be considered is the node associated with subproblem ILP_t corresponding to the linear programming relaxation with the current best objective function value, i.e.

$$\mathrm{ILP}_t = \arg\min \left\{ z^*_{\mathrm{ILP}_h\text{-c}} \mid h \in Q \right\}.$$

The algorithm stops as soon as $Q = \emptyset$. This technique has the advantage of generating a small number of nodes, but rarely goes to very deep levels in the branching tree.

1.1.3. *General-purpose ILP solvers*

The techniques described in the previous section, among others, are implemented as components of general-purpose ILP solvers that may be applied to any ILP. Examples of such ILP solvers include IBM ILOG CPLEX [IBM 16], Gurobi [GUR 15] and SCIP [ACH 09]. The advantage of these solvers is that they are implemented in an incredibly efficient way and they incorporate all cutting-edge technologies. However, for some CO problems it might be more efficient to develop a specific B&B algorithm, for example.

1.1.4. *Dynamic programming*

Dynamic programming is an algorithmic framework for solving CO problems. Similar to any divide and conquer scheme, it is based on the principle that it is possible to define an optimal solution to the original problem in terms of some combination of optimal solutions to its subproblems. Nevertheless, in contrast to the divide and conquer strategy, dynamic programming does not partition the problem into disjointed subproblems. It applies when the subproblems overlap, i.e. when subproblems share themselves. More formally, two subproblems (ILP_h) and (ILP_k) overlap if they can be divided into the following subproblems:

$$(ILP_h) = \{(ILP_{h1}), (ILP_{h2}), \dots, (ILP_{hi})\}$$

$$(ILP_k) = \{(ILP_{k1}), (ILP_{k2}), \dots, (ILP_{kj})\}$$

$$\{(ILP_{h1}), (ILP_{h2}), \dots, (ILP_{hi})\} \cap \{(ILP_{k1}), (ILP_{k2}), \dots, (ILP_{kj})\} \neq \emptyset,$$

where (ILP_h) and (ILP_k) share at least one subproblem.

A CO ILP problem can be solved by the application of a dynamic programming algorithm if it exhibits the following two fundamental characteristics:

1) ILP exhibits an optimal substructure, i.e. an optimal solution to ILP contains optimal solutions to its subproblems. This characteristic guarantees there is a formula that correctly expresses an optimal solution to ILP as combination of optimal solutions to its subproblems.

2) ILP must be divisible into overlapping subproblems. From a computational point of view, any dynamic programming algorithm takes advantage of this characteristic. It solves each subproblem, ILP_l, only once and stores the optimal solution in a suitable data structure, typically a table. Afterwards, whenever the optimal solution to ILP_l is needed, this optimal solution is looked up in the data structure using constant time per lookup.

When designing a dynamic programming algorithm for a CO ILP problem, the following three steps need to be taken:

1) Verify that ILP exhibits an optimal substructure.

2) Recursively define the optimal objective function value as combination of the optimal objective function value of the subproblems (*recurrence equation*). In this step, it is essential to identify the *elementary* subproblems, which are those subproblems that are not divisible into further subproblems and thus are immediately solvable (*initial conditions*).

3) Write an algorithm based on the recurrence equation and initial conditions stated in step 2.

1.2. Approximate methods: metaheuristics

In contrast to complete (or exact) techniques as outlined in the previous section, metaheuristics [BLU 03, GEN 10a] are approximate methods for solving optimization problems. They were introduced in order to provide high-quality solutions using a moderate amount of computational resources such as computation time and memory. Metaheuristics are often described as "generally applicable recipes" for solving optimization problems. The inspiration for specific metaheuristics are, taken from natural processes, such as the annealing of glass or metal that give rise to a metaheuristic known as *simulated annealing* (see section 1.2.5) and the shortest path-finding behavior of natural ant colonies that inspired the ant colony optimization (ACO) metaheuristic (see section 1.2.1). Many ideas originate from the way of visualizing the search space of continuous and CO problems in terms of a landscape with hills and valleys. When a maximization problem is considered, the task is then to find the highest valley in the search landscape.

The general idea of a *local search*, for example, is to start the search process at some point in the search landscape and then move uphill until the peak of a mountain is reached. In analogy, an alternative expression for a search procedure based on a local search is *hill-climber*. Several metaheuristics are extensions of a simple local search, equipped with strategies for moving from the current hill to other (possibly neighboring) hills in the search landscape. In any case, during the last 40–50 years, metaheuristics have gained a strong reputation for tackling optimization problems to which complete methods cannot be applied – for example, due to the size of the problem considered – and for problems for which simple greedy heuristics do not provide solutions of sufficient quality.

As mentioned above, several metaheuristics are extensions of a simple local search. To formally define a local search method, the notion of a so-called *neighborhood* must be introduced. Given a CO problem $(\mathcal{S}, f)$, where $\mathcal{S}$ is the search space – that is, the set of all valid solutions to the problem – and $f : \mathcal{S} \mapsto \mathbb{R}^+$ is the objective function that assigns a positive cost value to each valid solution $S \in \mathcal{S}$, a neighborhood is defined as a function, $N : \mathcal{S} \mapsto 2^{\mathcal{S}}$. In other words, a neighborhood assigns to each solution $S \in \mathcal{S}$ a subset $N(S) \subseteq \mathcal{S}$ which is called the *neighborhood of S*. Any solution S such that $f(S) \leq f(S')$ for all $S' \in N(S)$ is called a *local minimum* with respect to N. Moreover, a solution S^* such that $f(S^*) \leq f(S')$ for all $S' \in \mathcal{S}$ is called a *global minimum*. Note that any global minimum is a local minimum with respect to any neighborhood at the same time.

Algorithm 1.2. Local search

  input: initial solution S, neighborhood N
  while S is not a local minimum w.r.t. N **do**
    $S' := \mathsf{ChooseImprovingNeighbor}(N(S))$
    $S := S'$
  end while
  output: a local minimum S

Given a neighborhood N, a simple local search method can be defined as follows; see also Algorithm 1.2. First, an initial solution S must be generated. This may be done randomly, or by means of a greedy heuristic. Then, at each step a solution $S' \in N(S)$ is chosen in function ChooseImproving Neighbor $(N(S))$ such that $f(S') < f(S)$. Solution S is then replaced by S' and the algorithm proceeds to the next iterations. There are at least two standard ways of implementing function ChooseImproving Neighbor $(N(S))$. In the first one – henceforth, referred to as *best-improvement local search* – S' is chosen as follows:

$$S' := \mathbf{argmin}\{f(S'') \mid S'' \in N(S)\} \tag{1.6}$$

The second standard way of implementing this function is *first-improvement local search*. In first-improvement local search, the solutions to $N(S)$ are ordered in some way. They are then examined in the order they are produced and the first solution that has a lower objective function value than S (if any) is returned.

In general, the performance of a local search method depends firmly on the choice of the neighborhood N. It is also interesting to note that a local search algorithm partitions the search space into so-called *basins of attraction* of local minima. Hereby, the basin of attraction $B(S)$ of a local minimum $S \in \mathcal{S}$ is a subset of the search space, i.e. $B(S) \subseteq \mathcal{S}$. In particular, when starting the local search under consideration from any solution $S' \in B(S)$, the local minimum at which the local search method stops is S. In relation to constructive heuristics, it can be stated that constructive heuristics are often faster than local search methods, yet they frequently return solutions of inferior quality.

In the following section, we will describe some important metaheuristics. With the exception of evolutionary algorithms (see section 1.2.2), all these metaheuristics are either extensions of constructive heuristics or of a local search. The order in which the metaheuristics are described is alphabetical.

1.2.1. Ant colony optimization

ACO [DOR 04] is a metaheuristic which was inspired by the observation of the shortest-path finding behavior of natural ant colonies. From a technical perspective, ACO algorithms are extensions of constructive heuristics. Valid solutions to the problem tackled are assembled as subsets of the complete set C of solution components. In the case of the traveling salesman problem

(TSP), for example, C may be defined as the set of all edges of the input graph. At each iteration of the algorithm, a set of n_a solutions are probabilistically constructed based on greedy information and on so-called *pheromone information*. In a standard case, for each solution with components $c \in C$, the algorithm considers a *pheromone value* $\tau_c \in \mathcal{T}$, where $\mathcal{T}$ is the set of all pheromone values. Given a partial solution, $S^p \subseteq C$, the next component $c' \in C$ to be added to S^p is chosen based on its pheromone value $\tau_{c'}$ and the value $\eta(c')$ of a greedy function $\eta(\cdot)$. Set $\mathcal{T}$ is commonly called the *pheromone model*, which is one of the central components of any ACO algorithm. The solution construction mechanism together with the pheromone model and the greedy information define a probability distribution over the search space. This probability distribution is updated at each iteration (after having constructed n_a solutions) by increasing the pheromone value of solution components that appear in good solutions constructed in this iteration or in previous iterations.

In summary, ACO algorithms attempt to solve CO problems by iterating the following two steps:

– candidate solutions are constructed by making use of a mechanism for constructing solutions, a pheromone model and greedy information;

– candidate solutions are used to update the pheromone values in a way that is deemed to bias future sampling toward high-quality solutions.

In other words, the pheromone update aims to lead the search towards regions of the search space containing high-quality solutions. The reinforcement of solution components depending on the quality of solutions in which they appear is an important ingredient of ACO algorithms. By doing this, we implicitly assume that good solutions consist of good solution components. In fact, it has been shown that learning which components contribute to good solutions can – in many cases – help to assemble them into better solutions. A high-level framework of an ACO algorithm is shown in Algorithm 1.3. Daemon actions (see line 5 of Algorithm 1.3) mainly refer to the possible application of local search to solutions constructed in the AntBasedSolutionConstruction() function.

A multitude of different ACO variants have been proposed over the years. Among the ones with the best performance are (1) MAX–MIN Ant System

(MMAS) [STÜ 00] and (2) Ant Colony System (ACS) [DOR 97]. For more comprehensive information, we refer the interested reader to [DOR 10].

Algorithm 1.3. Ant colony optimization (ACO)

1: **while** termination conditions not met **do**
2:    **ScheduleActivities**
3:       AntBasedSolutionConstruction()
4:       PheromoneUpdate()
5:       DaemonActions() {optional}
6:    **end ScheduleActivities**
7: **end while**

1.2.2. Evolutionary algorithms

Evolutionary algorithms (EAs) [BÄC 97] are inspired by the principles of natural evolution, i.e. by nature's capability to evolve living beings to keep them well adapted to their environment. At each iteration, an EA maintains a *population* P of *individuals*. Generally, individuals are valid solutions to the problem tackled. However, EAs sometimes also permit infeasible solutions or even partial solutions. Just as in natural evolution, the driving force in EAs is the *selection* of individuals based on their *fitness*, which is – in the context of combinatorial optimization problems – usually a measure based on the objective function. Selection takes place in two different operators of an EA. First, selection is used at each iteration to choose *parents* for one or more *reproduction* operators in order to generate a set, P^{off}, of *offspring*. Second, selection takes place when the individuals in the population of the next iteration are chosen from the current population P and the offspring generated in the current iteration. In both operations, individuals with higher fitness have a higher probability of being chosen. In natural evolution this principle is known as *survival of the fittest*. Note that reproduction operations, such as *crossover*, often preserve the solution components that are present in the parents. EAs generally also make use of *mutation* or *modification* operators that cause either random changes or heuristically-guided changes in an individual. This process described above is pseudo-coded in Algorithm 1.4.

A variety of different EAs have been proposed over the last decades. To mention all of them is out of the scope of this short introduction. However, three major lines of EAs were independently developed early on. These are *evolutionary programming* (EP) [FOG 62, FOG 66], *evolutionary strategies* (ESs) [REC 73] and *genetic algorithms* (GAs) [HOL 75, GOL 89]. EP, for example, was originally proposed to operate on discrete representations of finite state machines. However, most of the present variants are used for CO problems. The latter also holds for most current variants of ESs. GAs, however are still mainly applied to the solution of CO problems. Later, other EAs – such as *genetic programming* (GP) [KOZ 92] and *scatter search* (SS) [GLO 00b] – were developed. Despite the development of different strands, EAs can be understood from a unified point of view with respect to their main components and the way in which they explore the search space. This is reflected, for example, in the survey by Kobler and Hertz [HER 00].

Algorithm 1.4. Evolutionary algorithm (EA)

1: $P :=$ GenerateInitialPopulation()
2: **while** termination conditions not met **do**
3:    $P^s :=$ Selection(P)
4:    $P^{off} :=$ Recombination(P^s)
5:    $P' :=$ Mutation(P^{off})
6:    $P :=$ Replacement(P, P')
7: **end while**

1.2.3. *Greedy randomized adaptive search procedures*

The *greedy randomized adaptive search procedure* (GRASP) [RES 10a] is a conceptually simple, but often effective, metaheuristic. As indicated by the name, the core of GRASP is based on the probabilistic construction of solutions. However, while ACO algorithms, for example, include a memory of the search history in terms of the pheromone model, GRASP does not make use of memory. More specifically, GRASP – as pseudo-coded in Algorithm 1.5 – combines the randomized greedy construction of solutions with the subsequent application of a local search. For the following discussion let us assume that, given a partial solution S^p, set $Ext(S^p) \subseteq C$ is the set of solution components that may be used to extend S^p. The probabilistic construction of a solution using GRASP makes use of a so-called *restricted candidate list L*, which is a subset of $Ext(S^p)$, at each step. In fact, L is determined to contain the best solution components from $Ext(S^p)$ with respect to a greedy function. After generating L, a solution component $c^* \in L$ is chosen uniformly at random. An important parameter of GRASP is α, which is the length of the restricted candidate list L. If $\alpha = 1$, for example, the solution construction is deterministic and the resulting solution is equal to the greedy solution. In the other extreme case – that is, when choosing $\alpha = |Ext(S^p)|$ – a random solution is generated without any heuristic bias. In summary, α is a critical parameter of GRASP which generally requires a careful fine-tuning.

Algorithm 1.5. Greedy randomized adaptive search procedure (GRASP)

while termination conditions not met **do**
  $S := \mathsf{ConstructGreedyRandomizedSolution}()$
  $S := \mathsf{LocalSearch}(S)$
end while

As mentioned above, the second component of the algorithm consists of the application of local search to the solutions constructed. Note that, for this purpose, the use of a standard local search method such as the one from Algorithm 1.2 is the simplest option. More sophisticated options include, for example, the use of metaheuristics based on a local search such as simulated annealing. As a rule of thumb, the algorithm designer should take care that: (1) the solution construction mechanism samples promising regions of the search space: and (2) the solutions constructed are good starting points for a local search, i.e. the solutions constructed fall into basins of attraction for high-quality local minima.

1.2.4. *Iterated local search*

Iterated local search (ILS) [LOU 10] is – among the metaheuristics described in this section – the first local search extension. The idea of ILS is simple: instead of repeatedly applying local search to solutions generated independently from each other, as in GRASP, ILS produces the starting solutions for a local search by randomly *perturbing* the incumbent solutions. The requirements for the perturbation mechanism are as follows. The perturbed solutions should lie in a different basin of attraction with respect to the local search method utilized. However, at the same time, the perturbed solution should be closer to the previous incumbent solution than a randomly generated solution.

More specifically, the pseudo-code of ILS – as shown in Algorithm 1.6 – works as follows. First, an initial solution is produced in some way in the GenerateInitialSolution() function. This solution serves as input for the first application of a local search (see ApplyLocalSearch(S) function in line 2 of the pseudo-code). At each iteration, first, the perturbation mechanism is applied to the incumbent solution S; see Perturbation(S,$history$) function. The parameter $history$ refers to the possible influence of the search history on this process. The perturbation mechanism is usually non-deterministic in order to avoid *cycling*, which refers to a situation in which the algorithm repeatedly returns to solutions already visited. Moreover, it is important to choose the perturbation strength carefully. This is, because: (1) a perturbation that causes very few changes might not enable the algorithm to escape from the current basin of attraction; (2) a perturbation that is too strong would make the algorithm similar to a random-restart local search. The last algorithmic component of ILS concerns the choice of the incumbent solution for the next iteration; see function Choose($S, S', history$). In most cases, ILS algorithms simply choose the better solution from among S and S'. However, other criteria – for example, ones that depend on the search history – might be applied.

Algorithm 1.6. Iterated local search (ILS)

1: S := GenerateInitialSolution()
2: S := ApplyLocalSearch(S)
3: **while** termination conditions not met **do**
4:    S' := Perturbation($S, history$)
5:    S' := ApplyLocalSearch(S')
6:    S := Choose($S, S', history$)
7: **end while**

1.2.5. *Simulated annealing*

Simulated annealing (SA) [NIK 10] is another metaheuristic that is an extension of local search. SA has – just like ILS – a strategy for escaping from the local optimal of the search space. The fundamental idea is to allow moves to solutions that are worse than the incumbent solution. Such a move is generally known as an *uphill move*. SA is inspired by the annealing process of metal and glass. When cooling down such materials from the fluid state to a solid state, the material loses energy and finally assumes a crystal structure. The perfection – or optimality – of this crystal structure depends on the speed at which the material is cooled down. The more carefully the material is cooled down, the more perfect the crystal structure. The first times that SA was presented as a search algorithm for CO problems was in [KIR 83] and in [CER 85].

SA works as shown in Algorithm 1.7. At each iteration, a solution $S' \in N(S)$ is randomly selected. If S' is better than S, then S' replaces S as incumbent solution. Otherwise, if S is worse than S' – that is, if the move from S to S' is an uphill move – S' may still be accepted as new incumbent solution with a positive probability that is a function of a temperature parameter T_k – in analogy to the natural inspiration of SA – and the difference between the objective function value of S' and that of S ($f(s') - f(s)$). Usually this probability is computed in accordance with Boltzmann's distribution. Note that when SA is running, the value of T_k gradually decreases. In this way, the probability of accepting an uphill move decreases during run time.

Algorithm 1.7. Simulated annealing (SA)

1: $S :=$ GenerateInitialSolution()
2: $k := 0$
3: $T_k :=$ SetInitialTemperature()
4: **while** termination conditions not met **do**
5:     $S' :=$ SelectNeighborAtRandom $(N(S))$
6:     **if** $(f(S') < f(S))$ **then**
7:         $S := S'$
8:     **else**
9:         accept S' as new solution with a probability $\mathbf{p}(S' \mid T_k, S)$
10:     **end if**
11:     $T_{k+1} :=$ AdaptTemperature (T_k, k)
12:     $k := k + 1$
13: **end while**

Note that the SA search process can be modeled as a *Markov chain* [FEL 68]. This is because the trajectory of solutions visited by SA is such that the next solution is chosen depending only on the incumbent solution. This means that – just like GRASP – basic SA is a memory-less process.

1.2.6. *Other metaheuristics*

Apart from the five metaheuristics outlined in the previous sections, the literature offers a wide range of additional algorithms that fall under the metaheuristic paradigm. Examples are established metaheuristics, such as *Tabu search* [GLO 97, GEN 10b], *particle swarm optimization* [KEN 95, JOR 15], *iterated greedy algorithms* [HOO 15] and *variable neighborhood search* (VNS) [HAN 10]. More recent metaheuristics include *artificial bee colony* optimization [KAR 07, KAR 08] and *chemical reaction optimization* [LAM 12].

1.2.7. *Hybrid approaches*

Quite a large number of algorithms have been reported in recent years that do not follow the paradigm of a single traditional metaheuristic. They combine various algorithmic components, often taken from algorithms from various different areas of optimization. These approaches are commonly referred to as *hybrid metaheuristics*. The main motivation behind the hybridization of different algorithms is to exploit the complementary character of different optimization strategies, i.e. hybrids are believed to benefit from *synergy*. In fact, choosing an adequate combination of complementary algorithmic concepts can be the key to achieving top performance when solving many hard optimization problems. This has also seen to be the case in the context of string problems in bioinformatics, for example in the context of longest common subsequence problems in Chapter 3. In the following section, we will mention the main ideas behind two generally applicable hybrid metaheuristics from the literature: large neighborhood search (LNS), and construct, merge, solve & adapt (CMSA). A comprehensive introduction into the field of hybrid metaheuristics is provided, for example, in [BLU 16e].

1.2.7.1. *Large neighborhood search*

The LNS Algorithm (see [PIS 10] for an introduction) was introduced based on the following observation. As complete solvers are often only efficient for small to medium size problems, the following general idea might work very well. Given a problem for which the complete solver under consideration is no efficient longer, we generate a feasible solution in some way – for example, by means of a constructive heuristic – and try to improve this solution in the following way. First, we partially destroy the solution by removing some components of the solution. This can either be done in a purely random way or guided by a heuristic criterion. Afterwards, the complete solver is applied to the problem of finding the best valid solution to the original problem that includes all solution components of the given partial solution. As a partial solution is already given, the complexity of this problem is significantly lower and the complete solver might be efficiently used to solve it. This procedure is iteratively applied to an incumbent solution. In this way, LNS still profits from the advantages of the complete solver, even in the context of large problems.

The pseudo-code of a general LNS algorithm is provided in Algorithm 1.8. First, in line 2 of Algorithm 1.8, an initial incumbent solution S_{cur} is generated in the GenerateInitialSolution() function. This solution (S_{cur}) is then partially destroyed at each iteration, for example by removing some of its components. The number (or percentage) of components to be removed, as well as how these components are chosen, are important design decisions. The resulting partial solution $S_{partial}$ is fed to a complete solver; see function ApplyCompleteSolver($S_{partial}$, t_{max}) in line 6 of Algorithm 1.8. This function includes the current partial solution $S_{partial}$ and a time limit t_{max}. Note that the complete solver is forced to include $S_{partial}$ in any solution considered. The complete solver provides the best valid solution found within the computation time available t_{max}. This solution, denoted by S'_{opt}, may or may not be the optimal solution to the subproblem tackled. This depends on the given computation time limit t_{max} for each application of the complete solver. Finally, the last step of each iteration consists of a choice between S_{cur} and S'_{opt} to be the incumbent solution of the next iteration. Possible options are: (1) selecting the better one among the two; or (2) applying a probabilistic choice criterion.

1.2.7.2. Construct, merge, solve and adapt

The CMSA algorithm was introduced in [BLU 16b] with the same motivation that had already led to the development of LNS as outlined in the previous section. More specifically, the CMSA algorithm is designed in order to be able to profit from an efficient complete solver even in the context of problem that are too large to be directly solved by the complete solver. The general idea of CMSA is as follows. At each iteration, solutions to the problem tackled are generated in a probabilistic way. The components found in these solutions are then added to a sub-instance of the original problem. Subsequently, an exact solver such as, for example, CPLEX is used to solve the sub-instance to an optimal level. Moreover, the algorithm is equipped with a mechanism for deleting seemingly useless solution components from the sub-instance. This is done such that the sub-instance has a moderate size and can be quickly and optimally solved.

Algorithm 1.8. Large neighborhood search (LNS)

1: **input:** problem instance $\mathcal{I}$, time limit $t_{\max}$ for the complete solver

2: $S_{\text{cur}} \leftarrow$ GenerateInitialSolution()

3: $S_{\text{bsf}} \leftarrow S_{\text{cur}}$

4: **while** CPU time limit not reached **do**

5:    $S_{\text{partial}} \leftarrow$ DestroyPartially(S_{cur})

6:    $S'_{\text{opt}} \leftarrow$ ApplyCompleteSolver($S_{\text{partial}}, t_{\max}$)

7:    **if** S'_{opt} is better than S_{bsf} **then** $S_{\text{bsf}} \leftarrow S'_{\text{opt}}$

8:    $S_{\text{cur}} \leftarrow$ ApplyAcceptanceCriterion($S'_{\text{opt}}, S_{\text{cur}}$)

9: **end while**

10: **return** S_{bsf}

The pseudo-code of the CMSA algorithm is provided in Algorithm 1.9. Each algorithm iteration consists of the following actions. First, the best-so-far solution S_{bsf} is set to NULL, indicating that no such solution yet exists. Moreover, the restricted problem, C', which is simply a subset of the complete set, C, of solution components is set to the empty set[2]. Then, at each iteration, n_{a} solutions are probabilistically generated in function ProbabilisticSolutionGeneration(C); see line 6 of Algorithm 1.9. The components found in the solutions constructed are then added to C'. The so-called age of each of these solution components ($age[c]$) is set to 0. Next, a complete solver is applied in function ApplyExactSolver(C') to find a possible

---

2 In the context of the famous TSP for example, the complete set of solution components might consist of all the edges of the input graph.

optimal solution S'_{opt} to the restricted problem C'. If S'_{opt} is better than the current best-so-far solution S_{bsf}, solution S'_{opt} is taken as the new best-so-far solution. Next, sub-instance C' is adapted on the basis of solution S'_{opt} in conjunction with the age values of the solution components; see function Adapt(C', S'_{opt}, age_{max}) in line 14. This is done as follows. First, the age of each solution component in $C' \setminus S'_{\text{opt}}$ is incremented while the age of each solution component in $S'_{\text{opt}} \subseteq C'$ is re-set to zero. Subsequently, those solution components from C' with an age value greater than age_{max} – which is a parameter of the algorithm – are removed from C'. This means that solution components that never appear in solutions derived by the complete solver do not slow down the solver in subsequent iterations. Components which appear in the solutions returned by the complete solver should be maintained in C'.

Algorithm 1.9. Construct, merge, solve & adapt (CMSA)

1: **given:** problem instance $\mathcal{I}$, values for parameters n_{a} and age_{max}
2: $S_{\text{bsf}} \leftarrow$ NULL; $C' \leftarrow \emptyset$
3: $age[c] \leftarrow 0$ for all $c \in C$
4: **while** CPU time limit not reached **do**
5:     **for** $i \leftarrow 1, \dots, n_{\text{a}}$ **do**
6:         $S \leftarrow$ ProbabilisticSolutionGeneration(C)
7:         **for all** $c \in S$ **and** $c \notin C'$ **do**
8:             $age[c] \leftarrow 0$
9:             $C' \leftarrow C' \cup \{c\}$
10:         **end for**
11:     **end for**
12:     $S'_{\text{opt}} \leftarrow$ ApplyExactSolver(C')
13:     **if** S'_{opt} is better than S_{bsf} **then** $S_{\text{bsf}} \leftarrow S'_{\text{opt}}$
14:     Adapt(C', S'_{opt}, age_{max})
15: **end while**
16: **return** S_{bsf}

1.3. Outline of the book

The techniques outlined in the previous sections have been used extensively over recent decades to solve CO problems based on strings in the field of bioinformatics. Examples of such optimization problems dealing with strings include the longest common subsequence problem and its variants [HSU 84, SMI 81], string selection problems [MEN 05, MOU 12a, PAP 13], alignment problems [GUS 97, RAJ 01a] and similarity search [RAJ 01b]. We will focus on a collection of selected string problems and recent techniques for solving them in this book:

– Chapter 2 is concerned with a CO problem known as the *unbalanced minimum common string partition* (UMCSP) problem. This problem is a generalization of the *minimum common string partition* (MCSP) problem. First, an ILP model for the UMCSP problem is presented. Second, a simple greedy heuristic initially introduced for the MCSP problem is adapted to be applied to the UMCSP problem. Third, the application of the hybrid metaheuristic, CMSA (see section 1.2.7.2 for a general description of this technique), to the UMCSP problem is described. The results clearly show that the CMSA algorithm outperforms the greedy approach. Moreover, they show that the CMSA algorithm is competitive with CPLEX for small and medium problems whereas it outperforms CPLEX for larger problems.

– Chapter 3 deals with a family of string problems that are quite common in bio-informatics applications: longest common subsequence (LCS) problems. The most general problem from this class is simply known as the LCS problem. Apart from the general LCS problem, there is a whole range of specific problems that are mostly restricted cases of the general LCS problem. In this chapter we present the best available algorithms for solving the general LCS problem. In addition, we will deal with a specific restriction known as the repetition-free longest common subsequence (RFLCS) problem. An important landmark in the development of metaheuristics for LCS problems was the application of beam search to the general LCS problem in 2009 [BLU 09]. This algorithm significantly outperformed any other algorithm that was known at this time. Moreover, most algorithms proposed afterwards are based on this original beam search approach. After a description of the original beam search algorithm, Chapter 3 presents a hybrid metaheuristic called Beam–ACO. This algorithm is obtained by combining the ACO metaheuristic with beam search. Subsequently, the current state-of-the-art metaheuristic for the RFLCS problem is described. This algorithm is also a hybrid metaheuristic obtained by combining probabilistic solution construction with the application of an ILP solver to solve sub-instances of the original problem (see section 1.2.7.2 for a general description of this technique).

– Chapter 4 deals with an NP-hard string selection problem known as the *most strings with few bad columns* (MSFBC) problem. This problem models the following situation: a set of DNA sequences from a heterogeneous population consisting of two subgroups: (1) a large subset of DNA sequences that are identical apart from at most k positions at which mutations may have occurred; and (2) a subset of outliers. The goal of the MSFBC problem is to separate the two subsets. First, an ILP model for the MSFBC problem is described. Second, two variants of a rather simple greedy strategy are outlined. Finally, the current state-of-the-art metaheuristic for the MSFBC problem, which is a LNS approach, is described. The LNS algorithm makes use of the ILP solver CPLEX as a sub-routine in order to find, at each iteration, the best neighbor in a large neighborhood of the current solution. A comprehensive experimental comparison of these techniques shows that LNS, generally, outperforms both greedy strategies. While LNS is competitive with the stand-alone application of CPLEX for small and medium size problems, it outperforms CPLEX in the context of larger problems.

– Chapter 5 provides an overview over the best metaheuristic approaches for solving string selection and comparison problems, with a special emphasis on so-called *consensus string problems*. The intrinsic properties of the problems are outlined and the most popular solution techniques overviewed, including some recently-proposed heuristic and metaheuristic approaches. It also proposes a simple and efficient ILP-based heuristic that can be used for any of the problems considered. Future directions are discussed in the last section.

– Chapter 6 deals with the pairwise and the multiple alignment problems. Solution techniques are discussed, with special emphasis on the CO perspective, with the goal of providing conceptual insights and referencing literature produced by the broad community of researchers and practitioners.

– Finally, the last chapter describes the best metaheuristic approaches for some other string problems that are not dealt with in this book in more detail, such as several variants of DNA sequencing and the founder sequence reconstruction problem.

2

Minimum Common
String Partition Problem

This chapter deals with a combinatorial optimization (CO) problem from computational biology known as the *unbalanced minimum common string partition* (UMCSP) problem. The UMCSP problem includes the *minimum common string partition* (MCSP) problem as a special case. First, an ILP model for the UMCSP problem is described. Second, a greedy heuristic initially introduced for the MCSP problem is adapted for application to the UMCSP problem. Third, the application of a general hybrid metaheuristic labeled construct, merge, solve and adapt (CMSA) to the UMCSP problem is described. The CMSA algorithm is based on the following principles. At each iteration, the incumbent sub-instance is modified by adding solution components found in probabilistically constructed solutions to the problem tackled. Moreover, the incumbent sub-instance is solved to optimality (if possible) by means of an ILP solver such as CPLEX. Finally, seemingly useless solution components are removed from the incumbent sub-instance based on an ageing mechanism. The results obtained indicate that the CMSA algorithm outperforms the greedy approach. Moreover, they show that the CMSA algorithm is competitive with CPLEX for small and medium problems, whereas it outperforms CPLEX for larger problems. Note that this chapter is based on [BLU 13].

2.1. The MCSP problem

Given that the special case – that is, the MCSP problem – is easier to describe than the UMCSP, we will first describe the MCSP problem. The MCSP problem was introduced in [CHE 05] due to its association with genome rearrangement. It has applications in biological questions such as: may a given DNA string be obtained by rearranging another DNA string? There are two input strings s^1 and s^2 of length n over a finite alphabet Σ. The two strings need to be *related*, which means that each letter appears the same number of times in each of them. This definition implies that s^1 and s^2 are the same length n. A valid solution to the MCSP problem is obtained by partitioning s^1 into a set P_1 of non-overlapping substrings, and s^2 into a set P_2 of non-overlapping substrings, such that $P_1 = P_2$. Moreover, the goal is to find a valid solution such that $|P_1| = |P_2|$ is minimum.

Consider the following example with the DNA sequences $s^1 = $ **AGACTG** and $s^2 = $ **ACTAGG**. As **A** and **G** appear twice in both input strings, and **C** and **T** appear once, the two strings are related. A trivial valid solution can be obtained by partitioning both strings into substrings of length 1, i.e. $P_1 = P_2 = \{\textbf{A}, \textbf{A}, \textbf{C}, \textbf{T}, \textbf{G}, \textbf{G}\}$. The objective function value of this solution is 6. However, the optimal solution, with objective function value 3, is $P_1 = P_2 = \{\textbf{ACT}, \textbf{AG}, \textbf{G}\}$.

2.1.1. *Technical description of the UMCSP problem*

The more general UMCSP problem [BUL 13] can technically be described as follows with an input string s^1 of length n_1 and an input string s^2 of length n_2, both over the same finite alphabet Σ. A valid solution to the UMCSP problem is obtained by partitioning s^1 into a set P_1 of non-overlapping substrings, and s^2 into a set P_2 of non-overlapping substrings, such that a subset $S_1 \subseteq P_1$ and a subset $S_2 \subseteq P_2$ exist with $S_1 = S_2$ and no letter $a \in \Sigma$ is simultaneously present in a string $x \in P_1 \setminus S_1$ and a string $y \in P_2 \setminus S_2$. Henceforth, given P_1 and P_2, let us denote the largest subset $S_1 = S_2$ such that the above-mentioned condition holds by S^*. The objective function value of solution (P_1, P_2) is then $|S^*|$. The goal consists of finding solution (P_1, P_2) where $|S^*|$ is minimum.

Consider the following example with the DNA sequences $s^1 = \textbf{AAGACTG}$ and $s^2 = \textbf{TACTAG}$. Again, a trivial valid solution can be obtained by partitioning both strings into substrings of length 1, i.e. $P_1 = \{\textbf{A}, \textbf{A}, \textbf{A}, \textbf{C}, \textbf{T}, \textbf{G}, \textbf{G}\}$ and $P_2 = \{\textbf{A}, \textbf{A}, \textbf{C}, \textbf{T}, \textbf{T}, \textbf{G}\}$. In this case, $S^* = \{\textbf{A}, \textbf{A}, \textbf{C}, \textbf{T}, \textbf{G}\}$, and the objective function value is $|S^*| = 5$. However, the optimal solution, with objective function value 2, is $P_1 = \{\textbf{ACT}, \textbf{AG}, \textbf{A}, \textbf{G}\}$, $P_2 = \{\textbf{ACT}, \textbf{AG}, \textbf{T}\}$ and $S^* = \{\textbf{ACT}, \textbf{AG}\}$.

Note that the only difference between the UMCSP and the MCSP is that the UMCSP does not require the input strings to be related.

2.1.2. Literature review

The MCSP problem that was first studied in the literature, has been shown to be non-deteministic polynomial time (NP)-hard even in very restrictive cases [GOL 05]. The MCSP has been considered quite extensively by researchers dealing with the approximability of the problem. In [COR 07], for example, the authors proposed an $O(\log n \log^* n)$-approximation for the *edit distance with moves* problem, which is a more general case of the MCSP problem. Shapira and Storer [SHA 02] extended this result. Other approximation approaches to the MCSP problem have been proposed in [KOL 07]. In this context, the authors of [CHR 04] studied a simple greedy approach to the MCSP problem, showing that the approximation ratio concerning the 2-MCSP problem is 3 and for the 4-MCSP problem the approximation ratio is $\Omega(\log n)$. Note, in this context, that the notation k-MCSP refers to a restricted version of the MCSP problem in which each letter occurs at most k times in the input strings. In case of the general MCSP problem, the approximation ratio is between $\Omega(n^{0.43})$ and $O(n^{0.67})$, assuming that the input strings use an alphabet of size $O(\log n)$. Later, in [KAP 06] the lower bound was raised to $\Omega(n^{0.46})$. The authors of [KOL 05] proposed a modified version of the simple greedy algorithm with an approximation ratio of $O(k^2)$ for the k-MCSP. Recently, the authors of [GOL 11] proposed a greedy algorithm for the MCSP problem that runs in $O(n)$ time. Finally, in [HE 07] a greedy algorithm aiming to obtain better average results was introduced.

The first ILP model for the MCSP problem, together with an ILP-based heuristic, was proposed in [BLU 15b]. Later, more efficient ILP models were proposed in [BLU 16d, FER 15]. Regarding metaheuristics, the MCSP problem has been tackled by the following approaches:

1) a MAX–MIN Ant System (MMAS) by Ferdous and Sohel Rahman [FER 13a, FER 14];

2) a probabilistic tree search algorithm by Blum *et al.* [BLU 14a].

3) a CMSA algorithm by Blum *et al.* [BLU 16b].

As mentioned above, the UMCSP problem [BUL 13] is a generalization of the MCSP problem [CHE 05]. In contrast to the MCSP, the UMCSP has not yet been tackled by means of heuristics or metaheuristics. The only existing algorithm is a fixed-parameter approximation algorithm described in [BUL 13].

2.1.3. *Organization of this chapter*

The remaining parts of the chapter is organized as follows. The first ILP model in the literature for the UMCSP problem is described in section 2.2. In section 2.4, the application of CMSA to the UMCSP problem is outlined. Finally, section 2.5 provides an extensive experimental evaluation and section 2.6 presents a discussion on promising future lines of research concerning UMCSP.

2.2. An ILP model for the UMCSP problem

As a first step in the development of an ILP model, the UMCSP problem is re-phrased by making use of the *common block* concept. Given input strings s^1 and s^2, a *common block* b_i is denoted as a triplet (t_i, k_i^1, k_i^2), where t_i is a string which can be found starting at position $1 \leq k_i^1 \leq n_1$ in string s^1 and starting at position $1 \leq k_i^2 \leq n_2$ in string s^2. Let $B = \{b_1, \ldots, b_m\}$ be the complete set of common blocks. Moreover, let us assume that the blocks appear in B in no particular order. In addition, given a string t over alphabet Σ, let $n(t, a)$ denote the number of occurrences of letter $a \in \Sigma$ in t. That is $n(s^1, a)$, and respectively $n(s^2, a)$, denote the number of occurrences of letter $a \in \Sigma$ in input string s^1, and s^2 respectively. Then, a subset S of B corresponds to a valid solution to the UMCSP problem if and only if the following conditions hold:

1) $\sum_{b_i \in S} n(t_i, a) = \min\{n(s^1, a), n(s^2, a)\}$ for all $a \in \Sigma$. That is, the sum of the occurrences of a letter $a \in \Sigma$ in the common blocks present in S must be less than or equal to the minimum number of occurrences of letter a in s^1 and s^2.

2) For any two common blocks $b_i, b_j \in S$, $i \neq j$ the corresponding strings do not overlap in s^1 nor in s^2.

A possible ILP model for the UMCSP problem for each common block $b_i \in B$ uses a binary variable x_i, indicating whether or not the corresponding common block forms part of the solution. In other words, if $x_i = 1$, the corresponding common block b_i is selected for the solution, and if $x_i = 0$, common block b_i is not selected.

$$\min \sum_{i=1}^{m} x_i \tag{2.1}$$

$$\text{s.t.} \sum_{i \in \{1,\dots,m \mid k_i^1 \leq j < k_i^1 + |t_i|\}} x_i \leq 1 \qquad \text{for } j = 1, \dots, n_1 \tag{2.2}$$

$$\sum_{i \in \{1,\dots,m \mid k_i^2 \leq j < k_i^2 + |t_i|\}} x_i \leq 1 \qquad \text{for } j = 1, \dots, n_2 \tag{2.3}$$

$$\sum_{i=1}^{m} n(t_i, a) x_i = \min\{n(s^1, a), n(s^2, a)\} \qquad \text{for } a \in \Sigma \tag{2.4}$$

$$x_i \in \{0, 1\} \qquad \text{for } i = 1, \dots, m$$

Objective function [2.1] minimizes the number of common blocks selected. Equations [2.2] ensure that the strings corresponding to the common blocks selected do not overlap with respect to s^1 and equations [2.3] ensure the same with respect to s^2. Finally, equations [2.4] ensure that the number of occurrences of each letter in the selected strings is equal to the minimum number of occurrences of this letter in s^1 and s^2.

2.3. Greedy approach

The following greedy heuristic, henceforth called GREEDY, is an extension of the greedy heuristic from [HE 07] which was introduced for the MCSP problem. It starts with the empty partial solution and chooses at each construction step exactly one common block and adds it to the valid partial solution under construction. Therefore, $S \subset B$ is called a valid partial solution if the substrings corresponding to the common blocks in S do not overlap for s^1 or s^2. Furthermore, let set $Ext(S) \subset B \setminus S$ denote the set of common blocks that may be used to extend S such that the result is again a valid (partial) solution. Note that when $Ext(S) = \emptyset$, S corresponds to a complete solution. At each step GREEDY chooses the common block with the longest substring from $Ext(S)$. The pseudo-code of GREEDY is provided in Algorithm 2.1.

Algorithm 2.1. GREEDY

1: **given:** B
2: $S := \emptyset$
3: **while** $|Ext(S)| > 0$ **do**
4:     choose b_i such that $|t_i| \geq |t_j|$ for all $b_j \in Ext(S)$
5:     $S := S \cup \{b_i\}$
6: **end while**
7: **return** complete solution S

2.4. Construct, merge, solve and adapt

The drawback of exact solvers in the context of CO problems – especially for problems from computational biology – is often that they are not applicable to problems of realistic size. When small problems are considered, however, exact solvers are often extremely efficient. This is because a considerable amount of time, effort and expertise has gone into the development of exact solvers. Examples include general-purpose ILP solvers such as CPLEX and Gurobi. Having this in mind, recent research efforts have focused on ways of making use of exact solvers within heuristic frameworks even in the context of large problems. A recently-proposed algorithm labeled CMSA [BLU 16b, BLU 15a] falls into this line of research. A general description of this algorithm is provided in section 1.2.7.2. In short, the algorithm works as follows. At each iteration, solutions to the problem tackled are generated in a probabilistic way. The components found in these solutions are then added to an incumbent sub-instance of the original problem. Subsequently, an exact solver – CPLEX, in the case of this chapter – is used to optimally solve the incumbent sub-instance. Moreover, the algorithm makes use of a mechanism for deleting seemingly useless components from the incumbent sub-instance. This is done in order to prevent these solution components slowing down the exact solver when applied to the sub-instance.

More specifically, the CMSA algorithm applied to the UMCSP problem, whose pseudo-code is given in Algorithm 2.2, works as follows. It maintains an incumbent sub-instance B', which is a subset of the complete set B of common blocks. Moreover, each common block $b_i \in B$ has a non-negative age value denoted by $age[b_i]$. At the start of the algorithm, the best-so-far solution S_{bsf} is set to NULL, indicating that no such solution yet exists, and the sub-instance B' is set to the empty set. Then, at each iteration, a number of n_a solutions is probabilistically generated, see function ProbabilisticSolutionGeneration(B) in line 6 of Algorithm 2.2. The common blocks that form part of these solutions are added to B' and their age is re-set to 0. Afterwards, the ILP solver CPLEX is applied to optimally solve sub-instance B'. Note that if this is not possible within the given CPU time limit, CPLEX simply returns the best solution found so far; see function ApplyExactSolver(B') in line 12 of Algorithm 2.2. If S'_{opt} is better than the current best-so-far solution S_{bsf}, solution S'_{opt} replaces the best-so-far solution (line 13). Next, sub-instance B' is updated. This is done based on solution S'_{opt} and on the age values of the common blocks; see function Adapt(B', S'_{opt}, age_{max}) in line 14. The functions of this algorithm are comprehensively described in the following:

– ProbabilisticSolutionGeneration(B) function: to generate a solution in a probabilistic way, this function (see line 6 of Algorithm 2.2) makes use of the GREEDY algorithm described in section 2.3. However, instead of choosing, at each construction step, the common block with maximum sub-string length from $Ext(S)$, the choice of a common block $b_i \in Ext(S)$ is made as follows. First, a value $\delta \in [0, 1)$ is chosen uniformly at random. In case $\delta \leq d_{\text{rate}}$, b_i is chosen such that $|t_i| \geq |t_j|$ for all $b_j \in Ext(S)$, i.e. one of the common blocks whose substring is of maximum size is chosen. Otherwise, a candidate list L containing the (at most) l_{size} longest common blocks from $Ext(S)$ is built and

b_i is chosen from L uniformly at random. In other words, the greediness of this procedure depends on the values of two input parameters: (1) the determinism rate (d_{rate}); and (2) the candidate list size (l_{size}).

Algorithm 2.2. CMSA for the UMCSP problem

1: **given:** set B corresponding to the tackled problem instance, values for parameters n_a and $age_{\max}$

2: $S_{\text{bsf}} := \text{NULL}; \ B' := \emptyset$

3: $age[b_i] := 0$ for all $b_i \in B$

4: **while** CPU time limit not reached **do**

5:    **for** $i = 1, \ldots, n_a$ **do**

6:      $S := \text{ProbabilisticSolutionGeneration}(B)$

7:      **for all** $b_i \in S$ **and** $b_i \notin B'$ **do**

8:        $age[b_i] := 0$

9:        $B' := B' \cup \{b_i\}$

10:      **end for**

11:    **end for**

12:    $S'_{\text{opt}} := \text{ApplyExactSolver}(B')$

13:    **if** $|S'_{\text{opt}}| < |S_{\text{bsf}}|$ **then** $S_{\text{bsf}} := S'_{\text{opt}}$

14:    $\text{Adapt}(C', S'_{\text{opt}}, age_{\max})$

15: **end while**

16: **return** S_{bsf}

– ApplyExactSolver(B') function: CPLEX is used in order to find the best solution contained in a sub-instance B'. The ILP model outlined in section 2.2 is used for this purpose after replacing all occurrences of B in this ILP model with B' and by replacing m with $|B'|$.

– Adapt(B', S'_{opt}, $age_{\max}$) function: this function initially increases the age of all common blocks in $B' \setminus S'_{\text{opt}}$. Moreover, the age of all common blocks in $S'_{\text{opt}} \subseteq B'$ is re-set to zero. Then, those common blocks from B' whose age has reached the maximum component age ($age_{\max}$) are deleted from B'. This removes common blocks that never form part of the optimal solution to B' after some time in order to prevent them slowing down the ILP solver.

Algorithm 2.3. ProbabilisticSolutionGeneration(B) function

1: **given:** B, d_{rate}, l_{size}
2: $S := \emptyset$
3: **while** $|Ext(S)| > 0$ **do**
4:   choose a random number $\delta \in [0, 1]$
5:   **if** $\delta \leq d_{\text{rate}}$ **then**
6:     choose b_i such that $|t_i| \geq |t_j|$ for all $b_j \in Ext(S)$
7:     $S := S \cup \{b_i\}$
8:   **else**
9:     let $L \subseteq Ext(S)$ contain the (at most) l_{size} longest common blocks from $Ext(S)$
10:     choose b_i from L uniformly at random
11:     $S := S \cup \{b_i\}$
12:   **end if**
13: **end while**
14: **return** complete solution S

2.5. Experimental evaluation

We now present an experimental comparison between the two techniques presented so far in this chapter – namely GREEDY and CMSA. IBM ILOG CPLEX v12.2 is applied to each problem considered. The application of CPLEX is henceforth referred to as CPLEX. All code was implemented in ANSI C++ using GCC 4.7.3 to compile the software. In the context of CMSA and CPLEX, CPLEX was used in single-threaded mode. The experimental evaluation was performed on a cluster of PCs with Intel(R) Xeon(R) CPU 5670 CPUs of 12 nuclei of 2933 MHz and at least 40 GB of RAM. Note that the fixed- parameter approximation algorithm described in [BUL 13] was not included in the comparison because, according to the authors of this work, the algorithm is only applicable to very small problem.

In the following, first, the set of benchmarks that were generated to test the solution methods considered are described. Then, the tuning experiments that were performed in order to determine a proper setting for the parameters of CMSA are outlined. Finally, an exhaustive experimental evaluation is presented.

2.5.1. Benchmarks

A set of 600 benchmarks was generated for the comparison of the three solutions considered. The benchmark set consists of 10 randomly generated instances for each combination of *base-length* $n \in \{200, 400, \ldots, 1800, 2000\}$, alphabet size $|\Sigma| \in \{4, 12\}$, and *length-difference* $ld \in \{0, 10, 20\}$. Each letter of Σ has the same probability of appearing at any of positions in input strings s^1 and s^2. Given a value for the base-length n and the length-difference ld, the length of s^1 is determined as $n + \lfloor (ld \cdot n)/100 \rfloor$ and the length of s^2 as $n - \lfloor (ld \cdot n)/100 \rfloor$. In other words, ld refers to the difference in length between s^1 and s^2 (in percent) given a certain base-length, n.

2.5.2. Tuning CMSA

There are several parameters involved in CMSA for which well-working values must be found: (n_a) the number of solution constructions per iteration, (age_{max}) the maximum allowed age of common blocks, (d_{rate}) the determinism rate, (l_{size}) the candidate list size, and (t_{max}) the maximum time in seconds allowed for CPLEX per application to a sub-instance. The last parameter is necessary, because even when applied to reduced problems, CPLEX might still need too much computation time to optimally solve such sub-instances. CPLEX always returns the best feasible solution found within the given computation time.

n	n_a	age_{max}	d_{rate}	l_{size}	t_{max}
200	50	10	0.0	10	480
400	50	10	0.0	10	120
600	50	10	0.0	10	240
800	50	5	0.5	10	120
1000	50	10	0.7	10	60
1200	50	5	0.5	10	120
1400	50	10	0.9	10	480
1600	50	5	0.9	10	480
1800	50	5	0.9	10	480
2000	50	10	0.9	10	480

Table 2.1. *Results of tuning CMSA for the UMCSP problem using irace*

The automatic configuration tool irace [LÓP 11] was used to tune the five parameters. In fact, irace was applied to tune separately CMSA for each *base-length*, which – after initial experiments – seemed to be the parameter with the most influence on algorithm performance. For each of the 10 base-length values considered, 12 tunings were randomly generated: two for each of the six combinations of Σ and ld. The tuning process for each alphabet size was given a budget of CMSA 1,000 runs, where each run was given a computation time limit of $3,600$ CPU seconds. Finally, the following parameter value ranges were chosen for the five parameters of CMSA:

– $n_a \in \{10, 30, 50\}$;

– $age_{max} \in \{1, 5, 10, inf\}$, where *inf* means that no common block is ever removed from sub-instance B';

– where a value of 0.0 means that the selection of the next common block to be added to the partial solution under construction is always done randomly from the candidate list, while a value of 0.9 means that solution constructions are nearly deterministic;

– $l_{size} \in \{3, 5, 10\}$;

– $t_{max} \in \{60, 120, 240, 480\}$ (in seconds).

The tuning runs with irace produced the configurations of CMSA shown in Table 2.1. The most important tendencies that can be observed are the following ones. First, with growing base-length, the greediness of the solution constructed grows, as indicated by the increasing value of d_{rate}. Second, the number of solutions constructed per iteration is always high. Third, the time limit for CPLEX does not play any role for smaller instances. However, for larger instances the time limit of 480 seconds is consistently chosen.

2.5.3. Results

The numerical results concerning all instances with $|\Sigma| = 4$ are summarized in Table 2.2, and concerning all instances with $|\Sigma| = 12$ in Table 2.3. Each table row presents the results averaged over 10 problems of the same type. For each of the three methods in the comparison (at least) the first column (with the heading *mean*) provides the average values of the best solutions obtained over 10 problems, while the second column (*time*) provides the average computation time (in seconds) necessary to find the corresponding solutions. In the case of CPLEX, this column provides two values in the form X/Y, where X corresponds to the (average) time at which CPLEX was able to find the first valid solution, and Y to the (average) time at which CPLEX found the best solution within 3,600 CPU seconds. An additional column with the heading *gap* in the case of CPLEX provides the average optimality gaps (in percent), i.e. the average gaps between the upper bounds and the values of the best solutions when stopping a run. A third additional column in the case of CMSA (*size (%)*) provides the average size of the sub-instances considered in CMSA as a percentage of the original problem size, i.e. the sizes of the complete sets B of common blocks. Finally, note that the best result for each table row is marked with a gray background. The numerical results are presented graphically in Figures 2.1 and 2.2 in terms of the improvement of CMSA over CPLEX and GREEDY (in percent).

The results allow us to make the following observations:

– applying CPLEX to the original problems, the alphabet size has a strong influence on the problem difficulty. Where $|\Sigma| = 4$, CPLEX is only able to provide feasible solutions within 3,600 CPU seconds for input string lengths of up to 800. When $|\Sigma| = 12$, CPLEX provides feasible solutions for input string lengths of up to 1,600 (for $ld \in \{0, 10\}$). When $ld = 20$, CPLEX is able to provide feasible solutions for all problem instances;

– in contrast to CPLEX, CMSA provides feasible solutions for all problems. Moreover, CMSA outperforms GREEDY in all cases. In those cases in which CPLEX is able to provide feasible (or even optimal) solutions, CMSA is either competitive or not much worse than CPLEX. CMSA is never more than 3% worse than CPLEX.

a) Results for instances where $ld = 0$.

n	GREEDY		CPLEX			CMSA		
	mean	time	mean	time	gap	mean	time	size (%)
200	67.0	< 1.0	55.3	4/21	0.0	55.3	90.1	30.7
400	119.4	< 1.0	98.7	118/1445	2.1	99.4	1878.3	14.7
600	172.8	< 1.0	146.0	556/1865	6.7	145.7	2317.5	9.3
800	222.5	< 1.0	189.1	2136/3525	8.1	190.8	1837.3	5.0
1000	271.7	1.6	n.a	n.a.	n.a.	235.1	1320.3	6.1
1200	314.3	2.0	n.a	n.a.	n.a.	274.1	1837.9	3.5
1400	368.5	3.7	n.a	n.a.	n.a.	320.4	2455.8	2.6
1600	413.2	4.9	n.a	n.a.	n.a.	358.3	2875.8	2.0
1800	450.5	6.7	n.a	n.a.	n.a.	401.6	2802.1	1.7
2000	504.8	9.3	n.a	n.a.	n.a.	453.4	2166.7	1.5

b) Results for instances where $ld = 10$.

n	GREEDY		CPLEX			CMSA		
	mean	time	mean	time	gap	mean	time	size (%)
200	61.0	< 1.0	52.1	3/5	0.0	52.1	88.0	29.0
400	108.4	< 1.0	90.3	102/675	0.0	91.2	801.0	13.0
600	151.4	< 1.0	126.3	548/3018	2.5	127.3	1500.4	7.8
800	192.6	< 1.0	164.2	2038/3583	4.6	164.6	1513.2	3.6
1000	232.8	1.5	n.a.	n.a.	n.a.	198.3	2504.4	3.5
1200	269.8	1.9	n.a.	n.a.	n.a.	231.7	2334.2	2.2
1400	313.1	3.5	n.a.	n.a.	n.a.	267.6	2170.0	1.8
1600	346.6	4.6	n.a.	n.a.	n.a.	301.3	3114.6	1.3
1800	383.3	6.4	n.a.	n.a.	n.a.	330.9	2652.8	1.1
2000	423.1	8.8	n.a.	n.a.	n.a.	364.7	2512.3	1.0

c) Results for instances where $ld = 20$.

n	GREEDY		CPLEX			CMSA		
	mean	time	mean	time	gap	mean	time	size (%)
200	51.8	< 1.0	44.8	3/3	0.0	44.8	241.9	23.8
400	89.4	< 1.0	77.4	86/90	0.0	77.6	251.6	9.9
600	127.9	< 1.0	108.5	467/634	0.0	109.3	716.8	5.7
800	159.5	< 1.0	135.8	1941/2583	0.2	138.0	1009.4	2.8
1000	197.9	1.4	n.a.	n.a.	n.a.	169.6	1220.1	2.7
1200	229.9	1.7	n.a.	n.a.	n.a.	198.9	1659.6	1.7
1400	262.1	3.1	n.a.	n.a.	n.a.	229.2	2052.5	1.7
1600	294.4	4.1	n.a.	n.a.	n.a.	255.4	1830.2	1.2
1800	327.6	5.9	n.a.	n.a.	n.a.	284.5	2620.1	1.0
2000	359.0	8.1	n.a.	n.a.	n.a.	313.0	2160.0	1.0

Table 2.2. *Results for instances where* $|\Sigma| = 4$

a) Results for instances where $ld = 0$.

n	GREEDY		CPLEX			CMSA		
	mean	time	mean	time	gap	mean	time	size (%)
200	107.5	< 1.0	98.1	0/0	0.0	98.1	0.3	52.0
400	204.7	< 1.0	181.2	4/7	0.0	181.8	791.5	34.0
600	290.2	< 1.0	251.8	28/599	0.0	254.9	1710.8	23.2
800	379.5	< 1.0	328.1	134/1338	1.1	331.6	1020.8	18.3
1000	467.3	< 1.0	399.5	305/2413	1.6	403.7	1682.6	18.3
1200	537.5	1.0	468.7	672/2800	2.9	469.3	2057.3	12.7
1400	624.7	2.1	543.2	1089/2641	3.6	539.7	2108.7	10.3
1600	706.0	2.6	672.2	2193/2661	12.0	610.9	1875.5	8.7
1800	794.2	3.6	n.a.	n.a.	n.a.	694.2	2300.9	8.0
2000	876.3	5.1	n.a.	n.a.	n.a.	758.1	2356.0	7.4

b) Results for instances where $ld = 10$.

n	GREEDY		CPLEX			CMSA		
	mean	time	mean	time	gap	mean	time	size (%)
200	104.2	< 1.0	95.9	0/0	0.0	95.9	0.9	54.2
400	196.5	< 1.0	173.5	5/7	0.0	173.8	733.1	32.7
600	274.2	< 1.0	240.1	34/119	0.0	242.0	1275.3	22.7
800	354.1	< 1.0	304.9	109/903	0.2	308.3	605.0	16.0
1000	427.3	< 1.0	369.0	303/2035	0.3	373.9	1332.0	15.2
1200	502.6	1.0	433.3	550/2457	0.7	439.0	1615.6	10.8
1400	570.1	1.7	494.4	1011/2249	1.3	498.6	1146.7	9.4
1600	646.8	2.4	561.4	1738/3071	2.1	561.8	1493.3	7.1
1800	712.7	3.6	n.a.	n.a.	n.a.	621.0	1571.2	6.2
2000	776.5	4.3	n.a.	n.a.	n.a.	678.2	2079.4	5.6

c) Results for instances where $ld = 20$.

n	GREEDY		CPLEX			CMSA		
	mean	time	mean	time	gap	mean	time	size (%)
200	93.9	< 1.0	86.0	0/0	0.0	86.0	0.8	51.0
400	170.2	< 1.0	151.4	4/5	0.0	151.6	101.7	29.1
600	237.4	< 1.0	210.8	28/29	0.0	212.1	688.4	18.1
800	301.3	< 1.0	267.2	99/102	0.0	269.1	741.8	12.1
1000	365.6	< 1.0	323.1	250/277	0.0	326.2	425.6	11.6
1200	426.3	< 1.0	374.0	568/591	0.0	377.7	772.9	8.2
1400	484.4	1.4	426.6	997/1142	0.0	433.6	609.1	7.3
1600	542.0	2.0	477.1	1331/1640	0.2	484.7	792.4	5.5
1800	598.3	3.1	528.1	2043/2387	0.5	535.2	698.2	5.0
2000	663.2	4.1	680.5	2971/3132	7.1	587.7	518.5	5.2

Table 2.3. *Results for instances where* $|\Sigma| = 12$

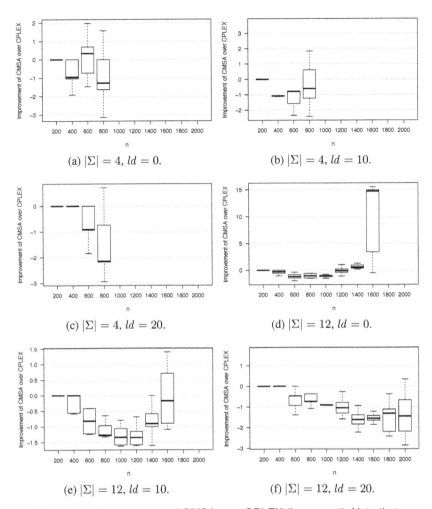

Figure 2.1. *Improvement of CMSA over CPLEX (in percent). Note that when boxes are missing, CPLEX was not able to provide feasible solutions within the computation time allowed*

In summary, CMSA is competitive when CPLEX is applied to the original ILP model when the size is rather small. The larger the size of the inputs, and the smaller the alphabet size, the greater the general advantage of CMSA over the other algorithms.

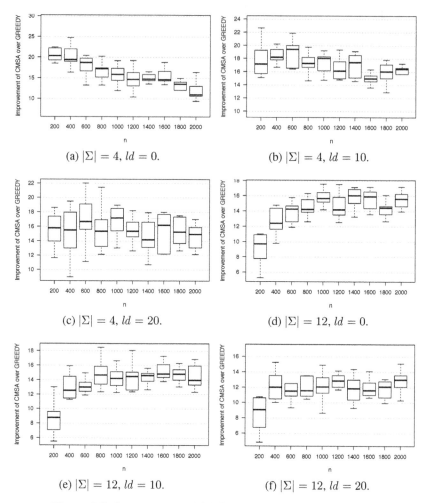

Figure 2.2. *Improvement of* CMSA *over* GREEDY *(in percent)*

Finally, the size of the sub-instances that are generated (and maintained) within CMSA in comparison to the size of the original problems are presented. These sub-instance sizes are provided in a graphical way in Figure 2.3. Note that these graphics show the sub-instance sizes averaged over all instances of the same alphabet size and the same ld value. In all cases, the x-axis ranges from instances with a small base-length (n) at the left, to instances with a large base-length at the right. Interestingly, when the base-length is rather small, the sub-instances tackled in CMSA are rather large (up to $\approx$ 55% of the size of the original problems). With growing base-length, the size of the sub-instances tackled decreases. The reason for this trend is as follows. As CPLEX is very efficient for problems created with rather small base-lengths, the parameter values of CMSA are chosen during the irace tuning process so that the sub-instance become quite large. With growing base-length, however, the parameter values chosen during tuning lead to smaller sub-instances, simply because CPLEX is not so efficient when applied to sub-instances that are not much smaller than the original problems.

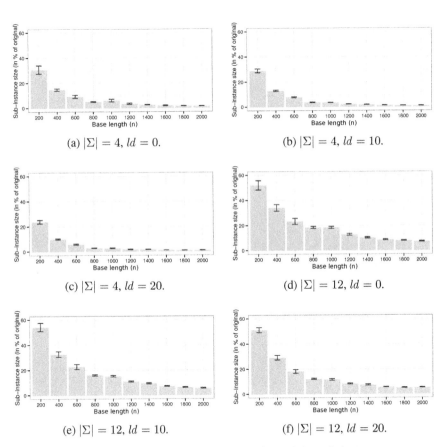

(a) $|\Sigma| = 4$, $ld = 0$.

(b) $|\Sigma| = 4$, $ld = 10$.

(c) $|\Sigma| = 4$, $ld = 20$.

(d) $|\Sigma| = 12$, $ld = 0$.

(e) $|\Sigma| = 12$, $ld = 10$.

(f) $|\Sigma| = 12$, $ld = 20$.

Figure 2.3. *Graphical presentation of the sizes of the sub-instances as a percentage of the size of the original problems*

2.6. Future work

For the UMCSP problem, pure metaheuristic approaches such as the MMAS algorithm from [FER 13a, FER 14] have been greatly outperformed by the application of CPLEX to the existing benchmarks. Understanding the reason for this will be an important step towards the development of pure metaheuristics – note that CMSA is a hybrid metaheuristic because it makes use of an ILP solver – for MCSP and UMCSP problems. This will be necessary as CPLEX and CMSA will reach their limits with growing problem size.

3

Longest Common Subsequence Problems

Longest common subsequence (LCS) problems frequently arise in bio-informatics applications. The most general problem in this class is simply known as the LCS problem. However, this problem class comprises a whole range of specific problems that are mostly restricted cases of the general LCS problem. Apart from the general LCS problem, we will also deal with one specific restriction known as the repetition-free longest common subsequence (RFLCS) problem in this chapter. An important landmark in the development of metaheuristics for LCS problems was the application of beam search to the general LCS problem in 2009. This algorithm significantly outperformed any other algorithm that was known at that time. Most approaches proposed thereafter have been based on beam search.

In this chapter, we will describe the original beam search approach to the general LCS problem. Moreover, we describe Beam–ACO, which is one of the more recent proposals based on beam search. This algorithm is obtained by combining the metaheuristic ant colony optimization (ACO) with beam search. After presenting the adaptation of the Beam–ACO algorithm to solve the RFLCS problem, we will describe current state-of-the-art metaheuristic for the RFLCS problem. This algorithm is a (IPL) hybrid metaheuristics obtained by combining probabilistic solution construction with the application of an integer linear programming of solver for sub-instances of the original problems. The general idea of this approach has been outlined in section 1.2.7.

3.1. Introduction

The classical LCS problem and some well-known restricted cases, including the RFLCS problem, are technically described in the following, followed by a literature review and an outline of the organization of this chapter.

3.1.1. *LCS problems*

First of all we introduce the general LCS problem. (S, Σ) of the LCS problem consists of a set $S = \{s_1, s_2, \ldots, s_n\}$ of n strings over a finite alphabet Σ. The problem consists of finding a longest string t^* that is a subsequence of all the strings in S. Such a string t^* is called the *longest common subsequence* of the strings in S. Note that string t is called a subsequence of string s if t can be produced from s by deleting characters. For example, *dga* is a subsequence of *adagtta*. As mentioned above, the problem has various applications in computational biology; see [SMI 81, JIA 02]. However, the problem has also been used in the context of more traditional computer science applications, such as data compression [STO 88], syntactic pattern recognition [LU 78], file comparison [AHO 83], text edition [SAN 83], query optimization in databases [SEL 88] and the production of circuits in field programmable gate arrays [BRI 04b].

The LCS problem was shown to be non-deterministic polynomial-time (NP)-hard [MAI 78] for an arbitrary number n of input strings. If n is fixed, the problem is polynomially solvable with dynamic programming [GUS 97]. Standard dynamic programming approaches for this problem require $O(l^n)$ of time and space, where l is the length of the longest input string and n is the number of strings. While several improvements may reduce the complexity of standard dynamic programming to $O(l^{n-1})$ ([BER 00] provide numerous references), dynamic programming quickly becomes impractical when n grows. An alternative to dynamic programming was proposed by Hsu and Du [HSU 84]. This algorithm was further improved in [EAS 07, SIN 07] by incorporating branch and bound (B&B) techniques. The resulting algorithm, called specialized branching (SB), has a complexity of $O(n|\Sigma||t^*|)$, where t^* is the LCS. According to the empirical results given by Easton and Singireddy [EAS 08], SB outperforms dynamic programming for large n and small l. Additionally, Singireddy [SIN 07] proposed an integer programming approach based on branch and cut.

Approximate methods for the LCS problem were first proposed by Chin and Poon [CHI 94] and Jiang and Li [JIA 95]. The long run (LR) algorithm [JIA 95] returns the longest common subsequence consisting of a single letter, which is always within a factor of $|\Sigma|$ of the optimal solution. The expansion algorithm (EXPANSION) proposed by Bonizzoni *et al.* [BON 01], and the Best-Next heuristic [FRA 95, HUA 04] also guarantee an approximation factor of $|\Sigma|$, however their results are typically much better than those of LR in terms of solution quality. Guenoche and Vitte [GUE 95] described a greedy algorithm that uses both forward and backward strategies and the resulting solutions are subsequently merged. Earlier approximate algorithms for the LCS problem can be found in Bergroth *et al.* [BER 98] and Brisk *et al.* [BRI 04b].

In 2007, Easton and Singireddy [EAS 08] proposed a large neighborhood search heuristic called time horizon specialized branching (THSB) that makes internal use of the SB algorithm. In addition, they implemented a variant of Guenoche and Vitte's algorithm [GUE 95], referred to as G&V, that selects the best solution obtained from running the original algorithm with four different greedy functions proposed by Guenoche [GUE 04]. Easton and Singireddy [EAS 08] compared their algorithm with G&V, LR and EXPANSION, showing that THSB was able to obtain better results than all the competitors in terms of solution quality. Their results also showed that G&V outperforms EXPANSION and LR with respect to solution quality, while requiring less computation time than EXPANSION and a computation time comparable to LR. Finally, Shyu and Tsai [SHY 09] studied the application of ACO to the LCS problem and concluded that their algorithm dominates both EXPANSION and Best-Next in terms of solution quality, while being much faster than EXPANSION.

A break-through both in terms of computation time and solution quality was achieved with the beam search (BS) approach described by Blum *et al.* in [BLU 09]. BS is an incomplete tree search algorithm which requires a solution construction mechanism and bounding information. Blum *et al.* used the construction mechanism of the Best-Next heuristic that was mentioned above and a very simple upper bound function. Nevertheless, the proposed algorithm was able to outperform all existing algorithms at that time. Later, Mousavi and Tabataba [MOU 12b] proposed an extended version of this BS algorithm in which they use a different heuristic function and a different pruning mechanism. Another extension of the BS algorithm from [BLU 09] is the so-called Beam–ACO approach that was proposed in [BLU 10]. Beam–ACO is a hybrid metaheuristic that combines the algorithmic framework of ACO with a probabilistic, adaptive, solution construction mechanism based on BS. Finally, Lozano and Blum [LOZ 10] presented another hybrid metaheuristic approach which is based on variable neighborhood search (VNS). This technique applies an iterated greedy algorithm in the improvement phase and generates the starting solutions by invoking either BS or a greedy randomized procedure.

3.1.1.1. *Restricted LCS problems*

Apart from the general LCS as mentioned above, various restricted problems have been tackled in the literature. Some of these are described in the following. Others are mentioned in survey papers such as [BON 10].

3.1.1.2. *Repetition-free longest common subsequence*

The repetition-free longest common sequence (RFLCS) problem is defined with two input strings s_1 and s_2 over a finite alphabet Σ. The goal is to find a longest common subsequence of s_1 and s_2 with the additional restriction that no letter may appear more than once in any valid solution. This problem was introduced in [ADI 08, ADI 10] as a comparison measure for two sequences of biological origin. In the same paper(s), the authors proposed three heuristics for solving this problem.

Three metaheuristic approaches were described in the literature for solving the RFLCS problem. The first one was the adaptation of the Beam–ACO algorithm [BLU 09] from the LCS problem to the RFLCS problem; see [BLU 14b]. A metaheuristic – particularly a genetic algorithm – specifically designed for the RFLCS problem can be found in [CAS 13]. Finally, the current state-of-the-art method is a construct, merge, solve and adapt (CMSA) approach that was presented by Blum and Blesa in [BLU 16a]. This last approach generates, at each iteration, sub-instances of the original problems and solves these by means of an integer linear programming (ILP) solver.

Bonizzoni *et al.* [BON 07] studied some variants of the RFLCS, such as the one in which some symbols are required to appear in the solution sought possibly more than once. They showed that these variants are approximable (APX)-hard and that, in some cases, the problem of deciding the feasibility of an instance is NP-complete.

3.1.1.3. *Constrained longest common subsequence*

The constrained longest common subsequence (C-LCS) problem was introduced in [TSA 03] for the case in which a longest common subsequence must be found for two input strings s_1 and s_2 over alphabet Σ that have a known common substructure. More specifically, given two input strings s_1 and s_2 and a third string s_c, the C-LCS seeks the longest common subsequence of s_1 and s_2 that is also a supersequence of s_c. Note that for this particular problem variant, polynomial time algorithms exist [TSA 03, CHI 04]. However, when the problem is generalized to a set of input strings, or to a set of constraint strings, the problem is NP-hard [GOT 08]. A dynamic programming algorithm for the problem is presented in [ZHU 15].

3.1.1.4. *Generalized constrained longest common subsequence*

This problem was tackled in [CHE 11b]. Given two input strings s_1 and s_2 over an alphabet Σ, and a third string t (called the pattern), the task is to find the longest common subsequence of s_1 and s_2 that includes (or excludes) t as a subsequence (or as a substring). The authors propose dynamic programming algorithms for solving the GC-LCS problem in $\mathcal{O}(nmr)$, where n is the length of s_1, m the length of s_2, and r the length of t.

3.1.2. *ILP models for LCS and RFLCS problems*

The LCS problem can be stated in terms of an integer linear program in the following way. Let us denote the length of any input string s_i by $|s_i|$. The positions in string s_i are numbered from 1 to $|s_i|$. The letter at position j of s_i is denoted by $s_i[j]$. The set Z of binary variables that is required for the ILP model is composed as follows. For each combination of indices $1 \leq k_i \leq |s_i|$ for all $i = 1, \ldots, n$ such that $s_1[k_1] = \ldots = s_n[k_n]$, set Z contains a binary variable $z_{k_1, \ldots, k_n}$. Consider, as an example, instance $I := (S = \{s_1, s_2, s_3\}, \Sigma = \{a, b, c, d\})$, where $s_1 = dbcadcc$, $s_2 = acabadd$ and $s_3 = bacdcdd$. In this case set Z would consist of 22 binary variables: three variables concerning letter a ($z_{4,1,2}$, $z_{4,3,2}$ and $z_{4,5,2}$), one variable concerning letter b ($z_{2,4,1}$), six variables concerning letter c (such as $z_{3,2,3}$ and $z_{6,2,5}$) and 12 variables concerning letter d (such as $z_{1,6,4}$ and $z_{5,7,4}$). Moreover, we say that two variables $z_{k_1,...,k_n} \neq z_{l_1,...,l_n}$ are in conflict, if and only if two indices exist $i \neq j$ such that $k_i \leq l_i$ and $k_j \geq l_j$. Concerning the problem mentioned above, variable pairs ($z_{4,1,2}, z_{4,3,2}$) and ($z_{4,5,2}, z_{3,2,3}$), are in conflict, whereas variable pair ($z_{4,1,2}, z_{6,2,5}$) is not in conflict. The LCS problem can then be rephrased as the problem of selecting the maximum number of non-conflicting variables from Z. With these notations, the ILP for the LCS problem is stated as follows:

$$\mathbf{max} \sum_{z_{k_1,...,k_n} \in Z} z_{k_1,...,k_n} \qquad [3.1]$$

subject to:

$$z_{k_1,...,k_n} + z_{l_1,...,l_n} \leq 1 \quad \text{for all } z_{k_1,...,k_n} \neq z_{l_1,...,l_n} \text{ being in conflict} \qquad [3.2]$$

$$z_{k_1,...,k_n} \in \{0,1\} \quad \text{for } z_{k_1,...,k_n} \in Z \qquad [3.3]$$

Therefore, constraints [3.2] ensure that selected variables are not in conflict.

In the case of the RFLCS problem, one set of constraints has to be added to the ILP model outlined above in order to ensure that a solution contains each letter from Σ a maximum of once. In this context, let $Z_a \subset Z$ denote the subset of Z that contains all variables z_{k_1,k_2} such that $s_1[k_1] = s_2[k_2] = a$, for all $a \in \Sigma$[1]. The ILP model for the RFLCS problem is then stated as follows:

$$\mathbf{max} \sum_{z_{k_1,k_2} \in Z} z_{k_1,k_2} \qquad [3.4]$$

subject to:

$$\sum_{z_{k_1,k_2} \in Z_a} z_{k_1,k_2} \leq 1 \quad \text{for } a \in \Sigma \qquad [3.5]$$

$$z_{k_1,k_2} + z_{l_1,l_2} \leq 1 \quad \text{for all } z_{k_1,k_2} \neq z_{l_1,l_2} \text{ being in conflict} \qquad [3.6]$$

$$z_{k_1,k_2} \in \{0,1\} \quad \text{for } z_{k_1,k_2} \in Z \qquad [3.7]$$

---

1 Remember that the RFLCS problem is only defined for two input strings: s_1 and s_2.

3.1.3. *Organization of this chapter*

This chapter is organized as follows. Section 3.2 presents the original BS algorithm for the LCS problem. Moreover, a Beam–ACO metaheuristic is described. This section concludes with an experimental evaluation of both algorithms on a benchmark set for the LCS problem. Algorithms for the RFLCS problem are outlined in section 3.3. We will describe CMSA, which is the current state-of-the-art technique for the RFLCS problem. This section concludes with an experimental evaluation. Finally, the chapter ends with conclusions and some interesting future lines of research.

3.2. Algorithms for the LCS problem

3.2.1. *Beam search*

BS is an incomplete derivative of B&B that was introduced in [RUB 77]. In the following sections, we will describe the specific variant of BS (from [BLU 09]) that was used to solve the LCS problem. The central idea behind BS is to allow the extension of partial solutions in several possible ways. In each step, the algorithm chooses at most $\lfloor \mu k_{bw} \rfloor$ feasible extensions of the partial solutions stored in a set B, which is called the *beam*. Therefore, k_{bw} is the *beam width* that serves as an upper limit for the number of partial solutions in B and $\mu \geq 1$ is a parameter of the algorithm. Feasible extensions are chosen in a deterministic way by means of a greedy function that gives a weight to each feasible extension. At the end of each step, a new beam B is obtained by selecting up to k_{bw} partial solutions from the set of chosen feasible extensions. For this purpose, BS algorithms calculate – in the case of maximization – an upper bound value for each chosen extension. Only the maximally k_{bw} best extensions – with respect to the upper bound – are added to the new B set. Finally, the best complete solution generated in this way is returned.

BS has been applied in quite a number of research papers in recent decades. Examples include scheduling problems [OW 88, SAB 99, GHI 05], berth allocation [WAN 07], assembly line balancing [ERE 05] and circular packing [AKE 09]. Crucial components of BS are: (1) the constructive heuristic that defines the feasible extensions of partial solutions; (2) the upper bound function for evaluating partial solutions. The application of BS to the LCS problem is described by focusing on these two crucial components.

3.2.1.1. *Constructive heuristic*

BEST-NEXT [FRA 95, HUA 04] is a fast heuristic for the LCS problem. It produces a common subsequence t from left to right, adding exactly one letter from Σ to the current subsequence at each construction step. The algorithm stops when no further letters can be added without producing an invalid solution. The pseudo-code is provided in Algorithm 3.1.

Algorithm 3.1. BEST-NEXT heuristic for the LCS problem

1: **input:** a problem $(\mathcal{S}, \Sigma)$
2: **initialization:** $t := \epsilon$ (where ϵ denotes the empty string)
3: **while** $|\Sigma_t^{\mathrm{nd}}| > 0$ **do**
4:     $a := \mathsf{Choose\_From}(\Sigma_t^{\mathrm{nd}})$
5:     $t := ta$
6: **end while**
7: **output:** common subsequence t

For a detailed technical description of how BEST-NEXT works, let us consider problem $I = (\mathcal{S} = \{s_1, s_2, s_3\}, \Sigma = \{a, b, c, d\})$, where $s_1 = dbcadcc$, $s_2 = acabadd$ and $s_3 = bacdcdd$. Given a partial solution t to problem $(\mathcal{S}, \Sigma)$, BEST-NEXT makes use of the following:

1) given a partial solution t, each input string s_i can be split into substrings x_i and y_i, i.e. $s_i = x_i \cdot y_i$, such that t is a subsequence of x_i and y_i is of maximum length;

2) given a partial solution t, for each $s_i \in \mathcal{S}$ we introduce a position pointer $p_i := |x_i|$, i.e. p_i points to the last character in x_i, assuming that the first character of a string has position one. The partition of input strings s_i into substrings as well as the corresponding position pointers are shown with respect to example I and the partial solution $t = ba$ in Figure 3.1;

3) the *position in which a letter first appears* $a \in \Sigma$ in a string $s_i \in \mathcal{S}$ after the position pointer p_i is well-defined and denoted by p_i^a. When letter $a \in \Sigma$ does not appear in y_i, p_i^a is set to ∞. This is also shown in Figure 3.1;

4) letter $a \in \Sigma$ is *dominated* if there is at least one letter $b \in \Sigma$, $a \neq b$, such that $p_i^b < p_i^a$ for $i = 1, \ldots, n$. Consider, for example, partial solution $t = b$ in the context of example I. In this case, a dominates d, as letter a always appears before letter d in y_i ($\forall\, i \in \{1, 2, 3\}$);

5) $\Sigma_t^{\mathrm{nd}} \subseteq \Sigma$ denotes the set of non-dominated letters with respect to partial solution t. Obviously letter $a \in \Sigma_t^{\mathrm{nd}}$ appears in each string s_i at least once after the position pointer p_i.

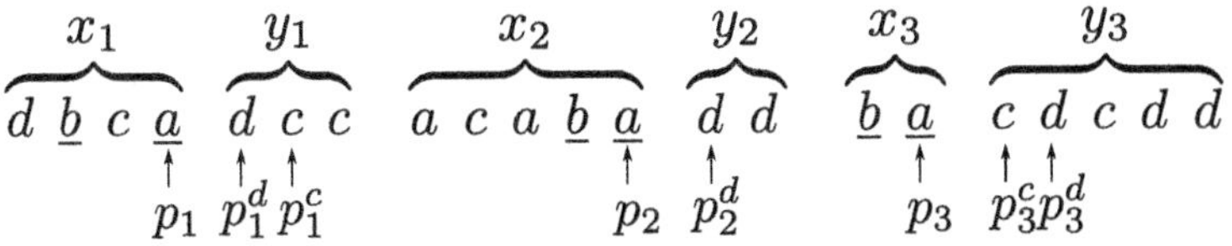

Figure 3.1. *Consider example $I := (S = \{s_1, s_2, s_3\}, \Sigma = \{a, b, c, d\})$, where $s_1 = dbcadcc$, $s_2 = acabadd$, and $s_3 = bacdcdd$. Let $t = ba$ be the current partial solution. Figures a), b), and c) show the separation of s_i into x_i and y_i. In addition, position pointers p_i and the next positions of the four letters in y_i are indicated. If, for some i, y_i does not contain a specific letter, the corresponding pointer is set to ∞. This happens, for example, in the case of letters a and b in y_1: $p_1^a := \infty$ and $p_1^b := \infty$*

In Function Choose_From(Σ_t^{nd}) – see line 4 of Algorithm 3.1 – exactly one letter is chosen from Σ_t^{nd} at each iteration. Subsequently, the chosen letter is appended to t. The choice of a letter is made by means of a *greedy function*. We then present the greedy function (labeled $\eta(.|.)$) that works well in the context of the problems considered in this chapter:

$$\eta(a|t) := \left(\sum_{i=1,\ldots,n} \frac{p_i^a - p_i}{|y_i|} \right)^{-1} , \forall\, a \in \Sigma_t^{\mathrm{nd}} \tag{3.8}$$

This greedy function calculates the average length of the remaining parts of all strings after the next occurrence of letter a after the position pointer. Function Choose_From(Σ_t^{nd}) chooses $a \in \Sigma_t^{\mathrm{nd}}$ such that $\eta(a|t) \geq \eta(b|t)$ for all $b \in \Sigma_t^{\mathrm{nd}}$. In the case of ties, the lexicographically smallest letter is taken.

3.2.2. Upper bound

In addition to the mechanism for extending partial solutions based on a greedy function, the second crucial aspect of BS is the upper bound function for evaluating partial solutions. Remember that any common subsequence t splits each string $s_i \in \mathcal{S}$ into a first part x_i and a second part y_i, i.e. $s_i = x_i \cdot y_i$. In this context, let $|y_i|_a$ denote the number of occurrences of letter $a \in \Sigma$ in y_i. The upper bound value of t is then defined as follows:

$$\mathrm{UB}(t) := |t| + \sum_{a \in \Sigma} \min\left\{|y_i|_a \mid i = 1, \ldots, n\right\} \qquad [3.9]$$

This upper bound is obtained by totalling $a \in \Sigma$ the minimum number (over $i = 1, \ldots, n$) of occurrences of each letter in y_i and adding the resulting sum to the length of t. Consider, as an example, partial solution $t = ba$ concerning the problems shown in Figure 3.1. As letters a, b and c do not occur in the remaining part of input string s_2, they do not contribute to the upper bound value. Letter d appears at least once in each y_i ($\forall\ i \in \{1,2,3\}$). Therefore, the upper bound value of ba is $|ba| + 1 = 2 + 1 = 3$.

Finally, note that this upper bound function can be computed efficiently by keeping appropriate data structures. Even though the resulting upper bound values are not very tight, experimental results have shown that it is capable of guiding the search process of BS effectively.

3.2.3. Beam search framework

The BS algorithm framework for the LCS problem, which is pseudo-coded in Algorithm 3.2, works roughly as follows. Apart from problem $(\mathcal{S}, \Sigma)$, the algorithm asks for values for two input parameters: (1) the *beam width* ($k_{\mathrm{bw}} \in \mathbb{Z}^+$; and (2) a parameter used to determine the number of extensions that can be chosen in each step ($\mu \in \mathbb{R}^+ \geq 1$). In each step of the algorithm, there is also a set B of subsequences called the *beam*. At the start of the algorithm, B contains only the empty string denoted by ϵ, i.e. $B := \{\epsilon\}$. Let E_B denote the set of all possible extensions of the partial solutions – i.e. common subsequences – from B. In this context, remember that a subsequence t is extended by appending exactly one letter from Σ_t^{nd}. At each step, the best $\lfloor \mu k_{\mathrm{bw}} \rfloor$ extensions from E_B are selected with respect to the greedy function $\eta(.|.)$. When a chosen extension is a complete solution, it is stored in set B_{compl}. When it is not, it is added to the beam of the next step. However, this is only done when its upper bound value, UB(), is greater than the length of the best solution so far t_{bsf}. At the end of each step, the new beam B is reduced (if necessary) to k_{bw} partial solutions. This is done by evaluating the subsequences in B by means of the upper bound function UB() and by selecting the k_{bw} subsequences with the greatest upper bound values.

Algorithm 3.2. BS for the LCS problem

1: **input:** a problem $(\mathcal{S}, \Sigma)$, k_{bw}, μ
2: $B_{\text{compl}} := \emptyset$, $B := \{\epsilon\}$, $t_{\text{bsf}} := \epsilon$
3: **while** $B \neq \emptyset$ **do**
4:     $E_B :=$ Produce_Extensions(B)
5:     $E_B :=$ Filter_Extensions(E_B)
6:     $B := \emptyset$
7:     **for** $k = 1, \ldots, \min\{\lfloor \mu k_{\text{bw}} \rfloor, |E_B|\}$ **do**
8:         $za :=$ Choose_Best_Extension(E_B)
9:         $t := za$
10:        **if** UB$(t) = |t|$ **then**
11:            $B_{\text{compl}} := B_{\text{compl}} \cup \{t\}$
12:            **if** $|t| > |t_{\text{bsf}}|$ **then** $t_{\text{bsf}} := t$ **end if**
13:        **else**
14:            **if** UB$(t) \geq |t_{\text{bsf}}|$ **then** $B := B \cup \{t\}$ **end if**
15:        **end if**
16:        $E_B := E_B \setminus \{t\}$
17:    **end for**
18:    $B :=$ Reduce(B, k_{bw})
19: **end while**
20: **output:** argmax $\{|t| \mid t \in B_{\text{compl}}\}$

The BS algorithm for the LCS problem uses four different functions. Given the current beam B as input, function Produce_Extensions(B) generates the set E_B of non-dominated extensions of all the subsequences in B. More specifically, E_B is a set of subsequences ta, where $t \in B$ and $a \in \Sigma_t^{\text{nd}}$.

The second function, Filter_Extensions(E_B), weeds out the dominated extensions from E_B. This is done by extending the non-domination relation that was defined in section 3.2.1.1 for two different extensions of one specific subsequence to the extensions of different subsequences of the same length. Formally, given two extensions $ta, zb \in E_B$, where $t \neq z$ but not necessarily $a \neq b$, ta dominates zb if and only if the position pointers concerning a appear before the position pointers concerning b in the corresponding remaining parts of the n strings.

The third function, Choose_Best_Extension(E_B), is used to choose extensions from E_B. Note that for the comparison of two extensions ta and zb from E_B, the greedy function is only useful where $t = z$, while it might be misleading where $t \neq z$. This problem is solved as follows. First, the weights assigned by the greedy function are replaced with the corresponding ranks. More specifically, given all extensions $\{ta \mid a \in \Sigma_t^{\text{nd}}\}$ of a subsequence t, the extension tb with $\eta(b|t) \geq \eta(a|t)$ for all $a \in \Sigma_t^{\text{nd}}$ receives rank 1, denoted by $r(b|t) = 1$. The extension with the second highest greedy weight receives rank 2, etc. The evaluation of an extension ta is then made on the basis of the sum of the ranks of the greedy weights that correspond to the steps performed to construct subsequence ta, i.e.

$$\nu(a|t) := r(t_1|\epsilon) + \left(\sum_{i=2}^{|t|} r(t[i]|t[1...i-1]) \right) + r(a|t) \qquad [3.10]$$

where $t[1...i]$ is the prefix of t from position 1 to position i and $t[i]$ the letter at position i of string t. Note that, in contrast to the greedy function weights, these newly defined $\nu()$ values can be used to compare extensions of different subsequences. In fact, a call of function Choose_Best_Extension(E_B) returns the extension from E_B with maximum $\nu()^{-1}$ value.

Finally, the last function used within the BS algorithm is Reduce(B, k_{bw}). Where $|B| > k_{\text{bw}}$, this function removes from B step-by-step those subsequences t that have an upper bound value UB(t) smaller or equal to the upper bound value of that are the other subsequences in B. The removal process stops once $|B| = k_{\text{bw}}$.

3.2.4. Beam–ACO

Beam–ACO, which is a general hybrid metaheuristic that was first introduced in [BLU 05], works roughly as follows. At each iteration, a probabilistic BS algorithm is applied, based both on greedy/pheromone information and on bounding information. The solutions constructed are used to update the pheromone values. In other words, the algorithmic framework of Beam–ACO is that of ACO; see section 1.2.1 for an introduction to ACO. However, instead of performing a number of sequential and independent solution constructions per iteration, a probabilistic BS algorithm is applied.

3.2.4.1. Pheromone model

One of the most important aspects of any ACO algorithm is the pheromone model, $\mathcal{T}$. In the case of the LCS problem, coming up with a pheromone model is not immediately intuitive. In [BLU 10], the authors finally defined a pheromone model, $\mathcal{T}$, that for each position j of a string $s_i \in S$ contains a pheromone value $0 \le \tau_{ij} \le 1$, i.e. $\mathcal{T} = \{\tau_{ij} \mid i = 1, \ldots, n, \ j = 1, \ldots, |s_i|\}$. Note that $\tau_{ij} \in \mathcal{T}$ represents the benefit of adding the letter at position j in the string s_i to the solution under construction: the greater τ_{ij}, the greater the aim of adding the corresponding letter. Based on this pheromone model, solutions in Beam–ACO – henceforth called ACO-solutions – can be represented in a specific way. Note that any common subsequence t of the strings in S – that is, any solution t – can be translated into a unique ACO-solution $T = \{T_{ij} \in \{0,1\} \mid i = 1, \ldots, n, \ j = 1, \ldots, |s_i|\}$ in a well-defined way which works as follows: for each string $s_i \in S$ the positions of the letters of t in s_i are determined in such a way that each letter is in the farthest left position possible. These positions j are set to 1 in T – that is, $T_{ij} = 1$ – and $T_{ij} = 0$ otherwise. For example, consider $S = \{dbcadcc, acabadd, bacdcdd\}$ from Figure 3.1 and a possible solution $t = bad$. This solution translates into the ACO-solution $T = \{0101100, 0001110, 1101000\}$.

3.2.4.2. Algorithm framework

In the following we outline the Beam–ACO approach for the LCS problem which was originally proposed in [BLU 10]. This Beam–ACO approach is based on a standard min-max ant system (MMAS) implemented in the hyper-cube framework (HCF); see [BLU 04]. The algorithm is pseudo-coded in Algorithm 3.3. The data structures of this algorithm are: (1) the best solution so far T^{bs}, i.e. the best solution generated since the start of the algorithm; (2) the *restart-best* solution T^{rb}, i.e. the best solution generated since the last restart of the algorithm; (3) the *convergence factor cf*, $0 \leq cf \leq 1$, which is a measure of the state of convergence of the algorithm; (4) the Boolean variable *bs_update*, which assumes the value TRUE when the algorithm reaches convergence.

Algorithm 3.3. Beam–ACO for the LCS problem

1: **input:** $k_{\mathrm{bw}}, \mu \in \mathbb{Z}^+$
2: $T^{\mathrm{bs}} :=$ NULL, $T^{\mathrm{rb}} :=$ NULL, $cf := 0$, *bs_update* := FALSE
3: $\tau_{ij} := 0.5$, $i = 1, \ldots, n, j = 1, \ldots, |s_i|$
4: **while** CPU time limit not reached **do**
5:    $T^{\mathrm{pbs}} :=$ ProbabilisticBeamSearch(k_{bw},μ) {see Alg. 3.2.}
6:    **if** $|t^{pbs}| > |t^{\mathrm{rb}}|$ **then** $T^{\mathrm{rb}} := T^{\mathrm{pbs}}$
7:    **if** $|t^{pbs}| > |t^{\mathrm{bs}}|$ **then** $T^{\mathrm{bs}} := T^{\mathrm{pbs}}$
8:    ApplyPheromoneUpdate(cf,*bs_update*,$\mathcal{T}$,T^{pbs},T^{rb},T^{bs})
9:    $cf :=$ ComputeConvergenceFactor($\mathcal{T}$)
10:    **if** $cf > 0.99$ **then**
11:      **if** *bs_update* = TRUE **then**
12:        $\tau_{ij} := 0.5$, $i = 1, \ldots, n, j = 1, \ldots, |s_i|$
13:        $T^{\mathrm{rb}} :=$ NULL
14:        *bs_update* := FALSE
15:      **else**
16:        *bs_update* := TRUE
17:      **end if**
18:    **end if**
19: **end while**
20: **output:** t^{bs} (that is, the string version of T^{bs})

After the initialization of the pheromone values to 0.5, each iteration consists of the following steps. First, the BS from section 3.2.1 is applied in a probabilistic way, guided by greedy information and pheromone values. This results in a solution, T^{pbs}. Second, the pheromone update is conducted in function ApplyPheromoneUpdate(cf, *bs_update*, $\mathcal{T}$, T^{pbs}, T^{rb}, T^{bs}). Third, a new value for the convergence factor cf is computed. Depending on this value, as well as on the value of the Boolean variable *bs_update*, a decision on whether or not to restart the algorithm is made. If the algorithm is restarted, all the pheromone values are reset to their initial value (i.e. 0.5). The algorithm is iterated until a maximum computation time limit is reached. Once terminated, the algorithm returns the string version t^{bs} of the best-so-far ACO-solution T^{bs}, the best solution found. We will describe the two remaining procedures in Algorithm 3.3 in more detail:

– ApplyPheromoneUpdate(cf,bs_update,$\mathcal{T}$,T^{pbs},T^{rb},T^{bs}):   as usual in MMAS algorithms implemented in the HCF, three solutions are used update pheromone values. These are solution T^{pbs} generated by BS, the restart-best solution T^{rb} and the best solution so far T^{bs}. The influence of each solution on pheromone update depends on the state of convergence of the algorithm, as measured by the convergence factor cf. Each pheromone value $\tau_{ij} \in \mathcal{T}$ is updated as follows:

$$\tau_{ij} := \tau_{ij} + \rho \cdot (\xi_{ij} - \tau_{ij}), \qquad\qquad [3.11]$$

where:

$$\xi_{ij} := \kappa_{pbs} \cdot T_{ij}^{pbs} + \kappa_{rb} \cdot T_{ij}^{rb} + \kappa_{bs} \cdot T_{ij}^{bs}, \qquad\qquad [3.12]$$

where κ_{pbs} is the weight (i.e. the influence) of solution T^{pbs}, κ_{rb} is the weight of solution T^{rb}, κ_{bs} is the weight of solution T^{bs} and $\kappa_{pbs} + \kappa_{rb} + \kappa_{bs} = 1$. After the pheromone update rule (equation [3.11]) is applied, pheromone values that exceed $\tau_{max} = 0.999$ are set back to τ_{max} and those pheromone values that fall below $\tau_{min} = 0.001$ are set back to τ_{min}. This is done in order to avoid a complete convergence of the algorithm, which is a situation that should be avoided. Equation [3.12] allows us to choose how to weight the relative influence of the three solutions used for updating the pheromone values. For application to the LCS problem, a standard update schedule as shown in Table 3.1 was used.

– ComputeConvergenceFactor($\mathcal{T}$): the convergence factor cf, which is a function of the current pheromone values, is computed as follows:

$$cf := 2 \left(\left(\frac{\displaystyle\sum_{\tau_{ij} \in \mathcal{T}} \max\{\tau_{max} - \tau_{ij}, \tau_{ij} - \tau_{min}\}}{|\mathcal{T}| \cdot (\tau_{max} - \tau_{min})} \right) - 0.5 \right)$$

Note that when the algorithm is initialized (or reset) it holds that $cf = 0$. When the algorithm has converged, then $cf = 1$. In all other cases, cf has a value in $(0, 1)$. This completes the description of the learning component of our Beam–ACO approach for the LCS problem.

| | $bs_update = $ FALSE | | | | bs_update |
	$cf < 0.4$	$cf \in [0.4, 0.6)$	$cf \in [0.6, 0.8)$	$cf \geq 0.8$	$=$ TRUE
κ_{pbs}	1	2/3	1/3	0	0
κ_{rb}	0	1/3	2/3	1	0
κ_{bs}	0	0	0	0	1
ρ	0.2	0.2	0.2	0.15	0.15

Table 3.1. *Setting of κ_{pbs}, κ_{rb}, κ_{bs}, and ρ depending on the convergence factor* cf *and the Boolean control variable bs_update*

Finally, we will describe the way in which BS is made probabilistic on the basis of the pheromone values. Function Choose_Best_Extension(E_B) in line 8 of Algorithm 3.2 is replaced by a function that chooses an extension $ta \in E_B$ (where t is the current partial solution and a is the letter appended to produce extension ta) based on the following probabilities:

$$
p(ta) = \frac{\left(\min_{i=1,\ldots,n} \{ \tau_{ip_i^a} \} \cdot \nu(t|a)^{-1} \right)}{\sum_{zb \in E_B} \left(\min_{i=1,\ldots,n} \{ \tau_{ip_i^b} \} \cdot \nu(b|z)^{-1} \right)}
\qquad [3.13]
$$

Remember in this context, that p_i^a was defined as the next position of letter a after position pointer p_i in string s_i. The intuition of choosing the minimum pheromone values corresponding to the next positions of a letter in the n given strings is as follows: if at least one of these pheromone values is low, the corresponding letter should not yet be appended to the partial solution because there is another letter that should be appended first. Finally, each application of the probabilistic choice function is either executed probabilistically or deterministically. This is decided with uniform probability. In the case of a deterministic choice, we simply choose the extension with the highest probability value. The probability for a deterministic choice, also called the *determinism rate*, is henceforth denoted by $d_{\mathrm{rate}} \in [0, 1]$.

3.2.5. *Experimental evaluation*

The three algorithms outlined in the previous sections – henceforth labeled Best-Next, BS and Beam–ACO – were implemented in ANSI C++ using GCC 4.7.3, without the use of any external libraries. Note that – in the case of the LCS problem – it is not feasible to solve the ILP models corresponding to the problems considered (see section 3.1.2) by means of an ILP solver such as CPLEX. The number of variables is simply too high. The experimental evaluation was performed on a cluster of PCs with Intel(R) Xeon(R) CPU 5670 CPUs of 12 nuclei of 2933 MHz and at least 40 GB of RAM. Initially, the set of benchmarks that were generated to compare the three algorithms considered are described. Then, the tuning experiments that were performed in order to determine a proper setting for the Beam–ACO parameters are outlined. Note that in the case of BS, a *low time* and a *high time* configuration, as in [BLU 09], was chosen manually. Finally, an exhaustive experimental evaluation is also presented.

3.2.5.1. *Problems*

Most algorithmic proposals for the LCS problem from the literature were evaluated using randomly-generated problems. This was also done for the experimental evaluation of Best-Next, BS and Beam–ACO. As many as 10 random instances were generated for each combination of the number of input strings $n \in \{10, 50, 100, 150, 200\}$, the length of the input stings $m \in \{100, 500, 1000\}$ and the alphabet size $|\Sigma| \in \{4, 12, 20\}$. This makes a total of 450 problems. All the results shown in forthcoming sections are averages over the 10 problems of each combination.

3.2.5.2. *Tuning*

The parameters involved in Beam–ACO – apart from the learning rate ρ which is not critical and which was set as shown in Table 3.1 – are basically those involved in the probabilistic beam search that is employed at each iteration: (1) the beam width (k_{bw}); (2) the parameter that controls the number of extensions that are chosen at each step of beam search (μ); and (3) the determinism rate (d_{rate}).

The automatic configuration irace tool [LÓP 11] was used for tuning the three parameters. In fact, irace was applied to tune Beam–ACO separately for each combination of input strings (n) and alphabet size ($|\Sigma|$). In preliminary experiments the length of the input strings did not seem to have a major influence on the performance of the algorithm. For each combination of n, $|\Sigma|$ and m, three tuning instances were randomly generated. This results in nine tuning instances per application of irace.

Each application of irace was given a budget of 1,000 runs of Beam–ACO, where each run was given a computation time limit of $\frac{m \cdot |\Sigma|}{100}$ CPU seconds. Finally, the following parameter value ranges were chosen concerning the three parameters considered for tuning:

- $k_{bw} \in \{5, 10, 30, 50, 100\}$;

- $\mu \in \{1.5, 2.0, 2.5, 3.0, 3.5, 4.0, 4.5, 5.0\}$;

- $d_{rate} \in \{0.0, 0.3, 0.6, 0.9\}$, where a value of 0.0 means that the choice of an extension is made uniformly at random with respect to their probabilities, while a value of 0.9 means that BS is nearly deterministic, in the sense that the extension with the highest probability is nearly always chosen deterministically.

The tuning runs with irace produced the configurations of Beam–ACO as shown in Table 3.2.

3.2.5.3. Experimental results

Four algorithms were included in the comparison. Apart from the Best-Next heuristic and Beam–ACO, BS was applied with two different parameter settings. The first setting, henceforth referred to as the *low time* setting, is characterized by $k_{bw} = 10$ and $\mu = 3.0$. The corresponding algorithm version is called BS-L. The second setting, which we refer to as the *high quality* setting, assumes $k_{bw} = 100$ and $\mu = 5.0$. This version of BS is referred to as BS-H. Additional experiments have shown that an additional increase in performance by increasing the value of any of these two parameters is rather minor and on the cost of much higher running times. Just like in the tuning phase, the maximum CPU time given to Beam–ACO for the application to each problem was $\frac{m \cdot |\Sigma|}{100}$ CPU seconds.

n	$\|\Sigma\|$	k_{bw}	μ	d_{rate}
10	4	100	1.5	0.3
	12	100	2.5	0.9
	20	50	2.5	0.6
50	4	50	1.5	0.3
	12	10	2.0	0.3
	20	10	2.5	0.9
100	4	50	1.5	0.9
	12	10	2.0	0.3
	20	10	3.0	0.6
150	4	30	2.0	0.9
	12	30	2.0	0.9
	20	30	3.0	0.0
200	4	30	2.0	0.3
	12	10	2.0	0.0
	20	30	2.5	0.6

Table 3.2. *Results of tuning Beam–ACO with irace*

The numerical results are presented in Tables 3.3, 3.4 and 3.5 in terms of one table per alphabet size. Each row presents the results averaged over 10 problems of the same type. The results of all algorithms are provided in two columns. The first one (**mean**) provides the result of the corresponding algorithm averaged over 10 problems, while the second column (**time**) provides the average computation time (in seconds) necessary to find the corresponding solutions. The best result for each row is marked with a gray background.

The following observations can be made:

– first of all, both BS variants – i.e. BS-L and BS-H – and Beam–ACO clearly outperform Best-Next. Moreover, the high-performance version of BS outperforms the low time version;

– for alphabet size $|\Sigma| = 4$ – particularly for larger instances – Beam–ACO seems to outperform the other algorithms. However, starting from an alphabet size of $|\Sigma| = 12$, BS-H has advantages over Beam–ACO;

– BS-H requires computation times that are comparable with those of Beam–ACO.

n	m	Best-Next		BS-L		BS-H		Beam–ACO	
		mean	time	mean	time	mean	time	mean	time
	100	29.2	0.0	32.8	0.0	33.8	0.4	33.1	0.6
10	500	160.5	0.0	169.7	0.1	175.8	2.4	175.0	13.0
	1000	329.3	0.0	342.4	0.2	355.9	4.8	354.1	24.0
	100	20.4	0.0	23.0	0.1	23.5	1.5	23.3	0.5
50	500	127.2	0.0	132.1	0.4	133.1	9.6	134.8	9.4
	1000	262.3	0.0	269.5	0.7	270.9	18.2	276.0	17.9
	100	19.6	0.0	20.9	0.1	21.3	2.5	21.0	0.6
100	500	118.0	0.0	124.2	0.7	124.9	17.0	126.3	7.3
	1000	247.8	0.0	255.4	1.4	256.3	30.2	261.1	15.5
	100	16.6	0.0	19.5	0.2	20.1	3.0	19.9	0.6
150	500	114.1	0.0	120.6	1.0	121.5	22.3	122.6	8.0
	1000	240.9	0.1	249.0	2.0	249.6	43.0	253.2	30.8
	100	16.6	0.0	19.1	0.2	19.4	3.7	19.5	1.3
200	500	110.9	0.0	118.2	1.3	118.8	29.3	119.2	10.2
	1000	234.9	0.1	245.5	2.6	245.9	51.1	247.7	22.7

Table 3.3. *Results for instances where* $|\Sigma| = 4$

n	m	Best-Next		BS-L		BS-H		Beam–ACO	
		mean	time	mean	time	mean	time	mean	time
	100	10.6	0.0	12.2	0.0	12.5	0.4	12.5	0.5
10	500	66.2	0.0	72.5	0.1	75.7	4.9	76.7	18.2
	1000	136.6	0.0	149.0	0.2	155.6	10.5	157.2	42.9
	100	5.4	0.0	6.4	0.1	6.8	0.6	6.5	0.1
50	500	43.0	0.0	46.5	0.3	47.3	10.3	47.1	15.2
	1000	92.3	0.0	97.4	0.6	98.2	20.6	98.4	42.8
	100	4.4	0.0	5.2	0.1	5.2	0.6	5.2	0.0
100	500	38.0	0.0	40.8	0.5	41.6	13.2	41.2	8.0
	1000	82.5	0.0	87.4	1.1	88.9	28.9	88.4	44.2
	100	3.5	0.0	4.1	0.1	4.7	0.5	4.6	0.4
150	500	34.0	0.0	38.5	0.8	39.2	16.7	39.2	7.9
	1000	78.0	0.1	83.0	1.6	84.3	37.3	84.7	20.8
	100	3.6	0.0	4.0	0.1	4.1	0.5	4.1	0.1
200	500	33.1	0.0	37.0	1.0	37.9	20.9	35.2	9.4
	1000	75.1	0.1	80.8	2.2	81.9	46.2	76.1	51.4

Table 3.4. *Results for instances where* $|\Sigma| = 12$

n	m	Best-Next		BS-L		BS-H		Beam–ACO	
		mean	time	mean	time	mean	time	mean	time
10	100	6.9	0.0	7.7	0.0	7.9	0.2	7.9	0.1
	500	43.0	0.0	48.1	0.2	49.8	6.7	49.6	11.5
	1000	89.0	0.0	98.6	0.3	103.4	15.5	102.6	64.5
50	100	2.4	0.0	3.0	0.0	3.0	0.1	3.0	0.0
	500	24.5	0.0	27.6	0.3	28.2	11.7	28.0	2.0
	1000	54.2	0.0	59.1	0.7	60.5	25.9	60.5	29.8
100	100	1.9	0.0	2.1	0.0	2.1	0.0	2.1	0.0
	500	20.9	0.0	23.6	0.6	24.0	15.3	24.0	2.2
	1000	47.4	0.1	51.8	1.3	53.0	35.1	53.1	30.4
150	100	1.5	0.0	1.9	0.0	1.9	0.0	1.9	0.0
	500	19.3	0.0	21.9	0.8	22.2	18.4	21.3	15.7
	1000	45.4	0.1	48.8	1.8	49.6	42.4	46.4	47.1
200	100	1.1	0.0	1.1	0.0	1.1	0.0	1.1	0.0
	500	18.8	0.0	20.6	1.0	21.1	22.2	21.0	5.6
	1000	43.0	0.1	47.2	2.4	47.9	52.3	47.8	54.0

Table 3.5. *Results for instances where* $|\Sigma| = 20$

Finally, the results are also presented in graphical form in terms of the improvement of Beam–ACO over the other three algorithms in Figures 3.2, 3.3 and 3.4. The labels on the x-axis indicate the number and length of the input strings of the corresponding instances. More specifically, a label is of the form X-Y, where X is the number of input strings and Y indicates their length.

3.3. Algorithms for the RFLCS problem

We will now present the best available algorithms for the RFLCS problem. The first one is a simple adaption of the Beam–ACO algorithm presented in section 3.2.4 for the general LCS problem. In fact, the extension to the RFLCS problem only concerns function Produce_ Extensions(B) and the calculation of the upper bound function ($UB(\cdot)$) in Algorithm 3.2. Remember that function Produce_Extensions(B) produces the set E_B of all extensions of the common subsequences $t \in B$, where B is the current beam. More specifically, E_B is the set of subsequences ta, where $t \in B$ and $a \in \Sigma_t^{nd}$. To adopt this function to the RFLCS problem, all letters that appear in a common subsequence $t \in B$ must be excluded from Σ_t^{nd}. Additionally, the upper bound function must be adapted. For any common subsequence t, the upper bound value in the context of the RFLCS problem is defined as follows:

$$\text{UB}(t) := |t| + \sum_{a \in \Sigma, a \notin t} \min\{|y_i|_a \mid i = 1, \dots, n\} \qquad [3.14]$$

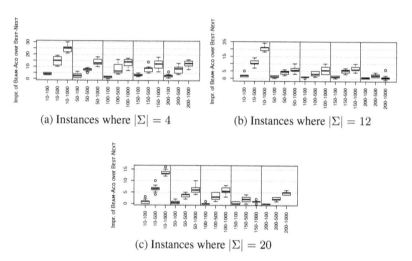

(a) Instances where $|\Sigma| = 4$

(b) Instances where $|\Sigma| = 12$

(c) Instances where $|\Sigma| = 20$

Figure 3.2. *Improvement of Beam–ACO over Best-Next. Each box shows the differences between the objective function value of the solution produced by Beam–ACO and the one of the solution produced by Best-Next for the 10 instances of the same type*

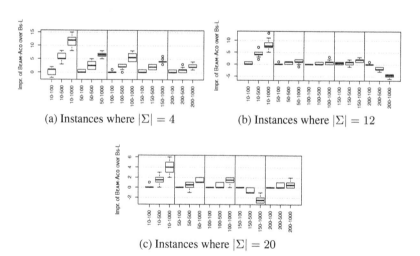

(a) Instances where $|\Sigma| = 4$

(b) Instances where $|\Sigma| = 12$

(c) Instances where $|\Sigma| = 20$

Figure 3.3. *Improvement of Beam–ACO over BS-L. Each box shows the differences between the objective function value of the solution produced by Beam–ACO and the one of the solution produced by BS-L for the 10 instances of the same type*

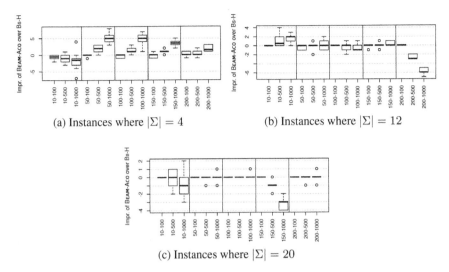

(a) Instances where $|\Sigma| = 4$

(b) Instances where $|\Sigma| = 12$

(c) Instances where $|\Sigma| = 20$

Figure 3.4. *Improvement of Beam–ACO over BS-H. Each box shows the differences between the objective function value of the solution produced by Beam–ACO and the one of the solution produced by BS-H for the 10 instances of the same type*

In addition to the Beam–ACO approach, the current state-of-the-art approach is outlined in the subsequent section.

3.3.1. CMSA

The application of the construct, merge, solve and adapt (CMSA) algorithm to the RFLCS problem was originally described in [BLU 16a]. As already described in section 1.2.7, the CMSA approach works as follows. At each iteration, solutions to the problem tackled are generated in a probabilistic way. The components found in these solutions are, then, added to a sub-instance of the original problem. Subsequently, an exact solver such as, for example, CPLEX is used to optimally solve the sub-instance. Moreover, the algorithm is equipped with a mechanism for deleting seemingly useless components from the sub-instance. This is done such that the sub-instance has a moderate size and can be solved quickly.

The pseudo-code of CMSA for the RFLCS problem is given in Algorithm 3.4. Note that in the context of this algorithm, solutions to the problem and sub-instances are both subsets of the complete set Z of variables that was described in section 3.1.2. If a solution S contains a variable z_{k_1,k_2}, the variable assumes a value of one in the corresponding solution.

CMSA starts by setting the best solution so far S_{bsf} to NULL and the restricted problem (Z_{sub}) to the empty set. The CMSA main loop is executed before the CPU time limit is reached. It consists of the following actions. First, a number of n_a solutions is probabilistically constructed in function ProbabilisticSolutionConstruction(Z) in line 6 of Algorithm 3.4. The variables that are found in these solutions are added to Z_{sub}. The age of a newly added variable z_{k_1,k_2} (age$[z_{k_1,k_2}]$) is set to 0. After the construction of n_a solutions, an ILP solver is applied to find the best solution S'_{opt} in the sub-instance Z_{sub} (see function ApplyILPSolver(Z_{sub}) in line 12 of Algorithm 3.4.). Where S'_{opt} is better than the current best solution so far S_{bsf}, solution S'_{opt} is stored as the new best solution so far (line 13). Next, sub-instance Z_{sub} is adapted, based on solution S'_{opt} and on the age of the variables. This is done in function Adapt(Z_{sub}, S'_{opt}, age$_{max}$) in line 14 as follows. First, the age of each variable in Z_{sub} is increased by one and, subsequently, the age of each variable in $S'_{opt} \subseteq Z_{sub}$ is re-set to zero. Finally, those solution components from Z_{sub} that have reached the maximum component age (age$_{max}$) are deleted from Z_{sub}. The motivation behind the aging mechanism is that variables which never appear in an optimal solution of Z_{sub} should be removed from Z_{sub} after a while, because they simply slow down the ILP solver. Components which appear in optimal solutions seem to be useful and should, therefore, remain in Z_{sub}.

The ILP solver used in function ApplyILPSolver(Z_{sub}) makes use of the ILP model for the RFLCS problem outlined in section 3.1.2. In order to apply this model to a sub-instance, Z_{sub}, all occurrences of Z in this model have to be replaced with Z_{sub}.

The remaining component in the application of CMSA to the RFLCS problem is the probabilistic construction of solutions in function ProbabilisticSolutionConstruction(Z). For this purpose, CMSA uses a probabilistic version of the Best-Next heuristic that was described in section 3.2.1.1 for the more general LCS problem. The probabilistic heuristic is described in terms of the variables used in the context of CMSA. The solution starts with an empty partial solution $S = \emptyset$. The first action at each step consists of generating the set C of variables that serve as options to be added to S. C is generated in order to contain for each letter $a \in \Sigma$, for which S does not yet contain a corresponding variable, the variable $z_{k_1,k_2} \in Z_a$ (if any) so that $k_1 < l_1$ and $k_2 < l_2$, $\forall z_{l_1,l_2} \in Z_a$. Assuming that z_{r_1,r_2} was the last variable added to S, all options $z_{k_1,k_2} \in C$ are assigned a weight value $w(z_{k_1,k_2}) := \left(\frac{k_1 - r_1}{|s_1| - r_1} + \frac{k_2 - r_2}{|s_2| - r_2} \right)^{-1}$. Only when $S = \emptyset$, does $r_1 = r_2 = 0$. Note that these weight values correspond exactly to the weight values assigned by greedy function $\eta()$ from section 3.2.1.1. At each step, exactly one variable is chosen from C and added to S. First, a value δ is chosen uniformly at random from $[0, 1]$. In the case $\delta \leq d_{\text{rate}}$, where d_{rate} is a parameter of the algorithm, the variable $z_{i,j} \in C$ with the greatest weight is deterministically chosen. Otherwise, a candidate list $L \subseteq C$ of size $\min\{l_{\text{size}}, |C|\}$ containing the options with the highest weight is generated and exactly one variable $z_{i,j} \in L$ is then chosen uniformly at random and added to S. Note that l_{size} is another parameter of the solution construction process. The construction of a complete (valid) solution is finished when the set of options is empty.

Algorithm 3.4. CMSA for the RFLCS problem

1: **input:** strings s_1 and s_2 over alphabet Σ, values for parameters n_a and $\text{age}_{\max}$

2: $S_{\text{bsf}} :=$ NULL, $Z_{\text{sub}} := \emptyset$

3: $\text{age}[z_{k_1,k_2}] := 0$ for all $z_{k_1,k_2} \in Z$

4: **while** CPU time limit not reached **do**

5:     **for** $i = 1, \ldots, n_a$ **do**

6:         $S :=$ ProbabilisticSolutionConstruction(Z)

7:         **for all** $z_{k_1,k_2} \in S$ and $z_{k_1,k_2} \notin Z_{\text{sub}}$ **do**

8:             $\text{age}[z_{k_1,k_2}] := 0$

9:             $Z_{\text{sub}} := Z_{\text{sub}} \cup \{z_{k_1,k_2}\}$

10:         **end for**

11:     **end for**

12:     $S'_{\text{opt}} :=$ ApplyILPSolver(Z_{sub})

13:     **if** $|S'_{\text{opt}}| > |S_{\text{bsf}}|$ **then** $S_{\text{bsf}} := S'_{\text{opt}}$

14:     Adapt($Z_{\text{sub}}, S'_{\text{opt}}, \text{age}_{\max}$)

15: **end while**

16: **output:** S_{bsf}

3.3.2. Experimental evaluation

We implemented both algorithms outlined earlier – henceforth labeled Beam–ACO and CMSA – in ANSI C++ using GCC 4.7.3, without the use of any external libraries. The ILP models of the original RFLCS and the sub-instances within CMSA, were solved with IBM ILOG CPLEX v12.2 in one-threaded mode. The experimental evaluation was performed on a cluster of PCs with Intel(R) Xeon(R) CPU 5670 CPUs of 12 nuclei of 2933 MHz and at least 40 GB of RAM. Initially, the set of benchmarks used to test the algorithms considered are described. Then, the tuning experiments performed in order to determine a proper setting for the algorithm parameters are outlined. Finally, an exhaustive experimental evaluation is presented.

3.3.2.1. Problems

Two different types of problems are proposed in the related literature (see [ADI 08, ADI 10]) for testing algorithms for the RFLCS problem. For the experimental evaluation of this chapter we chose type one instances. More specifically, the instances used in the following are generated on the basis of alphabet sizes $|\Sigma| \in \{32, 64, 128, 256, 512\}$ and the maximum repetition of each letter $rep \in \{3, 4, 5, 6, 7, 8\}$ in each input string. For each combination of $|\Sigma|$ and rep the instance set considered consists of 10 randomly generated problems, which makes a total of 300 problems. All the results shown in the forthcoming sections are averages over the 10 problems of each type.

3.3.2.2. Tuning of Beam–ACO

Remember that, the parameters involved in Beam–ACO – apart from the learning rate ρ which is not that critical and which was set to 0.1 – are basically those involved in the probabilistic BS that is employed at each iteration: (1) the beam width (k_{bw}); (2) the parameter that controls the number of extensions that are chosen at each step of beam search (μ); (3) the determinism rate (d_{rate}).

The automatic configuration tool irace [LÓP 11] was used for the tuning of the three parameters. In fact, irace was applied to tune Beam–ACO separately for instances concerning a specific alphabet size ($|\Sigma|$). This is because – as in the case of the LCS problem; see section 3.2.5.2 – the length of the input strings did not seem to have a major influence on the performance of the algorithm. For each combination of $|\Sigma|$ and rep, two tuning instances are randomly generated. This results in 12 tuning instances per application of irace.

$|\Sigma|$	k_{bw}	μ	d_{rate}
32	5	1.5	0.3
64	5	1.5	0.3
128	5	1.5	0.0
256	10	1.5	0.3
512	30	2.5	0.0

Table 3.6. *Results of Beam–ACO tuning for the RFLCS problem with irace*

$|\Sigma|$	n_a	age_{max}	d_{rate}	l_{size}	t_{max}
32	30	10	0.3	10	5.0
64	10	1	0.7	5	5.0
128	30	1	0.5	5	100.0
256	30	1	0.5	3	100.0
512	10	1	0.3	5	10.0

Table 3.7. *Results of CMSA tuning for the RFLCS problem with irace*

Each application of irace was given a budget of 1000 runs of Beam–ACO, where each run was given a computation time limit of $\frac{rep \cdot |\Sigma|}{10}$ CPU seconds. The parameter value ranges for the three parameters considered were chosen as in the case of the LCS problem; see section 3.2.5.2. The tuning runs with irace produced the Beam–ACO configurations shown in Table 3.6.

3.3.2.3. Tuning CMSA

There are several parameters involved in CMSA: (n_a) the number of solution constructions per iteration, (age_{max}) the maximum allowed age of solution components, (d_{rate}) the determinism rate, (l_{size}) the candidate list size and (t_{max}) the maximum time in seconds allowed for CPLEX per application to a sub-instance. The last parameter is necessary, because even when applied to reduced problems, CPLEX might still need too much computation time for optimal sub-instance solutions. In any case, CPLEX always returns the best feasible solution found within the given computation time.

As in the case of Beam–ACO, we made use of the automatic configuration tool irace [LÓP 11] to tune the five parameters. Again, irace was applied to tune CMSA separately for each alphabet size. The tuning instances were the same as the ones used to tune Beam–ACO. The tuning process for each alphabet size was given a budget of 1000 runs of CMSA, where each run was given a computation time limit of $\frac{rep\cdot|\Sigma|}{10}$ CPU seconds. Finally, the following parameter value ranges were chosen concerning the five parameters of CMSA:

– $n_a \in \{10, 30, 50\}$;

– $age_{max} \in \{1, 5, 10, inf\}$, where inf means that solution components are never removed from the incumbent sub-instance;

– $d_{rate} \in \{0.0, 0.3, 0.5, 0.7, 0.9\}$, where a value of 0.0 means that the selection of the component to be added to the partial solution under construction is always selected randomly from the candidate list, while a value of 0.9 means that solution constructions are nearly deterministic;

– $l_{size} \in \{3, 5, 10\}$;

– $t_{max} \in \{0.5, 1.0, 5.0\}$ (in seconds) for instances where $|\Sigma| \in \{32, 64\}$ and $t_{max} \in \{1.0, 10.0, 100.0\}$ for instances where $|\Sigma| > 64$.

Tuning with irace produced the CMSA configurations shown in Table 3.7.

3.3.2.4. Experimental results

Three solution techniques were included in the comparison. Apart from Beam–ACO and CMSA, CPLEX was additionally applied to all problems. In contrast to the LCS problem, this is feasible in the case of the RFLCS problem, at least for smaller problems. Just like in the tuning phase, the maximum CPU time given to all algorithms for the application to each problem was $\frac{rep\cdot|\Sigma|}{10}$ CPU seconds.

The numerical results are presented in Table 3.8. Each row presents the results averaged over 10 problems of the same type. The results of Beam–ACO and CMSA are provided in two columns. The first one (**mean**) provides the result of the corresponding algorithm averaged over 10 problems, while the second column (**time**) provides the average computation time (in seconds) necessary to find the corresponding solutions.

The same information is given for CPLEX. However in this case we will also provide the average optimality gaps (in percent), i.e. the average gaps between the upper bounds and the values of the best solutions when stopping a run.

$|\Sigma|$	$reps$	CPLEX			Beam–ACO		CMSA	
		mean	**time**	**gap (%)**	**mean**	**time**	**mean**	**time**
32	3	16.1	0.1	0.0	15.9	0.1	16.1	0.0
	4	19.2	0.3	0.0	19.0	0.0	19.2	0.0
	5	20.9	1.1	0.0	20.6	0.1	20.9	0.1
	6	24.4	4.6	0.0	24.0	2.6	24.4	0.3
	7	25.8	7.9	0.0	25.0	0.2	25.8	2.8
	8	25.5	15.6	13.7	26.8	0.9	27.3	4.2
64	3	24.9	1.4	0.00	24.8	2.8	24.9	0.7
	4	30.3	6.3	0.00	30.0	0.6	30.2	0.1
	5	28.3	20.3	67.2	34.5	0.6	34.6	1.0
	6	23.8	21.3	> 100	38.8	7.2	39.0	7.7
	7	22.6	9.7	> 100	43.1	7.9	43.8	6.2
	8	26.9	11.6	> 100	45.1	7.1	45.9	8.6
128	3	38.0	28.9	3.0	38.3	0.0	38.4	0.1
	4	21.5	14.3	> 100	45.2	3.1	45.1	0.5
	5	23.0	19.0	> 100	53.7	4.0	53.7	2.5
	6	18.1	45.3	> 100	60.1	7.6	61.2	17.3
	7	11.7	55.4	> 100	68.3	13.9	68.9	23.2
	8	n.a.	n.a.	n.a.	74.7	25.1	76.0	36.7
256	3	6.1	27.7	> 100	53.6	0.1	53.7	2.9
	4	0.1	61.4	> 100	67.0	10.3	67.2	8.6
	5	n.a.	n.a.	n.a.	80.0	7.3	81.0	7.4
	6	n.a.	n.a.	n.a.	90.8	27.6	92.2	55.7
	7	n.a.	n.a.	n.a.	101.4	60.7	102.7	60.0
	8	n.a.	n.a.	n.a.	110.0	46.1	110.8	132.3
512	3	n.a.	n.a.	n.a.	79.2	0.4	78.7	7.4
	4	n.a.	n.a.	n.a.	100.8	0.7	99.7	72.5
	5	n.a.	n.a.	n.a.	117.7	0.9	117.7	46.2
	6	n.a.	n.a.	n.a.	137.5	1.2	136.8	160.4
	7	n.a.	n.a.	n.a.	153.0	1.4	148.8	189.1
	8	n.a.	n.a.	n.a.	167.8	1.7	159.1	231.3

Table 3.8. *Experimental results concerning the RFLCS problem*

The following observations can be made:

– CPLEX is able to solve all instances where $|\Sigma| = 32$ and $reps < 8$ to optimality. Moreover, CPLEX is able to provide valid – although sometimes far from optimal – solutions up to instances where $|\Sigma| = 256$ and $reps \leq 4$; with the exception of instances where $|\Sigma| = 128$ and $reps = 8$;

– CMSA is the best-performing algorithm for instances where $|\Sigma| \leq 256$. Curiously, the performance of CMSA seems to degrade with growing alphabet size. More specifically, Beam–ACO outperforms CMSA for instances where $|\Sigma| = 512$. Moreover, the computation time required by Beam–ACO for doing so is almost negligible.

Finally, the results are also presented in graphical form in terms of the improvement of CMSA over the other two techniques in Figures 3.5 and 3.6. The labels of the x-axes of these figures provide information on the $reps$ parameter of the corresponding instances. Note that when a box shows negative values – i.e. negative improvements – the competitor algorithm was better than CMSA.

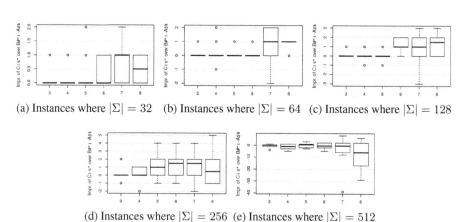

(a) Instances where $|\Sigma| = 32$ (b) Instances where $|\Sigma| = 64$ (c) Instances where $|\Sigma| = 128$

(d) Instances where $|\Sigma| = 256$ (e) Instances where $|\Sigma| = 512$

Figure 3.5. *Improvement of CMSA over Beam–ACO. Each box shows the differences between the objective function value of the solution produced by CMSA and the one of the solution produced by Beam–ACO for 10 instances of the same type*

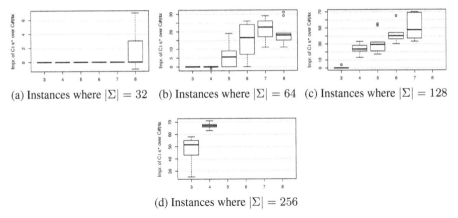

(a) Instances where $|\Sigma| = 32$ (b) Instances where $|\Sigma| = 64$ (c) Instances where $|\Sigma| = 128$

(d) Instances where $|\Sigma| = 256$

Figure 3.6. *Improvement of CMSA over CPLEX. Each box shows the differences between the objective function value of the solution produced by CMSA and that of the solution produced by CPLEX for 10 instances of the same type. Missing boxes indicate that CPLEX was not able to produce any valid solution*

3.4. Future work

In this chapter, after giving an introduction to the family of longest common subsequence problems, the current state-of-the-art metaheuristics for two specific longest common subsequence problems were presented. The first one was the most general LCS problem and the second one the RFLCS problem. The general impression is that the high-performance version of BS is a very strong algorithm for the LCS problem and that it will be difficult to significantly outperform this algorithm by means of some pure metaheuristic framework.

The situation for the RFLCS problem is a bit different. Although the CMSA algorithm works very well and better than Beam–ACO, in the context of small and medium size problems, the performance of CMSA seems to degrade with growing alphabet size. An interesting line for future research would be the combination of both techniques, i.e. using the Beam–ACO algorithm (or a simpler BS algorithm) to feed the sub-instance in the context of CMSA with new solution components. In other words, it might be beneficial to replace the simply probabilistic construction mechanism of CMSA with probabilistic BS or Beam–ACO.

4

The Most Strings With
Few Bad Columns Problem

This chapter deals with an non-deterministic polynomial-time (NP)-hard string selection problem known as the *most strings with few bad columns* (MSFBC) problem. The problem was originally introduced as a model for a set of DNA sequences from a heterogeneous population consisting of two subgroups: (1) a rather large subset of DNA sequences that are identical apart from mutations at maximal k positions; and (2) a smaller subset of DNA sequences that are outliers. The goal of the MSFBC problem is to identify the outliers. In this chapter, the first and foremost problem is modeled by means of integer linear programming (ILP). Second, two variants of a rather simple greedy strategy are outlined. Finally, a large neighborhood search (LNS) approach (see section 1.2.7.1 for a general introduction to LNS) for the MSFBC problem is described. This approach is currently the state-of-the-art technique. The LNS algorithm makes use of the ILP solver CPLEX as a sub-routine in order to find, at each iteration, the best possible neighbor in a large neighborhood of the current solution. A comprehensive experimental comparison among these techniques shows, first, that LNS generally outperforms both greedy strategies. Second, while LNS is competitive with the stand-alone application of CPLEX for small and medium size problems, it outperforms CPLEX in the context of larger problems. Note that the content of this chapter is based on [LIZ 16].

As already described in section 1.2.7.1, LNS algorithms are based on the following general idea. Given a valid solution to the problem tackled – also called the incumbent solution – first, destroy selected parts of it, resulting in a partial solution. Then apply some other, possibly exact, technique to find the best valid solution on the basis of the partial solution, i.e. the best valid solution that contains the given partial solution. Thus, the destroy-step defines a *large neighborhood*, from which the best (or nearly best) solution is determined not by naive enumeration but by the application of a more effective alternative technique. In the case of the MSFBC problem, the LNS algorithm makes use of the ILP-solver CPLEX to explore large neighborhoods. Therefore, the LNS approach can be labeled an ILP-based LNS.

4.1. The MSFBC problem

The MSFBC problem was originally introduced in [BOU 13]. It can, technically, be described as follows. A set I of n input strings of length m over a finite alphabet Σ, i.e. $I = \{s_1, \ldots, s_n\}$. The j-th position of a string s_i is, henceforth, denoted by $s_i[j]$ and has a $k < m$ fixed value. Set I together with parameter k define problem (I, k). The goal is to find a subset $S \subseteq I$ of maximal size such that the strings in S differ in at most k positions. In this context, the strings of a subset $S \subseteq I$ are said to differ in position $1 \leq j \leq m$ if, and only if, at least two strings $s_i, s_r \in S$ exist where $s_i[j] \neq s_r[j]$. A position j in which the strings from S differ is also called a *bad column*. This notation is derived from the fact that the set of input strings can conveniently be seen in the form of a matrix in which the strings are the rows.

4.1.1. *Literature review*

The authors of [BOU 13] showed that no polynomial-time approximation scheme (PTAS) exists for the MSFBC problem. Moreover, they state that the problem is a generalization of the problem of finding tandem repeats in a string [LAN 01]. In [LIZ 15], the authors introduced the first ILP model for the MSFBC problem (see section 4.2). They devised a greedy strategy which was tested in the context of a pilot method [VOß 05]. For problems of small and medium size, the best results were obtained by solving the ILP model by CPLEX, while the greedy-based pilot method scaled much better to large problems. On the downside, the greedy-based pilot method consumed a rather large amount of computation time.

4.2. An ILP model for the MSFBC problem

To describe the ILP model, let $\Sigma_j \subseteq \Sigma$ be the set of letters appearing at least once at the j-th position of the n input strings. In technical terms, $\Sigma_j :=$ $\{s_i[j] \mid i = 1, \ldots, n\}$. The proposed ILP model for the MSFBC problem makes use of several types of binary variable. First, for each input string s_i there is a binary variable x_i. Where $x_i = 1$, the corresponding input string s_i is part of the solution, otherwise not. Furthermore, for each combination of position j ($j = 1, \ldots, m$) and letter $a \in \Sigma_j$ the model makes use of a binary variable z_j^a, which is forced – by means of adequate constraints – to assume a value of one ($z_j^a = 1$) where at least one string s_i with $s_i[j] = a$ is chosen for the solution. Finally, there is a binary variable y_j for each position $j = 1, \ldots, m$. Variable y_j is forced to assume a value of one ($y_j = 1$) where the strings chosen for the solution differ at position j. Given these variables, the ILP can be formulated as follows:

$$\text{max} \quad \sum_{i=1}^{n} x_i \tag{4.1}$$

$$\text{s.t.} \quad x_i \leq z_j^{s_i[j]} \qquad\qquad \text{for } i = 1, \ldots, n \tag{4.2}$$
$$\text{and } j = 1, \ldots, m$$

$$\sum_{a \in \Sigma_j} z_j^a \leq 1 + |\Sigma_j| \cdot y_j \qquad\qquad \text{for } j = 1, \ldots, m \tag{4.3}$$

$$\sum_{j=1}^{m} y_j \leq k \tag{4.4}$$

$$x_i \in \{0, 1\} \qquad\qquad \text{for } i = 1, \ldots, n$$

$$z_j^a \in \{0, 1\} \qquad\qquad \text{for } j = 1, \ldots, m$$
$$\text{and } a \in \Sigma_j$$

$$y_j \in \{0, 1\} \qquad\qquad \text{for } j = 1, \ldots, m$$

The objective function [4.1] maximizes the number of strings chosen. Equations [4.2] ensure that, if a string s_i is selected ($x_i = 1$), the variable $z_j^{s_i[j]}$, which indicates that letter $s_i[j]$ appears at position j in at least one of the selected strings, has a value of one. Furthermore, equations [4.3] ensure that y_j is set to one when the selected strings differ at position j. Finally, constraint [4.4] ensures that no more than k bad columns are permitted.

4.3. Heuristic approaches

Given a non-empty partial solution to the problem, the authors of [LIZ 15] proposed the following greedy strategy to complete the partial solution given. In this context, $\mathrm{bc}(S^p)$ denotes the number of bad columns with respect to a given partial solution $S^p \subseteq I$. This measure corresponds to the number of columns j such that at least two strings $s_i, s_r \in S^p$ exist where $s_i[j] \neq s_r[j]$. A valid partial solution S^p to the MSWBC problem fulfills the following two conditions:

1) $\mathrm{bc}(S^p) \leq k$;

2) There is at least one string $s_l \in I \setminus S^p$ where $\mathrm{bc}(S^p \cup \{s_l\}) \leq k$.

It is not difficult to see that a valid complete solution S fulfills only the first of these conditions.

Algorithm 4.1. MakeSolutionComplete(S^p) procedure

1: **input:** a problem (I, k), a non-empty partial solution S^p
2: $E := \{s \in I \setminus S^p \mid \mathrm{bc}(S^p \cup \{s\}) \leq k\}$
3: **while** $E \neq \emptyset$ **do**
4:    $s^* := \mathrm{argmin}\{\mathrm{bc}(S^p \cup \{s\}) \mid s \in E\}$
5:    $S^p := S^p \cup \{s^*\}$
6:    $E := \{s \in I \setminus S^p \mid \mathrm{bc}(S^p \cup \{s\}) \leq k\}$
7: **end while**
8: **output:** a complete solution $S = S^p$

The pseudo-code of the MakeSolutionComplete(S^p) procedure for completing a given partial solution is provided in Algorithm 4.1. It works in an iterative way, whereby in each iteration exactly one of the strings from $I \setminus S^p$ is chosen. This is done by making use of a weighting function. The chosen string is then added to S^p. The weighting function concerns the number of bad columns. From $E := \{s \in I \setminus S^p \mid \mathrm{bc}(S^p \cup \{s\}) \leq k\}$ strings, the one with minimum $\mathrm{bc}(S^p \cup \{s\})$ is selected. In other words, at each iteration the string that causes a minimum increase in the number of bad columns is selected. In case of ties, the first one encountered is selected.

4.3.1. *Frequency-based greedy*

The authors of [LIZ 15] proposed two different ways of using the MakeSolutionComplete(S^p) procedure. In the first one, the initial partial solution contains exactly one string that is chosen based on a criterion related to letter frequencies. Let $fr_{j,a}$ for all $a \in \Sigma$ and $j = 1, \ldots, m$ be the frequency of letter a at position j in the input strings from I. If a appears, for example, in five out of n input strings at position j, then $fr_{j,a} = 5/n$. With this definition, the following measure can be computed for each $s_i \in I$:

$$\omega(s_i) := \sum_{j=1}^{m} fr_{j,s_i[j]}, \qquad [4.5]$$

where $s_i[j]$ denotes the letter at position j of string s_i. In words, $\omega(s_i)$ is calculated as the sum of the frequencies of the letters in s_i. The following string is, then, chosen to form the partial solution used as input for the MakeSolutionComplete(S^p) procedure:

$$s := \operatorname{argmax}\{\omega(s_i) \mid s_i \in I\} \qquad [4.6]$$

The advantages of this greedy algorithm – denoted by GREEDY-F – are to be found in its simplicity and low resource requirements.

4.3.2. *Truncated pilot method*

The MakeSolutionComplete(S^p) procedure was also used in [LIZ 15] in the context of a pilot method in which the MakeSolutionComplete(S^p) procedure was used at each level of the search tree in order to evaluate the respective partial solutions. The choice of a partial solution at each level was made on the basis of these evaluations. The computation time of such a pilot method is exponential in comparison to the basic greedy method. One way of reducing the computation time is to truncate the pilot method. Among several truncation options, the one with the best balance between solution quality and computation time in the context of the MSFBC problem is shown in Algorithm 4.2. For each possible string of $s_i \in I$, the resulting partial solution $S^p = \{s_i\}$ is fed in to the MakeSolutionComplete(S^p) procedure. The output of the truncated pilot method, henceforth called PILOT-TR, is the best of the n solutions constructed in this way.

Algorithm 4.2. Truncated pilot method

1: **input:** a problem (I, k)
2: $S_{bsf} := \emptyset$
3: **for** $i = 1, \ldots, n$ **do**
4:    $S^p := \{s_i\}$
5:    $S :=$ MakeSolutionComplete(S^p)
6:    **if** $|S| > |S_{bsf}|$ **then** $S_{bsf} := S$ **end if**
7: **end for**
8: **output:** Solution S_{bsf}

4.4. ILP-based large neighborhood search

In [LIZ 15], CPLEX was applied to a range of MSFBC problems. In this context, it was observed that CPLEX failed to provide near-optimal solutions for large problems. ILP-based LNS is a popular technique for profiting from CPLEX even with large problems are concerned. In the following, such an ILP-based LNS algorithm is described for application to the MSFBC problem. At each iteration, the current solution is initially partially destroyed. This may be done in a purely random way, or with some heuristic bias. The result, in any case, is a partial solution to the problem tackled. Then, CPLEX is applied to find the best valid solution that contains the partial solution obtained in the destruction step. Given a partial solution S^p, the best complete solution containing S^p is obtained by applying CPLEX to the ILP model from section 4.2, augmented by the following set of constraints:

$$x_i = 1 \quad \forall \ s_i \in S^p \qquad \qquad [4.7]$$

The pseudo-code of the ILP-based LNS algorithm is shown in Algorithm 4.3. First, in line 2, the first incumbent solution S_{bsf} is generated by applying heuristic GREEDY-F from section 4.3.1 to the problem tackled (I, k). Second, the current incumbent solution S_{bsf} is partially destroyed (see line 5) by removing a certain percentage $\mathbf{perc}_{dest}$ of the strings in S_{bsf}. This results in a partial solution S^p. After initial experiments it was decided to choose the strings to be removed uniformly at random. The precise number d of strings to be removed is calculated on the basis of $\mathbf{perc}_{dest}$ as follows:

$$d := \left\lfloor \frac{perc_{dest} \cdot |S_{cur}|}{100} \right\rfloor \qquad [4.8]$$

The last step of each iteration consists of applying the ILP solver CPLEX to produce the best solution, S'_{opt}, containing the partial solution S^p (see line 6). To avoid that this step taking too much computation time, CPLEX is given a computation time limit of t_{max} seconds. The output of CPLEX is, therefore, the best – possibly optimal – solution found within the computation time allowed.

Algorithm 4.3. ILP-based LNS for the MSFBC problem

1: **input:** a problem (I, k), values for the algorithm parameters
2: $S_{bsf} :=$ Result of applying GREEDY-F
3: $\mathbf{perc}_{dest} := \mathbf{perc}^l_{dest}$
4: **while** CPU time limit not reached **do**
5:     $S^p := \mathsf{DestroyPartially}(S_{bsf}, \mathbf{perc}_{dest})$
6:     $S'_{opt} := \mathsf{ApplyILPSolver}(S^p, t_{max})$
7:     **if** $|S'_{opt}| > |S_{bsf}|$ **then**
8:         $S_{bsf} := S'_{opt}$
9:         $\mathbf{perc}_{dest} := \mathbf{perc}^l_{dest}$
10:     **else**
11:         $\mathbf{perc}_{dest} := \mathbf{perc}_{dest} + 5$
12:         **if** $\mathbf{perc}_{dest} > \mathbf{perc}^u_{dest}$ **then**
13:             $\mathbf{perc}_{dest} := \mathbf{perc}^l_{dest}$
14:         **end if**
15:     **end if**
16: **end while**
17: **output:** S_{bsf}

To provide the algorithm with a way to escape from local optima, the percentage $\mathbf{perc}_{dest}$ of strings to be removed from the current solution is variable and depends on the search history. Two additional parameters are introduced for this purpose: a lower bound $\mathbf{perc}^l_{dest}$ and an upper bound $\mathbf{perc}^u_{dest}$. For the values of these bounds it holds that $0 \leq \mathbf{perc}^l_{dest} \leq \mathbf{perc}^u_{dest} \leq 100$.

Initially, the value of $\text{perc}_{\text{dest}}$ is set to the lower bound (see line 3 of Algorithm 4.3). Then, at each iteration, if the solution S'_{opt} produced by CPLEX is better than S_{bsf}, the value of $\text{perc}_{\text{dest}}$ is set to the lower bound $\text{perc}^l_{\text{dest}}$. If this is not the case, the value of $\text{perc}_{\text{dest}}$ is incremented by a certain amount. For the experimental evaluation presented in this chapter, this constant was set to five. If the value of $\text{perc}_{\text{dest}}$ exceeds the upper bound $\text{perc}^u_{\text{dest}}$, it is set to the lower bound $\text{perc}^l_{\text{dest}}$. This mechanism is described in lines 7–15 of the pseudo-code.

Note that the idea behind the dynamic change of the value of $\text{perc}_{\text{dest}}$ is as follows. As long as the algorithm is capable of improving the current solution $_{\text{bsf}}$ using a low destruction percentage, this percentage is kept low. In this way, the large neighborhood is rather small and CPLEX is faster in deriving the corresponding optimal solutions. Only when the algorithm does not seem to be able to improve over the current solution S_{bsf} is the destruction percentage is increased in a step-wise way.

4.5. Experimental evaluation

This section presents a comprehensive experimental evaluation of four algorithmic approaches: (1) the frequency-based greedy method GREEDY-F from section 4.3.1; (2) the truncated pilot method PILOT-TR from section 4.3.2; (3) the large neighborhood search (LNS) approach from section 4.4; and (4) the application of CPLEX to all problems. All approaches were implemented in ANSI C++ using GCC 4.7.3 to compile the software. Moreover, the original ILPs as well as the ILPs within LNS were solved with IBM ILOG CPLEX V12.2 (single-threaded execution). The experimental results that are presented were obtained on a cluster of computers with Intel® Xeon® CPU 5670 CPUs of 12 nuclei of 2933 MHz and (in total) 32 GB of RAM. A maximum of 4 GB of RAM was allowed for each run of CPLEX. In the following section, the set of benchmarks is described. A detailed analysis of the experimental results is presented thereafter.

4.5.1. Benchmarks

For the experimental comparison of the methods considered in this chapter, a set of random problems was generated on the basis of four different parameters: (1) the number of input strings (n); (2) the length of the input strings (m); (3) the alphabet size ($|\Sigma|$); and (4) the so-called *change probability* (p_c). Each random instance is generated as follows. First, a base string s of length m is generated uniformly at random, i.e. each letter $a \in \Sigma$ has a probability of $1/|\Sigma|$ to appear at any of the m positions of s. Then, the following procedure is repeated n times in order to generate n input strings of the problem being constructed. First, s is copied into a new string s'. Then, each letter of s' is exchanged with a randomly chosen letter from Σ with a probability of p_c. Note that the new letter does not need to be different from the original one. However, note that at least one change per input string was enforced.

The following values were used for the generation of the benchmark set:

– $n \in \{100, 500, 1000\}$;

– $m \in \{100, 500, 1000\}$;

– $|\Sigma| \in \{4, 12, 20\}$.

Values for p_c were chosen in relation to n:

1) If $n = 100$: $p_c \in \{0.01, 0.03, 0.05\}$;

2) If $n = 500$: $p_c \in \{0.005, 0.015, 0.025\}$;

3) If $n = 1000$: $p_c \in \{0.001, 0.003, 0.005\}$.

The three chosen values for p_c imply for any string length that, on average, 1%, 3% or 5% of the string positions are changed. Ten problems were generated for each combination of values for parameters n, m and $|\Sigma|$. This results in a total of 810 benchmarks. To test each instance with different limits for the number of bad columns allowed, values for k from $\{2, n/20, n/10\}$ were used.

	k = 2		k = n/20		k = n/10	
	(l,u)	t_{max}	(l,u)	t_{max}	(l,u)	t_{max}
100	(70,70)	20	(90,90)	10	(90,90)	10
500	(90,90)	10	(90,90)	15	(90,90)	20
1000	(90,90)	5	(90,90)	15	(90,90)	10

Table 4.1. *Parameter settings produced by irace for LNS concerning* $|\Sigma| = 4$

4.5.2. Tuning of LNS

The LNS parameters were tuned by means of the automatic configuration tool irace [LÓP 11]. The parameters subject to tuning were: (1) the lower and upper bounds – that is, $\mathbf{perc}_{\text{dest}}^{l}$ and $\mathbf{perc}_{\text{dest}}^{u}$ – of the percentage of strings to be deleted from the current incumbent solution S_{bsf}; and (2) the maximum time $t_{\max}$ (in seconds) allowed for CPLEX per application within LNS. irace was applied separately for each combination of values for n, $|\Sigma|$ and k, respectively. Note that no separate tuning was performed concerning the string length m and the percentage of character change $\mathbf{p}_c$. This is because, after initial runs, it was shown that parameters n, $|\Sigma|$ and k have as large an influence on the behavior of the algorithm as m and $\mathbf{p}_c$. irace was applied 27 times with a budget of 1,000 applications of LNS per tuning run. For each application of LNS, a time limit of $n/2$ CPU seconds was given. Finally, for each of irace run, one tuning instance for each combination of m and $\mathbf{p}_c$ was generated. This makes a total of 9 tuning instances per of irace run.

	k = 2		k = n/20		k = n/10	
	(l,u)	t_{max}	(l,u)	t_{max}	(l,u)	t_{max}
100	(80,80)	20	(90,90)	15	(40,40)	20
500	(90,90)	5	(90,90)	20	(90,90)	5
1000	(90,90)	15	(90,90)	20	(90,90)	20

Table 4.2. *Parameter settings produced by irace for LNS where* $|\Sigma| = 12$

Finally, the parameter value ranges that were chosen for the LNS tuning processes are as follows:

– for the lower and upper bound values of the percentage destroyed, the following value combinations were considered: $(\mathbf{perc}_{\text{dest}}^{l}, \mathbf{perc}_{\text{dest}}^{u}) \in$ {(10,10), (20,20), (30,30), (40,40), (50,50), (60,60), (70,70), (80,80), (90,90), (10,30), (10,50), (30,50), (30,70)}. Note that in the cases where both bounds have the same value, the percentage of deleted nodes is always the same;

– $t_{max} \in \{5.0, 10.0, 15.0, 20.0\}$.

The results of the tuning processes are shown in Tables 4.1, 4.2 and 4.3. The following observations can be made. First, in nearly all cases $(90, 90)$ is chosen for the lower and upper bounds of the percentage destroyed. This is surprising, because LNS algorithms generally require a lower of percentage destruction. At the end of section 4.5.3, some reasons will be outlined to explain this high percentage destruction in the MSFBC problem. No clear trend can be extracted from the settings chosen for t_{max}. The reason for this is related to the reason for choosing a high percentage destruction, which will be outlined later, as mentioned above.

	k = 2		k = n/20		k = n/10	
	(l,u)	t_{max}	(l,u)	t_{max}	(l,u)	t_{max}
100	(90,90)	10	(90,90)	20	(70,70)	20
500	90,90	15	(90,90)	10	(90,90)	5
1000	(90,90)	10	(90,90)	20	(90,90)	20

Table 4.3. *Parameter settings produced by irace for LNS where $|\Sigma| = 20$*

4.5.3. Results

The results are provided numerically in three tables: Table 4.4 provides the results for all instances with $|\Sigma| = 4$; Table 4.5 contains the results for all instances with $|\Sigma| = 12$; and Table 4.6 shows the results for instances with $|\Sigma| = 20$. The first three columns contain the number of input strings (n), string length (m) and the *probability* of change (p_c). The results of GREEDY-F, PILOT-TR, LNS and CPLEX are presented in the three blocks of columns, each one corresponding to one of the three values for k. In each of these blocks, the tables provide the average results obtained for 10 random instances in each row (columns with the heading "mean") and the corresponding average computation times in seconds (columns with the heading "time"). Note that LNS was applied with a time limit of $n/2$ CPU seconds for each problem. With CPLEX, which was applied with the same time limits as LNS, the average result (column with the heading "mean") and the corresponding average optimality gap (column with the heading "gap") is provided. Note that when the gap has a value of zero, the 10 corresponding problems were optimally solved within the computation time allowed. Finally, note that the best result in each row is marked in bold font.

n	m	p_c	\multicolumn{8}{c}{k = 2}								\multicolumn{8}{c}{k = n/20}								\multicolumn{8}{c}{k = n/10}							
			GREEDY-F mean	time	PILOT-TR mean	time	LNS mean	time	CPLEX mean	gap	GREEDY-F mean	time	PILOT-TR mean	time	LNS mean	time	CPLEX mean	gap	GREEDY-F mean	time	PILOT-TR mean	time	LNS mean	time	CPLEX mean	gap
100	100	0.01	29.0	0.0	31.0	0.1	32.1	0.1	32.1	0.0	33.5	0.0	35.3	0.0	39.6	0.1	39.6	0.0	42.2	0.0	43.8	0.0	49.7	1.7	49.7	0.0
		0.03	2.5	0.0	3.9	0.2	4.0	0.1	3.9	>99.9	4.4	0.0	7.6	0.1	8.2	0.1	7.5	>99.9	7.7	0.0	13.2	0.2	14.8	0.2	14.3	99.1
		0.05	1.9	0.0	2.1	0.1	2.1	0.0	1.6	>99.9	2.6	0.0	4.2	0.0	4.2	0.1	3.7	>99.9	4.2	0.0	8.0	0.1	8.0	0.1	6.9	>99.9
	500	0.01	1.4	0.0	1.4	0.1	1.4	0.0	1.0	>99.9	2.2	0.0	3.2	0.1	3.2	0.1	2.4	>99.9	3.6	0.0	5.8	0.4	5.8	0.1	4.5	>99.9
		0.03	1.0	0.0	1.0	0.1	1.0	0.0	1.0	>99.9	1.0	0.0	1.0	0.1	1.0	0.1	1.0	>99.9	1.0	0.0	1.0	0.1	1.0	0.0	1.0	>99.9
		0.05	1.0	0.0	1.0	0.1	1.0	0.0	1.0	>99.9	1.0	0.0	1.0	0.1	1.0	0.0	1.0	>99.9	1.0	0.0	1.0	0.0	1.0	0.0	1.0	>99.9
	1000	0.01	1.0	0.0	1.0	0.2	1.0	0.0	1.0	>99.9	1.1	0.0	1.1	0.2	1.1	1.0	1.0	>99.9	2.0	0.0	2.1	0.0	2.1	0.0	1.3	>99.9
		0.03	1.0	0.0	1.0	0.2	1.0	0.0	1.0	>99.9	1.0	0.0	1.0	0.2	1.0	1.0	1.0	>99.9	1.0	0.0	1.0	0.2	1.0	0.0	1.0	>99.9
		0.05	1.0	0.0	1.0	0.2	1.0	0.0	1.0	>99.9	1.0	0.0	1.0	0.2	1.0	0.0	1.0	>99.9	1.0	0.0	1.0	0.2	1.0	0.0	1.0	>99.9
500	100	0.005	139.3	0.0	143.0	2.0	147.0	1.7	147.0	0.0	244.5	0.0	248.2	16.4	284.9	5.2	284.9	0.0	346.7	0.0	350.6	20.4	390.0	2.7	390.0	0.0
		0.015	137.2	0.0	141.7	2.0	145.2	2.1	145.2	0.0	242.8	0.0	247.5	12.9	284.2	4.7	248.2	0.0	348.5	0.0	351.8	20.4	390.8	2.3	390.8	0.0
		0.025	39.4	0.0	44.9	1.8	45.8	1.5	45.8	77.4	118.5	0.0	129.1	16.6	160.7	21.6	160.3	29.6	228.4	0.0	243.7	28.7	285.6	19.2	286.1	4.9
	500	0.005	33.3	0.0	36.6	7.1	37.3	3.2	21.4	>99.9	56.8	0.0	69.7	79.5	86.9	13.9	75.8	89.9	84.5	0.0	104.0	114.0	135.1	14.4	127.2	38.8
		0.015	1.2	0.0	1.3	2.0	1.2	0.0	0.5	>99.9	6.3	0.0	12.3	20.7	12.3	8.7	0.3	>99.9	12.0	0.0	24.2	54.4	23.4	30.1	0.0	>99.9
		0.025	1.0	0.0	1.0	2.0	1.0	0.0	0.7	>99.9	3.7	0.0	5.4	8.6	5.2	13.8	0.4	>99.9	6.7	0.0	11.4	19.3	10.9	20.1	0.9	>99.9
	1000	0.005	2.2	0.0	2.3	4.0	2.3	0.0	0.4	>99.9	8.8	0.0	18.2	62.2	19.5	13.8	0.3	>99.9	16.1	0.0	32.6	113.8	34.7	13.9	0.1	>99.9
		0.015	1.0	0.1	1.0	3.9	1.0	0.0	0.1	>99.9	2.8	0.0	3.9	11.5	3.8	0.0	0.0	>99.9	5.1	0.0	7.9	26.6	7.6	5.1	0.0	>99.9
		0.025	1.0	0.1	1.0	3.9	1.0	0.0	0.4	>99.9	2.0	0.1	2.0	4.1	2.0	0.0	0.3	>99.9	3.0	0.1	4.0	12.3	4.0	0.0	0.0	>99.9
1000	100	0.001	270.4	0.0	276.9	10.6	281.9	15.9	282.6	0.0	664.3	0.1	668.8	87.1	733.0	25.4	733.0	0.0	1000	0.0	1000.0	106.5	1000.0	0.0	1000.0	0.0
		0.003	271.4	0.0	276.1	8.3	280.2	48.9	280.5	0.0	660.6	0.0	666.1	86.6	735.9	32.5	735.9	0.0	1000	0.0	1000.0	106.4	1000.0	0.0	1000.0	0.0
		0.005	265.8	0.0	274.4	8.3	280.4	32.6	280.4	0.0	666.0	0.0	671.9	87.4	737.1	27.3	737.1	0.0	1000	0.0	1000.0	106.2	1000.0	0.0	1000.0	0.0
	500	0.001	257.7	0.1	260.9	34.3	264.1	13.5	29.8	>99.9	372.0	0.1	375.8	463.0	446.9	22.2	397.8	>99.9	487.7	0.1	491.0	835.5	590.6	16.2	529.3	>99.9
		0.003	254.0	0.1	258.2	34.2	262.3	14.5	24.3	>99.9	372.0	0.1	375.9	470.7	444.5	35.7	399.3	>99.9	485.6	0.1	488.9	839.4	586.1	18.8	586.1	0.0
		0.005	63.6	0.1	68.7	30.1	69.8	5.8	6.6	>99.9	134.5	0.1	160.7	544.0	211.8	54.0	0.3	>99.9	221.7	0.1	257.2	1022.5	338.0	60.5	0.0	>99.9
	1000	0.001	253.0	0.1	256.3	61.4	259.1	17.1	127.9	>99.9	334.0	0.1	337.8	836.3	400.6	25.4	111.8	>99.9	422.3	0.1	425.4	1549.12	500.0	23.9	0.0	>99.9
		0.003	17.7	0.1	19.9	36.2	20.6	10.2	0.0	>99.9	45.5	0.1	75.6	833.0	93.5	51.6	0.0	>99.9	78.7	0.1	131.8	1586.8	158.2	60.2	0.0	>99.9
		0.005	3.0	0.1	3.6	17.3	3.6	0.9	0.0	>99.9	16.3	0.1	42.2	578.3	40.6	24.2	0.0	>99.9	32.8	0.1	74.0	1025.7	74.1	91.9	0.0	>99.9

Table 4.4. Experimental results for instances where $|\Sigma| = 4$

			k = 2								k = n/20								k = n/10							
			GREEDY-F		PILOT-TR		LNS		CPLEX		GREEDY-F		PILOT-TR		LNS		CPLEX		GREEDY-F		PILOT-TR		LNS		CPLEX	
n	m	p_c	mean	time	mean	time	mean	time	mean	gap	mean	time	mean	time	mean	time	mean	gap	mean	time	mean	time	mean	time	mean	gap
100	100	0.01	13.3	0.0	15.4	0.1	16.8	0.1	16.8	0.0	18.6	0.0	21.0	0.1	25.9	0.1	25.9	0.0	27.9	0.0	29.9	0.2	37.3	0.1	37.3	0.0
		0.03	1.6	0.0	1.9	0.0	1.8	5.0	1.9	0.0	2.7	0.0	4.4	0.1	4.4	0.1	4.3	0.0	4.5	0.9	8.8	0.1	8.7	0.3	8.8	0.0
		0.05	1.0	0.0	1.0	1.0	1.0	0.0	1.0	0.0	1.9	0.0	2.0	0.0	2.0	5.0	2.0	0.0	3.0	0.0	4.0	0.1	4.0	0.9	4.0	0.0
	500	0.01	1.0	0.0	1.0	1.0	1.0	0.0	1.0	0.0	1.5	0.0	1.7	0.5	1.5	0.0	1.7	87.3	2.7	0.0	3.2	0.2	3.2	0.0	3.1	>99.9
		0.03	1.0	0.0	1.0	1.0	1.0	0.0	1.0	0.0	1.0	0.0	1.0	0.0	1.0	0.0	1.0	>99.9	1.0	0.0	1.0	0.1	1.0	0.0	1.0	>99.9
		0.05	1.0	0.0	1.0	1.0	1.0	0.0	1.0	0.0	1.0	0.0	1.0	0.2	1.0	0.0	1.0	>99.9	1.0	0.0	1.0	0.1	1.0	0.0	1.0	>99.9
	1000	0.01	1.0	0.0	1.0	1.0	1.0	0.0	1.0	0.0	1.0	0.0	1.0	0.2	1.0	0.0	1.0	0.0	1.1	0.0	1.0	0.2	1.1	0.0	1.1	>99.9
		0.03	1.0	0.0	1.0	0.2	1.0	0.0	1.0	0.0	1.0	0.0	1.0	0.2	1.0	0.0	1.0	0.0	1.0	0.0	1.0	0.2	1.0	0.0	1.0	0.0
		0.05	1.0	0.0	1.0	0.2	1.0	0.0	1.0	>99.9	1.0	0.0	1.0	0.2	1.0	0.0	1.0	>99.9	1.0	0.0	1.0	0.2	1.0	0.0	1.0	0.0
500	100	0.005	51.2	0.0	56.6	2.1	60.5	6.7	60.5	0.0	180.2	0.0	184.9	15.8	224.4	7.2	224.4	0.0	307.8	0.0	310.9	25.8	352.1	3.4	352.1	0.0
		0.015	50.2	0.0	54.9	2.1	59.1	3.1	59.1	0.0	173.7	0.0	178.6	16.0	222.5	5.8	222.5	0.0	298.1	0.0	302.0	26.0	353.1	3.1	353.1	0.0
		0.025	7.4	0.0	11.4	1.3	11.4	6.2	10.9	>99.9	66.6	0.0	73.6	16.3	104.4	23.0	99.6	85.6	168.9	0.0	183.9	30.8	233.2	14.6	231.4	22.4
	500	0.005	5.8	0.0	7.9	6.0	8.4	2.2	2.0	>99.9	23.1	0.0	35.2	54.2	46.6	10.9	17.3	>99.9	44.8	0.0	64.6	102.2	84.3	34.8	72.7	>99.9
		0.015	1.0	0.0	1.0	2.6	1.0	0.0	1.0	>99.9	4.9	0.0	7.2	12.2	7.0	0.0	3.6	>99.9	8.9	0.0	15.0	26.6	14.6	10.1	10.1	>99.9
		0.025	1.0	0.0	1.0	2.0	1.0	0.0	0.3	>99.9	2.8	0.0	3.0	5.5	3.0	0.0	1.2	>99.9	5.3	0.0	5.3	12.7	6.9	6.9	1.6	>99.9
	1000	0.005	1.0	0.0	1.0	3.9	1.0	0.0	0.5	>99.9	6.3	0.0	10.5	35.7	10.5	13.0	0.0	>99.9	11.9	0.1	20.3	68.6	19.6	26.0	0.0	>99.9
		0.015	1.0	0.0	1.0	3.9	1.0	0.0	0.5	>99.9	2.0	0.0	2.1	7.7	2.1	0.0	0.3	>99.9	4.0	0.0	5.0	16.9	5.0	0.0	0.1	>99.9
		0.025	1.0	0.0	1.0	4.0	1.0	0.0	0.8	>99.9	1.0	0.0	1.0	4.0	1.0	0.0	0.5	>99.9	2.0	0.1	2.2	7.8	2.1	0.0	2.2	>99.9
1000	100	0.001	105.5	0.0	110.8	8.5	112.1	24.0	116.2	18.6	575.8	0.0	582.7	105.9	661.0	57.4	658.5	0.0	1000.0	0.0	1000.0	163.0	1000.0	0.1	1000.0	0.0
		0.003	100.2	0.0	107.4	8.5	111.7	26.2	113.4	19.1	572.9	0.0	578.9	105.9	660.5	47.4	660.5	0.0	1000.0	0.0	1000.0	130.4	1000.0	0.1	1000.0	0.0
		0.005	105.4	0.0	110.5	8.5	114.4	45.7	115.2	19.1	576.8	0.0	582.3	105.4	660.8	48.1	660.8	0.0	1000.0	0.0	1000.0	129.9	1000.0	0.1	1000.0	0.0
	500	0.001	88.3	0.1	93.9	37.0	95.0	13.6	72.2	>99.9	222.0	0.1	226.9	600.6	305.3	58.5	0.0	>99.9	355.7	0.1	360.5	1086.1	460.5	34.6	460.8	10.5
		0.003	91.3	0.1	95.4	36.9	100.8	17.3	55.8	>99.9	223.5	0.1	227.0	590.7	311.4	62.1	0.0	>99.9	358.1	0.1	361.9	1073.2	469.6	37.4	320.9	>99.9
		0.005	9.0	0.1	12.2	24.3	13.6	7.9	0.0	>99.9	59.0	0.1	82.1	492.0	120.9	65.4	0.0	>99.9	128.5	0.1	165.8	981.1	232.4	81.2	0.0	>99.9
	1000	0.001	91.6	0.2	95.0	70.5	94.3	29.6	34.8	>99.9	181.6	0.2	185.4	1382.6	250.7	65.7	0.0	>99.9	272.5	0.0	275.7	1966.1	366.0	27.3	0.0	>99.9
		0.003	2.1	0.2	2.7	17.6	2.4	0.7	0.0	>99.9	21.4	0.2	49.2	673.0	46.7	32.1	0.0	>99.9	44.4	0.2	93.1	1292.1	89.5	47.8	0.0	>99.9
		0.005	1.0	0.2	1.0	15.3	1.0	0.0	0.0	>99.9	12.4	0.2	23.7	323.6	21.7	10.4	0.0	>99.9	24.2	0.2	47.8	663.4	44.9	5.3	0.0	>99.9

Table 4.5. Experimental results for instances where $|\Sigma| = 12$

n	m	p_c	k = 2 GREEDY-F mean	time	PILOT-TR mean	time	LNS mean	time	CPLEX mean	gap	k = n/20 GREEDY-F mean	time	PILOT-TR mean	time	LNS mean	time	CPLEX mean	gap	k = n/10 GREEDY-F mean	time	PILOT-TR mean	time	LNS mean	time	CPLEX mean	gap
100	100	0.01	8.7	0.0	10.5	0.1	12.2	0.1	12.2	0.0	14.6	0.0	16.4	0.1	21.5	0.2	21.5	0.0	23.8	0.0	26.0	0.3	34.0	0.1	34.0	0.0
		0.03	1.5	0.0	1.5	0.0	1.5	0.0	1.5	0.0	2.9	0.0	3.8	0.0	3.8	0.1	3.9	0.0	4.9	0.0	8.4	0.1	8.3	0.2	8.4	0.0
		0.05	1.0	0.0	1.0	0.0	1.0	0.0	1.0	0.0	1.8	0.0	1.9	0.0	1.8	0.0	1.9	0.0	3.0	0.0	3.9	0.8	3.9	0.8	3.9	>99.9
	500	0.01	1.0	0.0	1.0	0.0	1.0	0.0	1.0	0.0	1.2	0.0	1.3	0.1	1.2	0.0	1.2	>99.9	2.5	0.0	3.0	0.2	3.0	0.0	2.9	>99.9
		0.03	1.0	0.0	1.0	0.0	1.0	0.0	1.0	0.0	1.0	0.0	1.0	0.0	1.0	0.0	1.0	>99.9	1.0	0.0	1.0	0.1	1.0	0.0	1.0	>99.9
		0.05	1.0	0.0	1.0	0.0	1.0	0.0	1.0	0.0	1.0	0.0	1.0	0.0	1.0	0.0	1.0	>99.9	1.0	0.0	1.0	0.0	1.0	0.0	1.0	>99.9
	1000	0.01	1.0	0.0	1.0	0.1	1.0	0.0	1.0	0.0	1.0	0.0	1.0	0.2	1.0	0.0	1.0	0.0	1.0	0.0	1.0	0.1	1.0	0.0	1.0	>99.9
		0.03	1.0	0.0	1.0	0.2	1.0	0.0	1.0	0.0	1.0	0.0	1.0	0.2	1.0	0.0	1.0	0.0	1.0	0.0	1.0	0.2	1.0	0.0	1.0	>99.9
		0.05	1.0	0.0	1.0	0.2	1.0	0.0	1.0	>99.9	1.0	0.0	1.0	0.2	1.0	0.0	1.0	>99.9	1.0	0.0	1.0	0.2	1.0	0.0	1.0	>99.9
500	100	0.005	35.3	0.0	39.7	2.0	44.1	9.3	44.1	0.0	161.9	0.0	166.4	16.3	214.8	9.8	214.8	0.0	295.4	0.0	299.1	26.7	350.1	4.3	350.1	0.0
		0.015	34.7	0.0	40.1	2.0	44.0	7.4	44.0	0.0	164.1	0.0	170.3	16.2	213.6	6.7	213.6	0.0	294.5	0.0	298.0	26.5	347.5	4.5	347.5	0.0
		0.025	3.4	0.0	7.4	1.1	7.3	2.2	7.5	>99.9	58.2	0.0	71.7	15.8	96.9	30.2	92.5	94.7	168.9	0.0	183.4	30.4	225.0	29.1	223.1	24.9
	500	0.005	3.2	0.1	5.3	5.0	5.7	3.8	1.2	0.0	17.9	0.0	31.7	52.0	41.0	11.1	8.4	>99.9	37.1	0.1	61.5	99.5	77.7	21.3	61.7	>99.9
		0.015	1.0	0.1	1.0	2.0	1.0	0.0	1.0	>99.9	4.1	0.1	6.1	10.2	6.0	6.0	4.0	>99.9	8.5	0.1	13.8	23.5	12.8	5.0	10.0	>99.9
		0.025	1.0	0.1	1.0	2.0	1.0	0.0	1.0	>99.9	2.3	0.1	3.0	4.5	3.0	0.0	1.6	>99.9	5.0	0.0	5.0	11.6	6.2	6.2	3.3	>99.9
	1000	0.005	1.0	0.1	1.0	3.8	1.0	0.0	0.1	>99.9	5.9	0.0	9.0	29.5	8.5	13.6	0.0	>99.9	11.1	0.1	18.1	61.5	17.4	15.9	0.0	>99.9
		0.015	1.0	0.1	1.0	3.9	1.0	0.0	0.4	>99.9	2.0	0.1	2.0	7.6	2.0	0.0	0.6	>99.9	4.0	0.1	4.5	15.4	4.2	0.0	0.4	>99.9
		0.025	1.0	0.1	1.0	5.1	1.0	0.0	0.7	>99.9	1.0	0.0	1.0	4.0	1.0	0.0	0.9	>99.9	2.0	0.1	2.0	7.8	2.0	0.0	0.8	>99.9
1000	100	0.001	71.3	0.0	77.6	8.4	80.6	29.6	82.2	24.4	560.0	0.0	565.8	109.2	645.0	52.0	645.0	0.0	1000.0	0.1	1000.0	134.8	1000.0	0.1	1000.0	0.0
		0.003	68.1	0.0	75.3	8.4	79.9	35.6	80.9	76.5	558.3	0.0	565.7	109.7	646.2	60.4	646.7	0.0	1000.0	0.1	1000.0	135.3	1000.0	0.1	1000.0	0.0
		0.005	66.9	0.0	76.1	8.4	82.0	39.3	83.6	21.4	561.4	0.0	566.2	110.6	648.2	61.4	648.2	0.0	1000.0	0.0	1000.0	135.0	1000.0	0.1	1000.0	0.0
	500	0.001	55.7	0.1	60.7	37.1	64.6	19.0	16.0	>99.9	188.2	0.1	193.3	653.3	281.7	55.1	29.4	>99.9	323.9	0.1	328.3	1127.6	443.6	31.2	208.5	>99.9
		0.003	53.4	0.1	56.4	37.1	59.9	19.7	15.5	>99.9	189.9	0.1	193.6	618.9	277.9	34.9	0.0	>99.9	324.7	0.1	328.9	1170.7	439.8	31.5	339.3	>99.9
		0.005	4.7	0.1	7.7	22.3	7.9	18.7	0.0	>99.9	47.7	0.1	72.7	476.4	102.5	87.9	0.0	>99.9	111.1	0.1	151.7	931.3	212.8	70.4	0.0	>99.9
	1000	0.001	54.1	0.2	58.0	69.8	59.8	33.6	17.8	>99.9	147.2	0.2	150.7	1111.7	217.0	61.1	0.0	>99.9	244.6	0.2	248.0	2840.9	342.0	22.2	0.0	>99.9
		0.003	2.0	0.2	2.1	16.1	2.0	0.0	0.0	>99.9	19.6	0.2	41.2	569.3	39.1	93.5	0.0	>99.9	40.3	0.2	81.6	1099.8	78.3	79.8	0.0	>99.9
		0.005	1.0	0.2	1.0	15.3	1.0	0.0	0.0	>99.9	11.9	0.2	20.2	275.1	18.8	0.1	0.0	>99.9	23.7	0.2	42.7	582.7	39.9	16.1	0.0	>99.9

Table 4.6. Experimental results for instances where $|\Sigma| = 20$

In addition to the numerical results, Figure 4.1 shows the improvement of LNS over PILOT-TR and Figure 4.2 shows the improvement of LNS over CPLEX. X, Y and Z take values from $\{S, M, L\}$, where S refers to *small*, M refers to *medium* and L refers to *large*. While X refers to the number of input strings, Y refers to their length and Z to the probability of change. In positions X and Y, S refers to 100, M to 500 and L to 1000, while in the case of Z, S refers to $\{0.01, 0.005, 0.001\}$, M to $\{0.03, 0.015, 0.003\}$ and L to $\{0.05, 0.025, 0.005\}$, depending on the value of n.

The following observations can be made on the basis of the results:

– alphabet size does not seem to play a role in the relative performance of the algorithms. An increasing alphabet size decreases the objective function values;

– PILOT-TR and LNS outperform GREEDY-F. It is beneficial to start the greedy strategy from n different partial solutions (each one containing exactly one of the n input strings) instead of applying the greedy strategy to the partial solution containing the string obtained by the frequency-based mechanism;

– LNS and PILOT-TR perform comparably for small problems. When large problems are concerned, especially in the case of $|\Sigma| = 4$, LNS generally outperforms PILOT-TR. However, there are some noticeable exceptions, especially for L-S-S and L-L-S in Figure 4.1(b) and L-L-S in Figure 4.1(c), i.e. when $k = 2$ and problems are large, PILOT-TR sometimes performs better than LNS;

– with LNS the relative behavior that is to be expected and CPLEX is displayed in Figure 4.2. LNS is competitive with CPLEX for small and medium instances all alphabet sizes and for all values of k. Moreover, LNS generally outperforms CPLEX in the context of larger problems. This is, again, with the exception of L-S-* in the case of $|\Sigma| \in \{12, 20\}$ for $k = 2$, where CPLEX performs slightly better than LNS;

– CPLEX requires substantially more computation time than LNS, GREEDY-R and PILOT-TR to reach solutions of similar quality.

In summary, LNS is currently the state-of-the-art method for the MSFBC problem. The disadvantages of LNS in comparison to PILOT-TR and CPLEX, for instance, where $|\Sigma| \in \{12, 20\}$ and $k = 2$, leave room for further improvement.

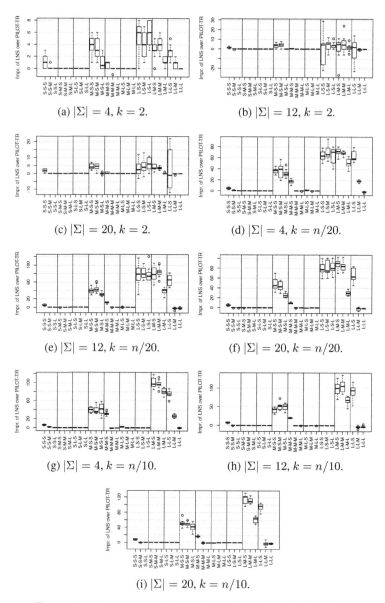

(a) $|\Sigma| = 4, k = 2.$ (b) $|\Sigma| = 12, k = 2.$

(c) $|\Sigma| = 20, k = 2.$ (d) $|\Sigma| = 4, k = n/20.$

(e) $|\Sigma| = 12, k = n/20.$ (f) $|\Sigma| = 20, k = n/20.$

(g) $|\Sigma| = 4, k = n/10.$ (h) $|\Sigma| = 12, k = n/10.$

(i) $|\Sigma| = 20, k = n/10.$

Figure 4.1. *Improvement of LNS over* PILOT-TR *(in absolute terms). Each box shows these differences for the corresponding 10 instances. Note that negative values indicate that* PILOT-TR *obtained a better result than LNS*

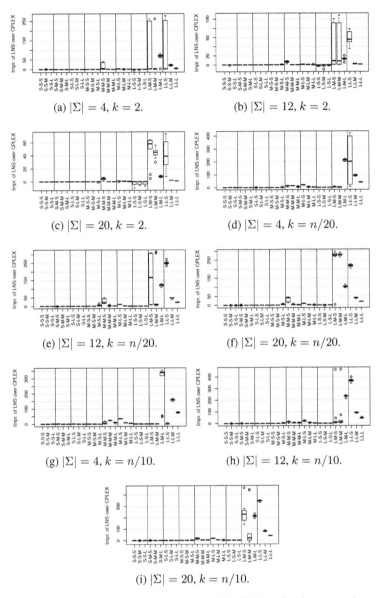

(a) $|\Sigma| = 4, k = 2$.

(b) $|\Sigma| = 12, k = 2$.

(c) $|\Sigma| = 20, k = 2$.

(d) $|\Sigma| = 4, k = n/20$.

(e) $|\Sigma| = 12, k = n/20$.

(f) $|\Sigma| = 20, k = n/20$.

(g) $|\Sigma| = 4, k = n/10$.

(h) $|\Sigma| = 12, k = n/10$.

(i) $|\Sigma| = 20, k = n/10$.

Figure 4.2. *Improvement of LNS over CPLEX (in absolute terms). Each box shows these differences for the corresponding 10 instances. Note that negative values indicate that CPLEX obtained a better result than LNS*

Finally, it is interesting to study the reasons that the tuning procedure (irace) has a very high percentage of destruction in nearly all cases. Remember that this is rather unusual for a LNS algorithm. To shed some light on this matter, LNS was applied for 100 iterations in two exemplary cases: (1) a problem with $n = 500$, $m = 100$, $p_c = 0.015$, $|\Sigma| = 4$; and $k = n/20$; and (2) a problem with $n = 1000$, $m = 500$, $p_c = 0.003$, $|\Sigma| = 4$ and $k = n/20$. This was done in both cases for fixed destruction over the whole range between 10% and 90%. In all runs, the average times needed by CPLEX to obtain optimal solutions when applied to the partial solution of each iteration was measured. The average times (together with the corresponding standard deviations) are displayed in Figure 4.3. It can be observed, in both cases, that CPLEX is very fast for any percentage destruction. In fact, the time difference betweens 10% and 90% destruction is nearly negligible. Moreover, note that CPLEX requires 18.1 seconds to solve the original problem optimally, whereas in the second case CPLEX is not able to find a solution with an optimality gap below 100 within 250 CPU seconds. This implies that in the case of the MSFBC problem, as long as a small partial solution is given, CPLEX is very fast in deriving the optimal solution that contains the respective partial solution. Moreover, there is hardly any difference in the computation time requirements with respect to the size of this partial solution. This is the main reason why irace chose a large destruction percentage in nearly all cases. This also implies that the computation time limit given to CPLEX within LNS hardly plays any role. In other words, all computation time limits considered were sufficient for CPLEX when applied within LNS. This is why no tendency can be observed in the values chosen by irace for $t_{\max}$.

4.6. Future work

Future work in the context of the MSFBC problem should exploit the following property: even when fed with very small partial solutions, CPLEX is often very fast in deriving the best possible solution containing a partial solution. In fact, a simple heuristic that profits from this property would start, for example, with the first string chosen by the frequency-based greedy method and would feed the resulting partial solution to CPLEX.

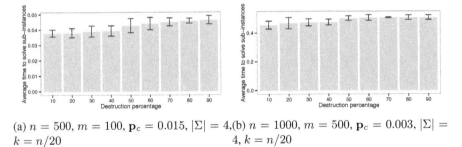

(a) $n = 500$, $m = 100$, $\mathbf{p}_c = 0.015$, $|\Sigma| = 4$,(b) $n = 1000$, $m = 500$, $\mathbf{p}_c = 0.003$, $|\Sigma| = $ $k = n/20$ 4, $k = n/20$

Figure 4.3. *Average time (in seconds) used by CPLEX within LNS for each application at each iteration. Two examples considering destruction between 10 and 90 percent*

Another line for future research includes the exploration of other, alternative, ways of combining metaheuristic strategies with CPLEX. One option concerns the use of CPLEX to derive a complete solution on the basis of a partial solution within the recombination operator of an evolutionary algorithm.

5

Consensus String Problems

This chapter provides an overview of some string selection and comparison problems, with special emphasis on *consensus string problems*. The intrinsic properties of the problems are studied and the most popular solution techniques given, including some recently-proposed heuristic and metaheuristic approaches. Finally, a simple and efficient ILP-based heuristic that can be used for any of the problems considered is presented. Future directions are discussed in the last section.

5.1. Introduction

Among string selection and comparison problems there is a class of problems known as consensus string problems, where a finite set of strings is given and one is interested in finding their consensus, i.e. a new string that agrees as much as possible with all the given strings. In other words, the objective is to determine a consensus string that once one or more criteria have been defined represents all the given strings. The idea of consensus can be related to several different objectives and prospectives. Some of them are considered in this chapter and are listed in the following:

1) the consensus is a new string whose total distance from all given strings is minimal (*closest string problem*);

2) the consensus is a new string close to most of the given strings (*close to most string problem*);

3) the consensus is a new string whose total distance from all given strings is maximal (*farthest string problem*);

4) the consensus is a new string far from most of the given strings (*far from most string problem*).

As a result of the linear coding of DNA and proteins, many molecular biology problems have been formulated as computational optimization (CO) problems involving strings and consisting of computing distance/proximity. Some biological applications require a region of similarity be discovered, while other applications use the reverse complement of the region, such as the designing of probes or primers. In the following, some relevant biological applications are listed.

5.1.1. *Creating diagnostic probes for bacterial infections*

Probes are strands of either DNA or RNA that have been modified (i.e. made either radioactive or fluorescent) so that their presence can be easily detected. One possible application of string problems arises in creating diagnostic probes for bacterial infections [LAN 04, MAC 90]. In this scenario, given a set of DNA strings from a group of closely-related pathogenic bacteria, the task is to find a substring that occurs in each of the bacterial strings (that is as close as possible) without occurring in the host's DNA. Probes are then designed to hybridize to these target strings, so that the detection of their presence indicates that at least one bacterial species is likely to be present in the host.

5.1.2. *Primer design*

Primers are short strings of nucleotides designed so that they hybridize to a given DNA string or to all of a given set of DNA strings with the aim of providing a starting point for DNA strand synthesis by polymerase chain reaction (PCR). The hybridization of primers depends on several conditions, including some thermodynamic rules, but it is largely influenced by the number of mismatching positions among the given strings, and this number should be as small as possible [GRA 03a, GRA 02, LI 99].

5.1.3. *Discovering potential drug targets*

Another biological application of string selection and comparison problems is related to discovering potential drug targets. Given a set of strings of orthologous genes from a group of closely-related pathogens, and a host (such as a human, crop, or livestock), the goal is to find a string fragment that is more conserved in all or most of the pathogens strings but not as conserved in the host. Information encoded by this fragment can then be used for novel antibiotic development or to create a drug that harms several pathogens with minimum effect on the host. All these applications involve finding a pattern that, with some error, occurs in one set of strings (closest string problem) and/or does not occur in another set (farthest string problem). The far from most string problem can help to identify a string fragment that distinguishes the pathogens from the host, so the potential exists to create a drug that harms several but not all pathogens [GRA 03a, GRA 02, LI 99].

5.1.4. Motif search

A motif is a string that is *approximately preserved* as a substring in some/several of the DNA strings of a given set. Approximately preserved means that the motif occurs with changes in at most t positions for a fixed non-negative integer t. The importance of a motif is that it is a candidate for substrings of non-coding parts of the DNA string that have functions related to, gene expression for instance [GRA 03a, GRA 02].

The general strings consensus problem was proved computationally intractable by Frances and Litman [FRA 97] and by Sim and Park [SIM 99, SIM 03]. For most consensus problems, Hamming distance is used instead of alternative measures, such as the editing distance. Given two strings s^1 and s^2 on an alphabet Σ: where $|s^1| = |s^2| = m$, $d_H(s^1, s^2)$ denotes their Hamming distance and is given by

$$d_H(s^1, s^2) = \sum_{j=1}^{|s^1|} \Phi(s_j^1, s_j^2),$$ [5.1]

where s_j^1 and s_j^2 denote the character at position j in string s^1 and in string s^2, respectively, and $\Phi : \Sigma \times \Sigma \to \{0, 1\}$ is a predicate function such that:

$$\Phi(a, b) = \begin{cases} 0, \text{ if } a = b; \\ 1, \text{ otherwise.} \end{cases}$$

For all consensus problems, each string s of length m over Σ is a valid solution. The biological reasons justifying the choice of the Hamming distance are very well described and motivated by Lanctot *et al.* in [LAN 99, LAN 03, LAN 04] and can be summarized with the claim that the "edit distance is more suitable to measure the *amount* of change that has happened, whereas the Hamming distance is more suitable to measure the *effect* of that change".

5.2. Organization of this chapter

The remainder of this chapter is organized as follows. Sections 5.3 and 5.4 are devoted to the closest string and the close to most string and the farthest string and the far from most string problem, respectively. All these problems are mathematically formulated and their properties analyzed. The most popular solutions are surveyed, along with the computational results obtained and analyzed in the literature. Section 5.5 describes a simple ILP-based heuristic that can be used for any of the problems considered. Concluding remarks and future directions are discussed in the last section.

5.3. The closest string problem and the close to most string problem

Given a finite set Ω of strings of length m over a finite alphabet Σ, the closest string problem (CSP) is to find a *center string* $s^* \in \Sigma^m$ such that the Hamming distance between s^* and all strings in Ω is minimal; in other words, s^* is a string to which a minimum value d corresponds such that:

$$d_H(s^*, s^i) \leq d, \quad \forall\, s^i \in \Omega.$$

The CSP can be seen as a special case of the close to most string problem (CTMSP), which consists of determining a string close to most of the strings in the input set Ω. This can be formalized by saying that, given a threshold t, a string s^* must be found maximizing the variable l such that:

$$d_H(s^*, s^i) \leq t, \text{ for } s^i \in P \subseteq \Sigma \text{ and } |P| = l.$$

5.3.1. *ILP models for the CSP and the CTMSP*

Let $\Sigma_k \subseteq \Sigma$ be the set of characters appearing at position k in any of the strings from Ω. The closest string problem can be formulated as an integer linear program (ILP) that uses $k = 1, 2, \ldots, m$ for each position and $c \in \Sigma_k$ for each character, the following binary variables:

$$x_{ck} = \begin{cases} 1, \text{ if character } c \in \Sigma_k \text{ is used at position } k \text{ of the solution;} \\ 0, \text{ otherwise.} \end{cases}$$

Then, the CSP can be formulated as follows:

$$\min \quad d \qquad\qquad\qquad\qquad\qquad\qquad\qquad\qquad\qquad [5.2]$$

$$\text{s.t.} \quad \sum_{c \in \Sigma_k} x_{ck} = 1 \qquad \text{for } k = 1, 2, \ldots, m \qquad\qquad [5.3]$$

$$m - \sum_{k=1}^{m} x_{s_k^i k} \leq d \qquad \text{for } i = 1, 2, \ldots, |\Omega| \qquad\qquad [5.4]$$

$$d \in \mathbb{N}^+ \qquad\qquad\qquad\qquad\qquad\qquad\qquad\qquad\quad [5.5]$$

$$x_{ck} \in \{0, 1\} \qquad \text{for } k = 1, 2, \ldots, m, \ \forall\, c \in \Sigma_k. \quad [5.6]$$

Objective function [5.2] minimizes d, i.e. the right-hand side of inequalities [5.4] which mean that if a character in a string s^i is not in the solution defined by the x-variables, then that character will contribute to increasing the Hamming distance from solution x to s^i. In this context, remember that s_k^i denotes the character at position k in $s^i \in \Omega$. d is forced to assume a non-negative integer value by [5.5]. Equalities [5.3] guarantee that only one character is selected for each position $k \in \{1, 2, \ldots, m\}$. Finally, [5.6] define the decision variables.

Besides the binary x-variables, to mathematically formulate the CTMSP a further binary vector $y \in \{0, 1\}^{|\Omega|}$ is introduced and the resulting ILP model can be stated as:

$$\max \quad \sum_{i=1}^{|\Omega|} y_i \qquad \qquad [5.7]$$

$$\text{s.t.} \quad \sum_{c \in \Sigma_k} x_{ck} = 1 \qquad \text{for } k = 1, 2, \ldots, m \qquad [5.8]$$

$$\sum_{k=1}^{m} x_{s_k^i k} \geq m \cdot y_i - t \qquad \text{for } i = 1, 2, \ldots, |\Omega| \qquad [5.9]$$

$$y_i \in \{0, 1\} \qquad \text{for } i = 1, 2, \ldots, |\Omega|, \qquad [5.10]$$

$$x_{ck} \in \{0, 1\} \qquad \text{for } k = 1, 2, \ldots, m, \ \forall \, c \in \Sigma_k. \quad [5.11]$$

Equalities [5.8] guarantee that only one character is selected for each position $k \in \{1, 2, \ldots, m\}$ for the CSP. Inequalities [5.4] ensure that y_i can only be set to 1 if and only if the number of differences between $s^i \in \Omega$ and the possible solution (as defined by setting of the x_{ck} variables) is less than or equal than t. The objective function [5.7] maximizes the number of y-variables set to 1. Finally, [5.10] and [5.11] define the decision variables.

5.3.2. Literature review

The CSP was first studied in the area of coding theory [ROM 92] and has been independently proven to be computationally intractable in [FRA 97] and in [LAN 99, LAN 03].

Since then, few exact and approximation algorithms and several heuristic procedures have been proposed. Despite its similarity with the CSP, the CTMSP instead has not been widely studied. In [BOU 13] it was proven that this problem has no polynomial-time approximation scheme (PTAS)[1] unless NP has randomized polynomial-time algorithms.

---

1 A PTAS is a special type of approximation algorithm that, for each $\epsilon > 1$, yields a performance guarantee of ϵ in polynomial time. Thus, this can be viewed as a way of getting solutions with guaranteed performance, for any desired threshold greater than one.

5.3.3. *Exact approaches for the CSP*

In 2004, Meneses *et al.* [PAR 04] used a linear relaxation of the ILP model of the problem to design a B&B algorithm. At each iteration, to generate the next node in the branching tree the best bound first strategy is adopted to select the next node and obtain an optimal fractional solution $x'_{ck} \in [0,1]$, $k = 1, 2, \ldots, m$, $\forall\, c \in \Sigma_k$, for the linear relaxation of the corresponding subproblem, and the algorithm branches on the fractional variable x_{ck} with maximum value of x'_{ck}. For the bounding phase, the authors computed an initial bound selecting one of the given input strings and modified it until a local optimal solution was found. They have empirically shown that their B&B algorithm is able to solve small-size instances with 10 to 30 strings, each of which is between 300 and 800 characters long in reasonable times.

Further exact methods proposed for the CSP are fixed-parameter algorithms [GRA 03b, MA 08, MA 09, WAN 09, PAP 13] that are applicable only when the maximum Hamming distance among pairs of strings is small. Since these algorithms are designed to solve the decision version of the problem, it is necessary to apply them multiple times to find an optimal solution that minimizes the Hamming distance.

In where the special case $|\Omega| = 3$ and $|\Sigma| = 2$, Liu *et al.* [LIU 11] designed an exact approach called distance first algorithm (DFA), whose basic idea is to let the Hamming distance $d_H(s^*, s^i)$, $i = 1, 2, 3$, be as small as possible. The algorithm decreases the distance between the string that is farthest from the other two strings and solution s^*, while increasing the distance between the string that is closest to the other two strings and solution s^*.

5.3.4. *Approximation algorithms for the CSP*

The first approximation algorithm for the CSP was proposed in 2003 by Lanctot *et al.* [LAN 03]. It is a simple purely random algorithm with a worst case performance ratio of 2. It starts from an empty solution and, until a complete solution is no obtained, it randomly selects the next element to be added to the solution being constructed.

Better performance approximation algorithms are based on the linear programming relaxation of the ILP model. The basic idea consists of solving the linear programming relaxation of the model, and in using the result to find an approximate solution to the original problem. Following this line, Lanctot *et al.* [LAN 03] proposed a $\frac{4}{3}(1 + \epsilon)$- approximation algorithm (for any small $\epsilon > 0$) that uses the randomized rounding technique to obtain an integer 0–1 solution from the continuous solution[2]. In 1999, Li *et al.* [LI 99] designed a PTAS that is also based on randomized rounding, refined to check results for a large (but polynomially bounded) number of subsets of indices. Unfortunately, a large number of iterations involves the solution of a linear relaxation of an ILP model, and this makes the algorithm impractical for solving large strings problems. To efficiently deal with real-world scenarios and/or medium to large problems, several heuristic and metaheuristic algorithms have been proposed.

5.3.5. *Heuristics and metaheuristics for the CSP*

In 2005, Lui *et al.* [LIU 05] designed a genetic algorithm and a simulated annealing algorithm, both in sequential and parallel versions. Genetic algorithms (GAs) (see also section 1.2.2) are population-based metaheuristics that have been applied to find optimal or near-optimal solutions to combinatorial optimization problems [GOL 89, HOL 75]. They implement the concept of *survival of the fittest*, making an analogy between a solution and an *individual* in a *population*. Each individual has a corresponding *chromosome* that encodes the solution. A chromosome consists of a string of *genes*. Each gene can take on a value, called an *allele*, from an alphabet. A chromosome has an associated *fitness level* which with correlates the corresponding objective function value of the solution it encodes. Over a number of iterations, called *generations*, GAs evolve a population of chromosomes. This is usually accomplished by simulating the process of natural selection through mating and mutation. For the CSP, starting from an initially randomly-generated population, at each generation $0 \le t \le$ number − generations of Liu *et al.*'s GA, a population $P(t)$ of popsize strings of length m evolves and the fitness function to be maximized is defined as the difference $m - d_{\max}$, where $d_{\max}$ is the largest Hamming distance between an individual of the population $P(t)$ and any string in Ω.

---

2 The randomized rounding technique works by defining the value of a Boolean variable $x \in \{0, 1\}$ as $x = 1$ with a certain probability y, where y is the value of the continuous variable corresponding to x in the relaxation of the original integer programming problem.

The production of offspring in a GA is done through the process of mating or crossover, and Liu *et al.* used a multi-point-crossover (MPX). At generic generation t, two parental individuals x and y in $P(t)$ are chosen randomly according to a probability proportional to their fitness. Then, iteratively until the offspring is not complete, x and y exchange parts at two randomly picked points. The strings in the resulting offspring have a different order, one part from the *first parent* and the other part from the *second parent*. Afterwards, a mutation in any individual in the current population $P(t)$ occurs with given probability. During this phase, two positions are randomly chosen and exchanged in the individual.

In their paper, Liu *et al.* proposed a simulated annealing (SA) algorithm for the CSP (see section 1.2.5 for a general introduction to SA). Originally proposed in [KIR 83], in the optimization and computer science research communities, SA is commonly said to be the "oldest" metaheuristic and one of the first techniques that had an explicit strategy to escape from local minima. Its fundamental idea is to allow moves resulting in poorer solutions in terms of objective function value (uphill moves). The origin of SA and the choice of the acceptance criterion of a better quality solution lie in the physical annealing process, which can be modeled by methods based on Monte Carlo techniques. One of the early Monte Carlo techniques for simulating the evolution of a solid in a heat bath to thermal equilibrium is due to [MET 53], who designed a method that iteratively (until a stopping criterion is met) generates a string of states at a generic iteration k, given a current solid state i (i.e. a current solution x) where:

– E_i is the energy of the solid in state i (objective function value $f(x)$);

– a subsequent state j (solution $\overline{x}$) is generated with energy E_j (objective function value $f(\overline{x})$) by applying a *perturbation mechanism* such as displacement of a single particle ($\overline{x}$ is a solution "close"to x);

– if $E_j - E_i < 0$ (i.e. $\overline{x}$ is a better quality solution), j ($\overline{x}$) is accepted; otherwise, j ($\overline{x}$) is accepted with probability given by

$$\exp\left(-\frac{E_j - E_i}{k_B T_k}\right) \qquad \left[\exp\left(-\frac{f(\overline{x}) - f(x)}{k_B \cdot T_k}\right)\right],$$

where T_k is the heat bath temperature and k_B is the Boltzmann constant.

As the number of iterations performed increases, the current temperature T_k decreases resulting in a smaller probability of accepting unimproved solutions. For the CSP, Liu *et al.*'s SA sets the initial temperature T_0 to $\frac{m}{2}$. The current temperature T_k is reduced every 100 iterations according to the "geometric cooling schedule" $T_{k+100} = \gamma \cdot T_k$, where $\gamma = 0.9$. When a current temperature less than or equal to 0.001 is reached, the stopping criterion is met. Despite the interesting ideas proposed in [LIU 05], the experimental analysis involves only small instances with up to 40 strings 40 characters in length.

More recently, [TAN 12] proposed a novel heuristic (TA) based on the Lagrangian relaxation of the ILP model of the problem that allows us to deconstruct the problem into subproblems, each corresponding to a position of the strings. The proposed algorithm combines a Lagrangian multiplier adjustment procedure to obtain feasibility and a Tabu search as local improvement procedure. In [CRO 12], Della Croce and Salassa described three relaxation-based procedures. One procedure (RA) rounds up the result of continuous relaxation, while the other two approaches (BCPA and ECPA) fix a subset of the integer variables in the continuous solution at the current value and let the solver run on the remaining (sub)problem. The authors also observed that all relaxation-based algorithms have been tested on *rectangular instances*, i.e. with $n \ll m$, and that the instances where $n \geq m$ are harder to solve due to the higher number of constraints imposed by the strings, which enlarge the portion of non-integer components in the continuous solution. In the attempt to overcome this drawback, [CRO 14] designed a multistart relaxation-based algorithm (called the selective fixing algorithm) that for a predetermined number of iterations, inputs a feasible solution and iteratively selects variables to be fixed at their initial value until the number of free variables is small enough that the remaining subproblem can be efficiently solved to optimality by an ILP solver. The new solution found by the solver can then be used as the initial solution for the next iteration. The authors have experimentally shown that their algorithm is much more robust than the state-of-the-art competitors and is able to solve a wider set of instances of different types, including those with $n \geq m$.

5.4. The farthest string problem and the far from most string problem

The farthest string problem (FSP) consists of finding a string $s^* \in \Sigma^m$ farthest from the strings in Ω; in other words, s^* is a string to which a maximum value d corresponds such that:

$$d_H(s^*, s^i) \geq d, \quad \forall s^i \in \Omega.$$

In biology, this type of string problem can be useful in situations such as finding a genetic string that cannot be associated with a given number of species. A problem closely related to the FSP is the far from most string problem (FFMSP). It consists of determining a string far from most of the strings in the input set Ω. This can be formalized by saying that, given a threshold t, a string s^* must be found that maximizes the variable l such that:

$$d_H(s^*, s^i) \geq t, \text{ for } s^i \in P \subseteq \Sigma \text{ and } |P| = l.$$

5.4.1. ILP models for the FSP and the FFMSP

The FSP can be formulated mathematically in the form of an ILP, where both decision variables and constraints are interpreted differently to the those in the CSP:

$$\max \quad d \qquad\qquad\qquad\qquad\qquad\qquad\qquad [5.12]$$

$$\text{s.t.} \quad \sum_{c \in \Sigma_k} x_{ck} = 1 \qquad \text{for } k = 1, 2, \ldots, m \qquad [5.13]$$

$$m - \sum_{k=1}^{m} x_{s_k^i k} \geq d \qquad \text{for } i = 1, 2, \ldots, |\Omega| \qquad [5.14]$$

$$d \in \mathbb{N}^+ \qquad\qquad\qquad\qquad\qquad\qquad\qquad [5.15]$$

$$x_{ck} \in \{0, 1\} \qquad \text{for } k = 1, 2, \ldots, m, \ \forall\, c \in \Sigma_k. \quad [5.16]$$

Here, the objective function [5.12] maximizes d, which is the right-hand side of inequalities [5.14].

To formulate the FFMSP mathematically in [BLU 14c], a further binary vector $y \in \{0, 1\}^{|\Omega|}$ has been defined and the resulting ILP model can be stated as follows:

$$\max \quad \sum_{i=1}^{|\Omega|} y_i \qquad\qquad\qquad\qquad\qquad\qquad [5.17]$$

$$\text{s.t.} \quad \sum_{c \in \Sigma_k} x_{ck} = 1 \qquad\qquad \text{for } k = 1, 2, \ldots, m \quad [5.18]$$

$$\sum_{k=1}^{m} x_{s_k^i k} \leq m - t \cdot y_i \qquad \text{for } i = 1, 2, \ldots, |\Omega| \quad [5.19]$$

$$y_i \in \{0, 1\} \qquad\qquad \text{for } i = 1, 2, \ldots, |\Omega|, \quad [5.20]$$

$$x_{ck} \in \{0, 1\} \qquad\qquad \text{for } k = 1, 2, \ldots, m, \ \forall\, c \in \Sigma_k. \quad [5.21]$$

Equalities [5.18] guarantee that only one character is selected for each position $k \in \{1, 2, \ldots, m\}$. Inequalities [5.19] ensure that y_i can only be set to 1 if and only if the number of differences between $s^i \in \Omega$ and the possible solution (as defined by the setting of x_{ck} variables) is greater than or equal to t. The target [5.17] is to maximize the number of y-variables set to 1.

5.4.2. Literature review

The FSP and the FFMSP are specular compared to the CSP and the CTMSP, respectively. Despite this similarity, they are both harder from a computational point of view, as proven in 2003 by Lanctot et al. [LAN 03], who demonstrated that the two problems remain complex even in the case of strings over an alphabet Σ with only two characters. Particularly, Lanctot et al. proved that with $|\Sigma| \geq 3$, approximating the FFMSP within a NP-hard polynomial factor. The reason why the FFMSP is more difficult to approximate than the FSP lies in the approximation preserving the reduction to FFMSP from the independent set, a classical and computationally intractable combinatorial optimization problem.

The mathematical formulation of FSP is similar to the one used for the CSP, with only a change in the optimization objective, and the inequality sign in the constraint:

$$m - \sum_{j=1}^{m} x_{s_j^i j} \geq d, \qquad i = 1, 2, \ldots, n.$$

This suggests that to solve the problem using an ILP formulation one can use similar techniques to those employed to solve the CSP. Zörnig [ZÖR 11, ZÖR 15] has proposed a few integer programming models for some variants of the FSP and the CSP. The number of variables and constraints is substantially less than the standard ILP model and the solution of the linear programming-relaxation contains only a small proportion of non-integer values, which considerably simplifies the subsequent rounding process and a B&B procedure.

For the FSP, Lanctot *et al.* [LAN 03] proposed a PTAS based on the randomized rounding of the relaxed solution of the ILP model. It uses the randomized rounding technique together with probabilistic inequalities to determine the maximum error possible in the solution computed by the algorithm.

For the FFMSP, given theoretical computational hardness results, polynomial-time algorithms can only yield solutions without a constant guarantee of approximation. In such cases, to find good quality solutions in reasonable running times and to overcome the inner intractability of the problem from a computational point of view, heuristic methods are recommended. Some of the most efficient heuristics are described in the subsequent sections.

5.4.3. *Heuristics and metaheuristics for the FFMSP*

The first attempt to design a heuristic approach was made in 2005 by Meneses *et al.* [MEN 05], who proposed a simple greedy construction followed by an iterative improvement phase. Later, in 2007, Festa [FES 07] designed a simple GRASP, improved in 2012 by Mousavi *et al.* [MOU 12a], who noticed that the search landscape of the FFMSP is characterized by many solutions with the same objective value. As a result, local search is likely to visit many sub-optimal local maxima. To avoid this efficiently, Mousavi *et al.* devised a new hybrid heuristic evaluation function to be used in conjunction with the objective function when evaluating neighbor solutions during the local search phase in the GRASP framework.

In 2013, Ferone *et al.* [FER 13b] designed the following pure and hybrid multistart iterative heuristics:

– a pure GRASP, inspired by [FES 07];

– a GRASP that uses forward path-relinking for intensification;

– a pure VNS;

– a VNS that uses forward path-relinking for intensification;

– a GRASP that uses VNS to implement the local search phase;

– a GRASP that uses VNS to implement the local search phase and forward path-relinking for intensification.

The algorithms were tested with several random instances and the results showed that the hybrid GRASP with VNS and forward path-relinking always found much better quality solutions compared with the other algorithms, but with higher running times than the pure GRASP and hybrid GRASP with forward path-relinking. In the last decade, several articles have been published on GRASP and path-relinking and related issues, showing that the path-relinking memory mechanism added to GRASP leads to a significant enhancement of the basic framework in terms of both solution time and quality [FES 13, DE 11, MOR 14b]. Following this recent trend, Ferone *et al.* [FER 16] have investigated the benefits with respect to computation time and solution quality of the integration of different path-relinking strategies in GRASP, when applied to solve the FFMSP.

The remaining section is devoted to the description of the GRASP proposed in [FER 13b] and the hybrid heuristic evaluation function proposed by Mousavi *et al.* [MOU 12a] that Ferone *et al.* in [FER 16] have integrated with GRASP local search. Several path-relinking strategies that can be integrated in GRASP are also discussed, along with a hybrid ant colony optimization approach (ACO) proposed by Blum and Festa [BLU 14c] and a simple ILP-based heuristic [BLU 16c] proposed for tackling all four consensus problems described in this chapter. Finally, the most significant and relevant experimental results on both a set of randomly-generated and a set of real-world problems will be analyzed and discussed.

5.4.3.1. GRASP for the FFMSP

GRASP is a multistart metaheuristic framework [FEO 89, FEO 95]. As introduced briefly in section 1.2.3, each GRASP iteration consists of a construction phase, where a solution is built adopting a *greedy, randomized* and *adaptive* strategy besides a local search phase which starts at the solution constructed and applies iterative improvement until a locally optimal solution is found. Repeated applications of the construction procedure yield diverse starting solutions for the local search, and the best overall local optimal solution is returned as the result. The reader can refer to [FES 02b, FES 09a, FES 09b] for annotated bibliographies of GRASP.

The construction phase iteratively builds a feasible solution, one element at a time. At each iteration, the choice of the element to be added next is determined by ordering all candidate elements (i.e. those that can be added to the solution) in a candidate list C with respect to a greedy criterion. The probabilistic component of a GRASP is characterized by randomly choosing one of the best candidates in the list, but not necessarily the top candidate. The list of best candidates is called the *restricted candidate list* (RCL). Algorithm 5.1 depicts the pseudo-code of the GRASP for the FFMSP proposed in [FER 13b]. The objective function to be maximized according to [5.17] is denoted by $f_t : \Sigma^m \mapsto \mathbb{N}$. For each position $j \in \{1, \ldots, m\}$ and for each character $c \in \Sigma$, $V_j(c)$ is the number of times c appears in position j in any of the strings in Ω. In line 2, the incumbent solution s_{best} is set to the empty solution with a corresponding objective function value $f_t(s_{best})$ equal to $-\infty$. The for-loop in lines 3–6 computes $V_j^{\min}$ and $V_j^{\max}$ as the minimum and the maximum function value $V_j(c)$ all over characters $c \in \Sigma$, respectively. Then, until the stopping criterion is no longer met, the while-loop in lines 7–13 computes a GRASP incumbent solution s_{best} which is returned as output in line 14.

Algorithm 5.2 shows a pseudo-code of the construction procedure that iteratively builds a sequence $s = (s_1, \ldots, s_m) \in \Sigma^m$, selecting one character at time. The greedy function is related to the occurrence of each character in a given position. To define the construction mechanism for the RCL, once $V_j^{\min}$

and $V_j^{\max}$ are known, a cut-off value $\mu = V_j^{\min} + \alpha \cdot (V_j^{\max} - V_j^{\min})$ is computed in line 5, where α is a parameter such that $0 \leq \alpha \leq 1$ (line 4). Then, the RCL is made up of all characters whose greedy function value is less than or equal to μ (line 8). A character is then selected, uniformly at random, from the RCL (line 11).

Algorithm 5.1. GRASP for the FFMSP

1: **input:** t, m, Σ, $f_t(\cdot)$, $\{V_j(c)\}_{j\in\{1,\ldots,m\}}^{c\in\Sigma}$, Seed
2: **initialization:** $s_{best}:=\emptyset$; $f_t(s_{best}):=-\infty$
3: **for** $j \leftarrow 1,\ldots,m$ **do**
4:     $V_j^{\min}:=\min_{c\in\Sigma} V_j(c)$
5:     $V_j^{\max}:=\max_{c\in\Sigma} V_j(c)$
6: **end for**
7: **while** stopping criterion not satisfied **do**
8:     $[s, \{\text{RCL}_j\}_{j=1}^m]:=\text{GrRand}(m, \Sigma, \{V_j(c)\}_{j\in\{1,\ldots,m\}}^{c\in\Sigma}, V_j^{\min}, V_j^{\max}, \text{Seed})$
9:     $s:=\text{LocalSearch}(t, m, s, f_t(\cdot), \{\text{RCL}_j\}_{j=1}^m)$
10:     **if** $(f_t(s) > f_t(s_{best}))$ **then**
11:         $s_{best}:=s$
12:     **end if**
13: **end while**
14: **output:** s_{best}

Algorithm 5.2. Function GRRAND of Algorithm 5.1

1: **input:** m, Σ, $\{V_j(c)\}_{j\in\{1,\ldots,m\}}^{c\in\Sigma}$, $V_j^{\min}$, $V_j^{\max}$, Seed
2: **for** $j \leftarrow 1,\ldots,m$ **do**
3:     $\text{RCL}_j:=\emptyset$
4:     $\alpha:=\text{Random}([0,1], \text{Seed})$
5:     $\mu:=V_j^{\min} + \alpha \cdot (V_j^{\max} - V_j^{\min})$
6:     **for all** $c \in \Sigma$ **do**
7:         **if** $(V_j(c) \leq \mu))$ **then**
8:             $\text{RCL}_j:=\text{RCL}_j\cup\{c\}$
9:         **end if**
10:     **end for**
11:     $s_j:=\text{Random}(\text{RCL}_j, \text{Seed})$
12: **end for**
13: **output:** s, $\{\text{RCL}_j\}_{j=1}^m$

The basic GRASP local search step consists of investigating all positions $j \in \{1, \ldots, m\}$ and changing the character in position j in the sequence s to another character in RCL_j. The current solution is replaced by the first improving neighbor and the search stops after all possible moves have been evaluated and no improving neighbor has been found, returning a locally optimal solution. The worst case computational complexity of the local search procedure is $O(n \cdot m \cdot |\Sigma|)$. In fact, since the objective function value is at most n, the while-loop in lines 2–14 runs at most n times. Each iteration costs $O(m \cdot |\Sigma|)$, since for each $j = 1, \ldots, m$, $|\text{RCL}_j| \leq |\Sigma| - 1$.

5.4.3.2. The hybrid heuristic evaluation function

The objective function of any instance of the FFMSP is characterized by large plateaus, since there are $|\Sigma|^m$ points in the search space with only n different objective values. To efficiently handle the numerous local maxima, Mousavi *et al.* [MOU 12a] proposed a new function to be used in the GRASP framework in conjunction with the objective function when evaluating neighbor solutions during the local search phase.

Given a candidate solution $s \in \Sigma^m$, the following further definitions and notations are needed:

– $Near(s) = \{s^j \in \Omega \mid d_H(s, s^j) \leq t\}$ is the subset of the input strings whose Hamming distance from s is at most t;

– for each input string $s^j \in \Omega$, its cost is defined as $c(s^j, s) = t - d_H(s, s^j)$;

– a *L-walk*, $L \in \mathbb{N}$, $1 \leq L \leq m$, is a walk of length L in the solution space. A L-walk from s leads to the replacement of s with a solution $\bar{s}$ so that $d_H(s, \bar{s}) = L$;

– given a L-walk from s to a solution $\bar{s}$ and an input string $s^j \in \Omega$, then $\Delta_j = d_H(\bar{s}, s^j) - d_H(s, s^j)$;

– a L-walk from s is *random* if $\bar{s}$ is equally likely to be any solution $\hat{s}$ where $d_H(s, \hat{s}) = L$.

In the case of a random L-walk, Δ_j is a random variable and $Pr_L(\Delta_j \leq k)$, $k \in \mathbb{Z}$, denotes the probability of $\Delta_j \leq k$ as a result of a random walk.

– where $s^j \in Near(s)$ and $L = c(s^j, s)$, the *potential gain* $g_j(s)$ of s^j with respect to s is defined as follows:

$$g_j(s) = 1 + \sum_{s^k \in \Omega,\, k \neq j} Pr_L(\Delta_k \geq c(s^k, s)).$$

– where $s^j \in Near(s)$ and $L = c(s^j, s)$:

- the *potential gain* $g_j(s)$ of s^j with respect to s is defined as follows:

$$g_j(s) = 1 + \sum_{s^k \in \Omega,\, k \neq j} Pr_L(\Delta_k \geq c(s^k, s)),$$

- the *Gain-per-Cost* $GpC(s)$ of s is defined as the average of the gain per cost of the sequences in $Near(s)$:

$$GpC(s) = \frac{1}{|Near(s)|} \cdot \sum_{s^j \in Near(s)} \frac{g_j(s)}{c(s^j, s)}.$$

Computing the gain-per-cost of candidate solutions requires knowledge of the probability distribution function of Δ_k for all possible lengths of random walks and this task has high computational complexity. To reduce the computational effort, Mousavi *et al.* proposed to approximate all these probability distribution functions with the probability distribution function for a unique random variable Δ corresponding to a random string as a representative of all the strings in Ω. With respect to a random L-walk, Δ is defined as $d_H(\hat{s}, \bar{s}) - d_H(\hat{s}, s)$, where $\hat{s}$ is a random string (and not an input string) and s and $\bar{s}$ are the source and destination of the random L-walk, respectively. Once the probability distribution function for the random variable Δ is known, to evaluate candidate solutions based on their likelihood of leading to better solutions, Mousavi *et al.* define the $\widetilde{GpC}$ as follows:

$$\widetilde{GpC}(s) = \frac{1}{|Near(s)|} \cdot \sum_{s^j \in Near(s)} \frac{\tilde{g}_j(s)}{c(s^j, s)},$$

where s is a candidate solution, and $\tilde{g}_j(s)$ is the *estimated gain* of s^j, with respect to s, defined as follows:

$$\tilde{g}_j(s) = 1 + \sum_{s^k \in \Omega, k \neq j} Pr_{c(s^j, s)}(\Delta \geq c(s^k, s)).$$

Then, they define a heuristic function $h_{f_t, \widetilde{GpC}}(\cdot)$ which takes into account both the objective function $f_t(\cdot)$ and the estimated gain-per-cost function $\widetilde{GpC}$.

Given two candidate solutions $\bar{s}, \hat{s} \in \Sigma^m$, $\bar{s} \neq \hat{s}$, function $h_{f_t, \widetilde{GpC}}(\cdot)$ must combine $f_t(\cdot)$ and $\widetilde{GpC}$ in such a way that:

$$h_{f_t, \widetilde{GpC}}(\bar{s}) > h_{f_t, \widetilde{GpC}}(\hat{s}),$$

if and only if either $f_t(\bar{s}) > f_t(\hat{s})$, or $f_t(\bar{s}) = f_t(\hat{s})$ and $\widetilde{GpC}(\bar{s}) > \widetilde{GpC}(\hat{s})$. In other words, according to function $h_{f_t, \widetilde{GpC}}(\cdot)$, the candidate solution $\bar{s}$ is considered better than $\hat{s}$ if it corresponds to a better objective function value or the objective function assumes the same value when evaluated in both solutions, but $\bar{s}$ has a higher probability of leading to better solutions. Based on proven theoretical results, Mousavi *et al.* proposed the following heuristic function $h_{f_t, \widetilde{GpC}}(s)$, where s is a candidate solution:

$$h_{f_t, \widetilde{GpC}}(s) = (n + 1)f_t(s) + \widetilde{GpC}(s).$$

Looking at the results of a few experiments conducted in [MOU 12a], it emerges that use of the hybrid heuristic evaluation function $h_{f_t, \widetilde{GpC}}(\cdot)$ in place of the objective function $f_t(\cdot)$ in the GRASP local search proposed by Festa [FES 07] results in a reduction in the number of local maxima. Consequently the algorithm's climb toward better solutions is sped up. On a large set of both real-world and randomly-generated test instances, Ferone *et al.* [FER 16] conducted a deeper experimental analysis to help determine whether the integration of the hybrid heuristic evaluation function $h_{f_t, \widetilde{GpC}}(\cdot)$ of Mousavi *et al.* in a GRASP is beneficial. The following two sets of problems were used:

– Set $\mathcal{A}$: this is the set of benchmarks introduced in [FER 13b], consisting of 600 random instances of different sizes. The number n of input sequences in Ω is $\{100, 200, 300, 400\}$ and the length m of each of the input sequences is $\{300, 600, 800\}$. In all cases, the alphabet consists of four letters, i.e. $|\Sigma| = 4$.

For each combination of n and m, the set $\mathcal{A}$ consists of 100 random instances. The threshold parameter t varies from 0.75 m to 0.85 m.

– Set $\mathcal{B}$: this set of problems was used in [MOU 12a]. Some instances were randomly generated, while the remaining are real-world instances from biology (*Hyaloperonospora parasitica* V 6.0 sequence data). In both randomly-generated and real-world instances, the alphabet as four letters, i.e. $|\Sigma| = 4$, the number n of input sequences in Ω is $\{100, 200, 300\}$ and the length m of each of the input sequence ranges from 100 to 1200. Finally, the threshold parameter t varies from 0.75 m to 0.95 m.

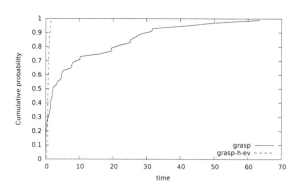

Figure 5.1. *Time to target distributions (in seconds) comparing* grasp *and* grasp-h-ev *for a random instance where* $n = 100$, $m = 600$, $t = 480$, *with a target value of* $\hat{z} = 0.68 \times n$

Looking at the results, Ferone *et al.* concluded that either the two algorithms find the optimal solution or the hybrid GRASP with the Mousavi *et al.* evaluation function finds better quality results. The further investigation performed by the authors that involves the study of the empirical distributions of the random variable *time-to-target-solution-value* (TTT-plots) considering the following instances is particulars interesting:

1) random instance where $n = 100$, $m = 600$, $t = 480$ and target value $\hat{z} = 0.68 \times n$ (Figure 5.1);

2) random instance where $n = 200$, $m = 300$, $t = 255$ and target value $\hat{z} = 0.025 \times n$ (Figure 5.2);

3) real instance where $n = 300$, $m = 1200$, $t = 1,020$ and target value $\hat{z} = 0.22 \times n$ (Figure 5.3).

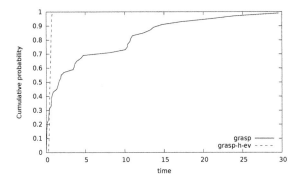

Figure 5.2. *Time to target distributions (in seconds) comparing* grasp *and* grasp-h-ev *for a random instance where* $n = 200$, $m = 300$, $t = 255$, *and a target value of* $\hat{z} = 0.025 \times n$

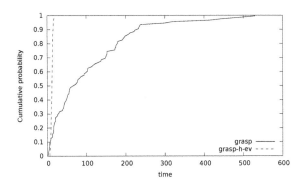

Figure 5.3. *Time to target distributions (in seconds) comparing* grasp *and* grasp-h-ev *for a real instance where* $n = 300$, $m = 1200$, $t = 1020$, *and a target value of* $\hat{z} = 0.22 \times n$

Ferone *et al.* performed 100 independent runs of each heuristic using 100 different random number generator seeds and recorded the time taken to find a solution at least as good as the target value $\hat{z}$. As in [AIE 02], to plot the empirical distribution, a probability $p_i = \frac{i-1/2}{100}$ is associated with the ith sorted running time (t_i) and the points $z_i = (t_i, p_i)$, for $i = 1, \ldots, 100$, are plotted. As shown in Figures 5.1–5.3, we can observe that the relative position of the curves implies that, given any fixed amount of run time, the hybrid GRASP with the Mousavi *et al.* evaluation function (grasp-h-ev) has a higher probability of finding a solution with an objective function value at least as good as the target objective function value than pure GRASP (grasp).

5.4.3.3. Path-relinking

Path-relinking is a heuristic proposed by Glover [GLO 96, GLO 00b] in 1996 as an intensification strategy exploring trajectories connecting elite solutions obtained by Tabu search or scatter search [GLO 00a, GLO 97, GLO 00b, RIB 12].

Starting from one or more elite solutions, paths in the solution space leading towards other guiding elite solutions are generated and explored in the search for better solutions. This is accomplished by selecting moves that introduce attributes contained in the guiding solutions. At each iteration, all moves that incorporate attributes of the guiding solution are analyzed and the move that best improves (or least deteriorates) the initial solution is chosen.

Algorithm 5.3 illustrates the pseudo-code of path-relinking for the FFMSP proposed by Ferone *et al.* in [FER 13b]. It is applied to a pair of sequences $(s', \hat{s})$. Their common elements are kept constant and the space spanned by this pair of solutions is searched with the objective of finding a better solution. This search is done by exploring a path in the space linking solution s' to solution $\hat{s}$. s' is called the *initial solution* and $\hat{s}$ the *guiding solution*.

Algorithm 5.3. Path-relinking for the FFMSP

1: **input:** t, m, $f_t(\cdot)$, s', $\hat{s}$, Seed
2: **initialization:** $f^* := \max\{f_t(s), f_t(\hat{s})\}$; $s^* := \arg\max\{f_t(s), f_t(\hat{s})\}$
3: $\Delta(s', \hat{s}) := \{i = 1, \ldots, m \mid s'_i \neq \hat{s}_i\}$
4: **while** $\Delta(s', \hat{s}) \neq \emptyset$ **do**
5:    $i^* := \arg\max\{f_t(s' \oplus i) \mid i \in \Delta(s', \hat{s})\}$
6:    $\Delta(s' \oplus i^*, \hat{s}) := \Delta(s', \hat{s}) \setminus \{i^*\}$
7:    $s' := s' \oplus i^*$
8:    **if** $(f_t(s') > f^*)$ **then**
9:       $f^* := f_t(s')$
10:       $s^* := s'$
11:    **end if**
12: **end while**
13: **output:** s^*

The procedure (line 3) computes the symmetric difference $\Delta(s', \hat{s})$ between the two solutions as the set of components for which the two solutions differ:

$$\Delta(s', \hat{s}) := \{i = 1, \ldots, m \mid s'_i \neq \hat{s}_i\}.$$

Note that, $|\Delta(s', \hat{s})| = d_H(s', \hat{s})$ and $\Delta(s', \hat{s})$ represents the set of moves needed to reach $\hat{s}$ from s', where a move applied to the initial solution s' consists of selecting a position $i \in \Delta(s', \hat{s})$ and replacing s'_i with $\hat{s}_i$.

Path-relinking generates a path of solutions $s'_1, s'_2, \ldots, s'_{|\Delta(s', \hat{s})|}$ linking s' and $\hat{s}$. The best solution s^* in this path is returned by the algorithm (line 13). The path of solutions is computed in the loop in lines 4 through 12. This is achieved by advancing one solution at a time in a greedy manner. At each iteration, the procedure examines all moves $i \in \Delta(s', \hat{s})$ from the current solution s' and selects the one which results in the highest cost solution (line 5), i.e. the one which maximizes $f_t(s' \oplus i)$, where $s' \oplus i$ is the solution resulting from applying move i to solution s'. The best move i^* is made, producing solution $s' \oplus i^*$ (line 7). The set of available moves is updated (line 6). If necessary, the best solution s^* is updated (lines 8–11). The algorithm stops when $\Delta(s', \hat{s}) = \emptyset$.

Given two solutions s' and $\hat{s}$, Ferone et al. adopted the following path-relinking strategies:

– *Forward PR*: the path emanates from s', which is the worst solution between s' and $\hat{s}$ (Algorithm 5.3);

– *Backward PR*: the path emanates from s', which is the best solution between s' and $\hat{s}$ (Algorithm 5.3);

– *Mixed PR*: two paths are generated, one emanating from s' and the other emanating from $\hat{s}$. The process stops as soon as an intermediate common solution is met (Algorithm 5.4);

– *Greedy Randomized Adaptive Forward PR*: the path emanates from the worst solution between s' and $\hat{s}$. At each iteration a move is made towards an intermediate solution selected at random from among a subset of top-ranked solutions (Algorithm 5.5);

– *Evolutionary PR*: a greedy randomized adaptive forward PR is performed at each iteration. At fixed intervals the elite pool is intensified. In fact, at each

EvIterations iteration, the algorithm Evolution is invoked (Algorithm 5.6) that performs path-relinking between each pair of current elite set solutions with the aim of eventually improving the current elite set.

Algorithm 5.4. Mixed-Path-relinking for the FFMSP [RIB 07]

1: **input:** t, m, $f_t(\cdot)$, s', $\hat{s}$, Seed
2: **initialization:** $f^* := \max\{f_t(s), f_t(\hat{s})\}$; $s^* := \arg\max\{f_t(s), f_t(\hat{s})\}$
3: $\Delta(s', \hat{s}) := \{i = 1, \ldots, m \mid s'_i \neq \hat{s}_i\}$
4: **while** $\Delta(s', \hat{s}) \neq \emptyset$ **do**
5: $\quad i^* := \arg\max\{f_t(s' \oplus i) \mid i \in \Delta(s', \hat{s})\}$
6: $\quad \Delta(s' \oplus i^*, \hat{s}) := \Delta(s', \hat{s}) \setminus \{i^*\}$
7: $\quad s' := s' \oplus i^*$
8: $\quad$ **if** $(f_t(s') > f^*)$ **then**
9: $\quad\quad f^* := f_t(s')$
10: $\quad\quad s^* := s'$
11: $\quad$ **end if**
12: $\quad$ **if** $(\Delta(s', \hat{s}) \neq \emptyset)$ **then**
13: $\quad\quad i^* := \arg\max\{f_t(\hat{s} \oplus i) \mid i \in \Delta(s', \hat{s})\}$
14: $\quad\quad \Delta(s', \hat{s} \oplus i^*) := \Delta(s', \hat{s}) \setminus \{i^*\}$
15: $\quad\quad \hat{s} := \hat{s} \oplus i^*$
16: $\quad\quad$ **if** $(f_t(\hat{s}) > f^*)$ **then**
17: $\quad\quad\quad f^* := f_t(\hat{s})$
18: $\quad\quad\quad s^* := \hat{s}$
19: $\quad\quad$ **end if**
20: $\quad$ **end if**
21: **end while**
22: **output:** s^*

5.4.3.4. Hybridizations of GRASP with path-relinking

Ferone *et al.* [FER 16] integrated a path-relinking intensification procedure in the hybrid GRASP grasp-h-ev described in section 5.4.3.1. The idea behind this integration was to add memory to GRASP and was first proposed in 1999 by Laguna and Martí [LAG 99]. It was followed by several extensions, improvements and successful applications [CAN 01, FES 06, FES 02a, RIB 12].

Algorithm 5.5. (GRAPR) Greedy Randomized Adaptive Path-relinking for FFMSP [FAR 05]

1: **input:** t, m, $f_t(\cdot)$, s', $\hat{s}$, Seed, α
2: **initialization:** $f^* := \max\{f_t(s'), f_t(\hat{s})\}$; $s^* := \arg\max\{f_t(s'), f_t(\hat{s})\}$
3: $\Delta(s', \hat{s}) := \{i = 1, \ldots, m \mid s'_i \neq \hat{s}_i\}$
4: **while** $\Delta(s', \hat{s}) \neq \emptyset$ **do**
5:    $i_{\min} := \arg\min\{f_t(s' \oplus i) \mid i \in \Delta(s', \hat{s})\}$
6:    $i_{\max} := \arg\max\{f_t(s' \oplus i) \mid i \in \Delta(s', \hat{s})\}$
7:    $\mu := i_{\min} + \alpha(i_{\max} - i_{\min})$
8:    $\text{RCL} := \{i \in \Delta(s', \hat{s}) \mid f_t(s' \oplus i) \geq \mu\}$
9:    $i^* := \text{Random}(\text{RCL}, \text{Seed})$
10:    $\Delta(s' \oplus i^*, \hat{s}) := \Delta(s', \hat{s}) \setminus \{i^*\}$
11:    $s' := s' \oplus i^*$
12:    **if** $(f_t(s') > f^*)$ **then**
13:       $f^* := f_t(s')$
14:       $s^* := s'$
15:    **end if**
16: **end while**
17: **output:** s^*

In the hybrid GRASP with path-relinking for the FFMSP, path-relinking is applied at each GRASP iteration to pairs $(s, \hat{s})$ of solutions, where s is the locally optimal solution obtained by the GRASP local search and $\hat{s}$ is randomly chosen from a pool with at most MaxElite high-quality solutions. The pseudo-code for the proposed hybrid GRASP with path-relinking is shown in Algorithm 5.7.

The pool of elite solutions $\mathcal{E}$ is empty (line 1) initially and, until $\mathcal{E}$ is no longer full, the current GRASP locally optimal solution s is inserted in $\mathcal{E}$. As soon as the pool becomes full ($|\mathcal{E}| = $ MaxElite), through the Choose-PR-Strategy procedure, the desired strategy for implementing path-relinking is chosen s and solution $\hat{s}$ are randomly chosen from $\mathcal{E}$. The best solution $\overline{s}$ found along the relinking trajectory is returned and considered as a candidate to be inserted into the pool. The AddToElite procedure evaluates its insertion into $\mathcal{E}$. If $\overline{s}$ is better than the best elite solution, then $\overline{s}$ replaces the worst elite solution. If the candidate is better than the worst elite solution, but not better than the best, it replaces the worst if it is *sufficiently different* from all elite solutions.

Algorithm 5.6. Evolutionary path-relinking for FFMSP [RES 10b, RES 04]

1: **input:** t, m, $f_t(\cdot)$, $\mathcal{E}$, Seed
2: **initialization:** $\hat{\mathcal{E}} := \emptyset$; $f^* := -\infty$
3: **for** all $s' \in \mathcal{E}$ **do**
4:   **for** all $s'' \in \mathcal{E}$, $s'' \neq s'$ **do**
5:     $s_{\min} := \arg\min(f(s'), f(s''))$
6:     $s_{\max} := \arg\max(f(s'), f(s''))$
7:     $\alpha := \mathrm{Random}([0, 1], \mathrm{Seed})$
8:     $s := \mathrm{grapr}(t, m, f_t(\cdot), s_{\min}, s_{\max}, \mathrm{Seed}, \alpha)$
9:     **if** $(f(s) > f^*)$ **then**
10:       $s^* := s$
11:       $f^* = f(s^*)$
12:     **end if**
13:     $\mathrm{AddToElite}(\hat{\mathcal{E}}, s)$
14:   **end for**
15: **end for**
16: **output:** $\hat{\mathcal{E}}, s^*$

Path-relinking is also applied as post-optimization phase (lines 27–34): at the end of all GRASP iterations, for each different pair of solutions s', $s'' \in \mathcal{E}$, if s' and s'' are *sufficiently different*, path-relinking is performed between s' and s'' by using the same strategy as the intensification phase.

With the same test instances described in section 5.4.3.2, Ferone *et al.* comprehensively analyzed of the computational experiments they conducted with the following hybrid GRASPs:

– grasp-h-ev, the hybrid GRASP that integrates Mousavi *et al.*'s evaluation function into the local search;

– grasp-h-ev_f, the hybrid GRASP approach that adds forward path-relinking to grasp-h-ev;

– grasp-h-ev_b, the hybrid GRASP that adds backward path-relinking to grasp-h-ev;

– grasp-h-ev_m, the hybrid GRASP approach that adds Mixed path-relinking to grasp-h-ev;

– grasp-h-ev_grapr, the hybrid GRASP that adds greedy randomized adaptive forward path-relinking to grasp-h-ev;

– grasp-h-ev_ev_pr, the hybrid GRASP that adds evolutionary path-relinking to grasp-h-ev.

For the best values to be assigned to several involved parameters, the authors proposed the following settings:

– setting the maximum number MaxElite of elite solutions to 50;

– inserting a candidate solution $\bar{s}$ in the elite set $\mathcal{E}$. If $\bar{s}$ is better than the best elite set solution or is better than the worst elite set solution but not better than the best and its Hamming distance to at least half of the solutions in the elite set is at least 0.75 m, solution $\bar{s}$ replaces the worst solution in the elite set;

– in the post-optimization phase, path-relinking is performed between s' and s'' if their Hamming distance is at least 0.75 m.

In terms of average objective function values and standard deviations, Ferone *et al.* concluded that grasp-h-ev_ev_pr finds slightly better quality solutions compared to the other variants when running for the same number of iterations, while grasp-h-ev_b finds better quality solutions within a fixed running time. To validate the good behavior of the backward strategy, in Figures 5.4 and 5.5, the empirical distributions of the *time-to-target-solution-value* random variable (TTT-plots) are plot, involving algorithms grasp-h-ev, grasp-h-ev_b and grasp-h-ev_ev_pr without performing path-relinking as post-optimization phase. The plots show that, given any fixed amount of computing time, grasp-h-ev_b has a higher probability than the other algorithms of finding a good quality target solution.

5.4.3.5. *Ant colony optimization algorithms*

ACO algorithms [DOR 04] are metaheuristics inspired by ant colonies and their shortest path-finding behavior. In 2014, Blum and Festa [BLU 14c] proposed a hybrid between ACO and a mathematical programming solver for the FFMSP. To describe this approach, the following additional notations are needed.

Algorithm 5.7. GRASP+PR for the FFMSP

1: **input:** t, m, Σ, $f_t(\cdot)$, $\{V_j(c)\}_{j \in \{1,\dots,m\}}^{c \in \Sigma}$, Seed, MaxElite, c, EvIterations
2: **initialization:** $s_{best}:=\emptyset$; $f_t(s_{best}):=-\infty$; $\mathcal{E} := \emptyset$; $iter:=0$
3: **for** $j \leftarrow 1,\dots,m$ **do**
4:     $V_j^{\min}:=\min_{c \in \Sigma} V_j(c)$
5:     $V_j^{\max}:=\max_{c \in \Sigma} V_j(c)$
6: **end for**
7: **while** stopping criterion not satisfied **do**
8:     $iter:=iter + 1$
9:     $[s, \{\text{RCL}_j\}_{j=1}^m]:=\text{GrRand}(m, \Sigma, \{V_j(c)\}_{j \in \{1,\dots,m\}}^{c \in \Sigma}, V_j^{\min}, V_j^{\max}, \text{Seed})$
10:     $s:=\text{LocalSearch}(t, m, s, f_t(\cdot), \{\text{RCL}_j\}_{j=1}^m)$
11:     **if** $(iter \leq \text{MaxElite})$ **then**
12:         $\mathcal{E} := \mathcal{E} \cup \{s\}$
13:         **if** $(f_t(s) > f_t(s_{best}))$ **then**
14:             $s_{best}:=s$
15:         **end if**
16:     **else**
17:         $s' := \text{Random}(\mathcal{E}, \text{Seed})$
18:         $\alpha := \text{Random}([0, 1], \text{Seed})$
19:         $(\mathcal{E}, \bar{s}) := \text{Choose-PR-Strategy}(c, s', s, t, m, f_t(\cdot), \mathcal{E}, \text{Seed}, \alpha, \text{EvIterations})$
20:         $\text{AddToElite}(\mathcal{E}, \bar{s})$
21:         **if** $(f_t(\bar{s}) > f_t(s_{best}))$ **then**
22:             $s_{best}:=\bar{s}$
23:         **end if**
24:     **end if**
25: **end while**
26: **for all** $s' \in \mathcal{E}$ **do**
27:     **for all** $s'' \in \mathcal{E}$, $s'' \neq s'$ **do**
28:         $\alpha := \text{Random}([0, 1], \text{Seed})$
29:         $(\mathcal{E}, \bar{s}) := \text{Choose-PR-Strategy}(c, s', s, t, m, f_t(\cdot), \mathcal{E}, \text{Seed}, \alpha, \text{EvIterations})$
30:         **if** $(f_t(\bar{s}) > f_t(s_{best}))$ **then**
31:             $s_{best}:=\bar{s}$
32:         **end if**
33:     **end for**
34: **end for**
35: **output:** s_{best}

Algorithm 5.8. CHOOSE-PR-STRATEGY – Function for selection of path-relinking strategy for FFMSP

1: **input:** choice, s', s'', t, m, $f_t(\cdot)$, $\mathcal{E}$, Seed, α, EvIterations
2: **initialization:** $s_{\min}$:= $\arg\min(f(s'), f(s''))$; $s_{\max}$:= $\arg\max(f(s'), f(s''))$
3: **if** (choice = FORWARD) **then**
4:    $s^* := \texttt{Path-relinking}(t, m, f_t(\cdot), s_{\min}, s_{\max}, \texttt{Seed})$
5: **else if** (choice = BACKWARD) **then**
6:    $s^* := \texttt{Path-relinking}(t, m, f_t(\cdot), s_{\max}, s_{\min}, \texttt{Seed})$
7: **else if** (choice = MIXED) **then**
8:    $s^* := \texttt{Path-relinking-mixed}(t, m, f_t(\cdot), s_{\min}, s_{\max}, \texttt{Seed})$
9: **else if** (choice = GRAPR) **then**
10:    $s^* := \texttt{grapr}(t, m, f_t(\cdot), s_{\min}, s_{\max}, \texttt{Seed}, \alpha)$
11: **else if** (choice = EVOLUTIONARY) **then**
12:    $s^* := \texttt{grapr}(t, m, f_t(\cdot), s_{\min}, s_{\max}, \texttt{Seed}, \alpha)$
13:    **if** (iteration mod EvIterations = 0) **then**
14:      $(\mathcal{E}, s^*) := \texttt{Evolution}(t, m, f_t(\cdot), \mathcal{E}, \texttt{Seed})$
15:    **end if**
16: **end if**
17: **output:** $(\mathcal{E}, s^*)$

Given any valid solution s to the FFMSP (i.e. any s of length m over Σ is a valid solution) and a threshold value $0 \le t \le m$, let $P^s \subseteq \Omega$ be the set defined as follows:

$$P^s := \{s^i \in \Omega \mid d_H(s^i, s) \ge t\}.$$

The FFMSP can be equivalently stated as the problem that consists of finding a sequence s^* of length m over Σ such that P^{s^*} is of maximum size. In other words, the objective function $f_t : \Sigma^m \mapsto \{1, \ldots, n\}$ can be equivalently evaluated as follows:

$$f_t(s) := |P^s|, \qquad \text{for any given solution } s. \qquad [5.22]$$

Moreover, for any given solution s set Q^s is defined as the set consisting of all sequences $s' \in \Omega$ that have a Hamming distance at least t with respect to s. Formally, the following holds:

$- |Q^s| = \max\{|P^s| + 1, n\}$;

$- d_H(s', s) \ge d_H(s'', s)$ for all $s' \in Q^s$ and $s'' \in \Omega \setminus Q^s$.

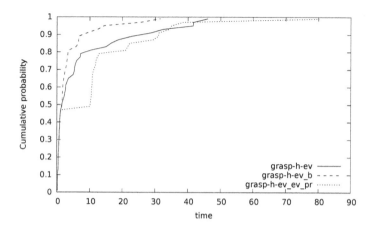

Figure 5.4. *Time-to-target distributions (in seconds) comparing* $grasp\text{-}h\text{-}ev$, $grasp\text{-}h\text{-}ev\_b$ *and* $grasp\text{-}h\text{-}ev\_ev\_pr$ *on the random instance where* $n = 100$, $m = 300$, $t = 240$, *and a target value of* $\hat{z} = 0.73 \times n$

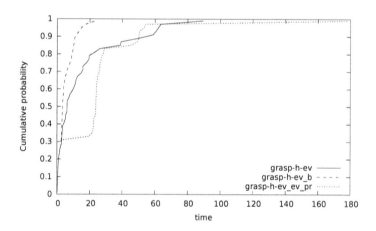

Figure 5.5. *Time-to-target distributions (in seconds) comparing* $grasp\text{-}h\text{-}ev$, $grasp\text{-}h\text{-}ev\_b$ *and* $grasp\text{-}h\text{-}ev\_ev\_pr$ *on the random instance where* $n = 200$, $m = 300$, $t = 240$, *and a target value of* $\hat{z} = 0.445 \times n$

Note that where $|P^s| < n$, set Q^s also contains the sequence $\hat{s} \in \Omega \setminus P^s$ that has, among all sequences in $\Omega \setminus P^s$, the largest Hamming distance with respect to s. To better handle the drawback related to the large plateaus of objective function, the authors proposed slightly modifying the comparison criterion between solutions. Solution s is considered better than solution s' ($s >_{\text{lex}} s'$) if and only if the following conditions hold in lexicographical order:

$$f(s) > f(s') \text{ or } \left(f(s) = f(s') \text{ and } \sum_{s'' \in Q^s} d_H(s'', s) > \sum_{s'' \in Q^{s'}} d_H(s'', s') \right).$$

In other words, the comparison between s and s' is done by considering first the corresponding objective function values and then, as a second criterion, the sum of the Hamming distances of the two solutions from the respective sets Q^s and $Q^{s'}$. It is intuitive to assume that the solution for which this sum is greater is somehow closer to a solution with a higher objective function value.

Algorithm 5.9. (Hybrid) ACO for the FFMSP

1: **input:** Ω, Σ, t, $tlim_{\text{ACO}}$, $runlim_{\text{ACO}}$, $tlim_{\text{CPLEX}}$
2: $s^{bs} :=$ NULL
3: $runs_{\text{ACO}} := 0$
4: **while** time limit $tlim_{\text{ACO}}$ not reached **and** $runs_{\text{ACO}} < runlim_{\text{ACO}}$ **do**
5:    $s :=$ RunACO(s^{bs})
6:    **if** $s >_{\text{lex}} s^{bs}$ **then**
7:       $s^{bs} := s$
8:       $runs_{\text{ACO}} := 0$
9:    **else**
10:      $runs_{\text{ACO}} := runs_{\text{ACO}} + 1$
11:   **end if**
12: **end while**
13: **if** time limit $tlim_{\text{CPLEX}}$ not reached **then**
14:   $s^{bs} :=$ SolutionPolishing(s^{bs}, $tlim_{\text{CPLEX}}$)
15: **end if**
16: **output:** the best-so-far solution s^{bs}

The hybrid ACO (Algorithm 5.9) consists of two phases. After setting the incumbent solution (the best solution found so far) to the empty solution, the first phase (lines 4–12) accomplishes the ACO approach. After this first phase, the algorithm possibly applies a second phase in which hybridization with a mathematical programming solver takes place (lines 13–15). The ACO-phase stops as soon as either a fixed running time limit ($tlim_{\text{ACO}}$) has been reached or the number of consecutive unsuccessful iterations (with no improvement of the incumbent solution) has reached a fixed maximum number of iterations ($runlim_{\text{ACO}}$).

Algorithm 5.10. RunACO(s^{bs}) function of Algorithm 5.9

1: **input:** s^{bs}
2: $s^{rb} :=$ NULL, $cf := 0$
3: Initialize all pheromone values of $\mathcal{T}$ to 0.5
4: **while** $cf < 0.99$ **do**
5:    $s^{ib} :=$ NULL
6:    **for** all n_a artificial ants **do**
7:       $s :=$ ConstructSolution($\mathcal{T}$)
8:       $s :=$ LocalSearch(s)
9:       **if** $s >_{\text{lex}} s^{ib}$ **then** $s^{ib} := s$
10:    **end for**
11:    $s^{ib} :=$ PathRelinking(s^{ib}, s^{bs})
12:    **if** $s^{ib} >_{\text{lex}} s^{rb}$ **then** $s^{rb} := s^{ib}$
13:    **if** $s^{ib} >_{\text{lex}} s^{bs}$ **then** $s^{bs} := s^{ib}$
14:    ApplyPheromoneUpdate($cf, \mathcal{T}, s^{ib}, s^{rb}$)
15:    $cf :=$ ComputeConvergenceFactor($\mathcal{T}$)
16: **end while**
17: **output:** the best-so-far solution s^{bs}

The ACO phase is pseudo-coded in Algorithm 5.10. The pheromone model $\mathcal{T}$ used consists of a pheromone value τ_{i,c_j} for each combination of a position $i = 1, \ldots, m$ in a solution sequence and a letter $c_j \in \Sigma$. Moreover, a greedy value, η_{i,c_j}, to each of these combinations is assigned which measures the desirability in reverse proportion letter c_j to position i. Intuitively, value η_{i,c_j} should be of assigning to the number of occurrences of letter, c_j, at position i in the $|\Omega| = n$ input sequences. Formally,

$$\eta_{i,c_j} := \frac{\left(n - |\{s \in \Omega \mid s_i = c_j\}|\right)}{n}.$$

The incumbent solution, s^{bs}, is input as the function which sets all pheromone values of $\mathcal{T}$ to 0.5. Then, it proceeds in iterations stopping as soon as the convergence factor value cf is greater than or equal to 0.99. At each iteration of the while-loop (lines 4–16), $n_a = 10$ solutions are constructed in the ConstructSolution($\mathcal{T}$) the function on basis of pheromone and greedy information. Starting from each of these solutions, a local search procedure (LocalSearch()) is applied producing a local optimal solution s^{ib} to which path-relinking is applied. Solution s^{ib} is also referred to as the *iteration-best* solution. Path-relinking is applied in the PathRelinking(s^{ib}, s^{bs}) function. Therefore, s^{ib} serves as the initial solution and the best-so-far solution s^{bs} serves as the guiding solution. After updating the best-so-far solution and the so-called *restart-best* solution, which is the best solution found so far during the current application of RunACO() (if necessary) the pheromone update is performed in function ApplyPheromoneUpdate($cf, \mathcal{T}, s^{ib}, s^{rb}$). At the end of each iteration, the new convergence factor value cf is computed in function ComputeConvergenceFactor($\mathcal{T}$).

ConstructSolution($\mathcal{T}$) is the function that in line 7 constructs a solution s on the basis of pheromone and greedy information. It proceeds in m iteration, and at each iteration it chooses the character to be inserted in the ith position of s. For each letter $c_j \in \Sigma$, a probability p_{i,c_j} position i will be chosen is calculated as follows:

$$\mathrm{p}_{i,c_j} := \frac{\tau_{i,c_j} \cdot \eta_{i,c_j}}{\sum_{c \in \Sigma} \tau_{i,c} \cdot \eta_{i,c}} \qquad [5.23]$$

Then, value z is chosen uniformly at random from $[0.5, 1.0]$. where $z \le d_{\text{rate}}$, the letter $c \in \Sigma$ with the largest probability value is chosen for position i. Otherwise, a letter $c \in \Sigma$ is chosen randomly with respect to the probability values. d_{rate} is a manually chosen parameter of the algorithm set to 0.8.

The local search and path-relinking procedures are those proposed by Ferone *et al.* [FER 13b] with solution s^{ib} playing the role of initial solution and solution s^{bs} that of the guiding solution.

The algorithm works with the following upper and lower bounds for them pheromone values: $\tau_{\text{max}} = 0.999$ and $\tau_{\text{min}} = 0.001$. Where pheromone values surpasses one of these limits, the value is set to the corresponding limit. This has the effect that complete convergence of the algorithm is avoided. Solutions s^{ib} and s^{rb} are used to update the pheromone values. The weight of each solution for the pheromone update is determined as a function of the convergence factor cf and the pheromone values τ_{i,c_j} are updated as follows:

$$\tau_{i,c_j} := \tau_{i,c_j} + \rho \cdot (\xi_{i,c_j} - \tau_{i,c_j}),$$ [5.24]

where

$$\xi_{i,c_j} := \kappa_{ib} \cdot \Delta(s_i^{ib}, c_j) + \kappa_{rb} \cdot \Delta(s_i^{rb}, c_j).$$ [5.25]

Function $\Delta(s, c_j)$ evaluates to 1 when character c_j is to be found at position i of solution s; otherwise it is given the value 0. Moreover, solution s^{ib} has weight κ_{ib}, while the weight of solution s^{rb} is κ_{rb} and it is required that $\kappa_{ib} + \kappa_{rb} = 1$. The weights that the authors have chosen are the standard ones shown in Table 5.1.

	$cf < 0.4$	$cf \in [0.4, 0.6)$	$cf \in [0.6, 0.8)$	$cf \geq 0.8$
κ_{ib}	1	$2/3$	$1/3$	0
κ_{rb}	0	$1/3$	$2/3$	1

Table 5.1. *Setting of κ_{ib} and κ_{rb} depending on the convergence factor cf*

Finally, ComputeConvergenceFactor($\mathcal{T}$) function computes the value of the convergence factor as follows:

$$cf := 2 \left(\left(\frac{\sum\limits_{\tau \in \mathcal{T}} \max\{\tau_{\max} - \tau, \tau - \tau_{\min}\}}{|\mathcal{T}| \cdot (\tau_{\max} - \tau_{\min})} \right) - 0.5 \right).$$

This implies that at the start of function RunACO(s^{bs}), cf has a value of zero. When all pheromone values are either at $\tau_{\min}$ or at $\tau_{\max}$, cf has a value of one. In general, cf moves in $[0, 1]$.

This hybrid ACO ($tlim_{\text{ACO}} = 60s$, $tlim_{\text{CPLEX}} = 90s$, $runlim_{\text{ACO}} = 10$) has been tested against the same set of benchmarks originally introduced in [FER 13b] and compared with a pure ACO ($tlim_{\text{ACO}} = 90s$, $tlim_{\text{CPLEX}} = 0s$, $runlim_{\text{ACO}} =$ very large integer) and the GRASP hybridized with path-relinking in [FER 13b]. The mathematical model of the problem was solved with IBM ILOG CPLEX V12.1 and the same version of CPLEX was used within the hybrid ACO approach. The (total) computation time limit for each run was set to 90 CPU seconds. The three algorithms are referred to as ACO, HyACO and GRASP+PR, and the results are summarized in Table 5.2. Note that for each combination of n, m and t, the given values are averages of the results of 100 problems. In each case, the best results are shown with a gray background. For the analysis of the results, since the performance of the algorithms significantly changes from one case to another, the three cases resulting from $t \in \{0.75 \ m, 0.8 \ m, 0.85 \ m\}$ are treated separately.

n, m, t	GRASP+PR	CPLEX	ACO	HyACO
$100, 300, t = 0.75 \ m$	100	100	100	100
$100, 300, t = 0.8 \ m$	79.61	69.21	73.55	77.84
$100, 300, t = 0.85 \ m$	13.18	22.08	24.64	28.3
$100, 600, t = 0.75 \ m$	100	100	100	100
$100, 600, t = 0.8 \ m$	80.13	66.95	69.12	72.97
$100, 600, t = 0.85 \ m$	4.98	19.38	20.82	22.82
$100, 800, t = 0.75 \ m$	100	100	100	100
$100, 800, t = 0.8 \ m$	82.64	67.28	67.43	70.94
$100, 800, t = 0.85 \ m$	1.84	18.3	19.84	21.66
$200, 300, t = 0.75 \ m$	200	200	199.38	200
$200, 300, t = 0.8 \ m$	100	75.32	104.3	104.17
$200, 300, t = 0.85 \ m$	11.9	19.16	27.1	28.59
$200, 600, t = 0.75 \ m$	200	200	199.99	200
$200, 600, t = 0.8 \ m$	88.49	59.29	85.53	85.02
$200, 600, t = 0.85 \ m$	2.42	18.12	21.03	21.9
$200, 800, t = 0.75 \ m$	200	200	199.99	200
$200, 800, t = 0.8 \ m$	73.08	54.31	78.54	77.95
$200, 800, t = 0.85 \ m$	0.21	18.56	19.14	20.4

Table 5.2. *Numerical results*

Looking at the results, it is evident that the most interesting case study is represented by those instances characterized by $t = 0.85 \ m$. In fact, it turns out that GRASP+PR, as proposed in [FER 13b], is not very effective and that HyACO consistently outperforms the pure ACO approach, which consistently outperforms CPLEX.

5.5. An ILP-based heuristic

Blum and Festa [BLU 16c] proposed a simple two-phase ILP-based heuristic. Since it is based on the ILP model of the problem, it is able to deal with all the four consensus problems described in this chapter.

Given a fixed running time t_{limit}, for $t_{\text{limit}}/2$ an ILP solver is used in the first phase to tackle the mixed integer linear problem (MILP) that is obtained by relaxing the x_{ck}-variables involved in all four ILP models. After $t_{\text{limit}}/2$ the ILP solver stops returning the incumbent solution, x', it found, and that can have some fractional components. In the second phase of the heuristic, the corresponding ILP models are solved in the remaining computation time $t_{\text{limit}}/2$, with the following additional constraints:

$$x_{ck} = 1 \text{ for } k = 1, \ldots, m, \ c \in \Sigma_k, \ x'_{ck} = 1.$$

In other words, whenever a variable x_{ck} in the best MILP solution-found has a value of 1, this value is fixed for the solution of the ILP model.

Using the same set of benchmarks originally introduced in [FER 13b], this simple heuristic has been compared with the ILP solver applied to the original mathematical models and a simple iterative pure greedy algorithm that builds a solution by adding $j = 1, \ldots, m$ the best ranked character at each iteration according to a greedy criterion that takes into account the number of times each character $c \in \Sigma$ appears in position j in any of the strings in Ω. The (M)ILP solver used in the experiments was IBM ILOG CPLEX V12.1 configured for single-threaded execution. Depending on the problems, two different computation time limits were used: $t_{\text{limit}} = 200$ seconds and $t_{\text{limit}} = 3600$ seconds per problem. The different applications of CPLEX and the ILP-based heuristic are named CPLEX-200, CPLEX-3600, HEURISTIC-200 and HEURISTIC-3600.

n	m	GREEDY		HEURISTIC-200		CPLEX-200		
		value	time	value	time	value	time	gap
100	300	228.55	< 0.009	213.33	10.79	213.48	10.53	0.88
100	600	446.91	< 0.009	422.90	7.36	423.06	5.22	0.47
100	800	590.08	< 0.009	562.40	6.86	562.52	7.19	0.36
200	300	235.02	< 0.009	219.99	12.74	220.03	33.42	1.38
200	600	457.19	< 0.009	434.33	14.03	434.36	67.29	0.78
200	800	604.49	< 0.009	576.95	11.59	577.01	87.03	0.60

Table 5.3. *Numerical results for the CSP*

The numerical results for the CSP are shown in Table 5.3. They are presented as averages over 100 instances for each combination of n (the number of input strings) and m (the length of the input strings). For all three algorithms, the table reports the values of the best solutions found (averaged over 100 problem instances) and the computation time at which these solutions were found. In the case of CPLEX-200, the average optimality gap is also provided. The results clearly show that HEURISTIC-200 outperforms both GREEDY and CPLEX-200. Similar conclusions can be drawn in the case of the FSP, for which the results are presented in Table 5.4. Except for one case ($n = 200$, $m = 300$) HEURISTIC-200 outperforms both GREEDY and CPLEX-200.

n	m	GREEDY		HEURISTIC-200		CPLEX-200		
		value	time	value	time	value	time	gap
100	300	221.67	< 0.009	236.53	4.46	236.41	9.34	0.68
100	600	455.15	< 0.009	476.55	7.13	476.39	7.10	0.38
100	800	611.61	< 0.009	636.58	10.13	636.45	9.09	0.27
200	300	215.74	< 0.009	230.11	9.29	230.14	25.72	1.24
200	600	443.88	< 0.009	465.68	10.81	465.59	53.41	0.67
200	800	596.41	< 0.009	622.81	10.52	622.72	60.49	0.51

Table 5.4. *Numerical results for the FSP*

For the CTMSP and the FFMSP, Blum and Festa noticed that the value of t has a significant impact on the hardness of both problems. For the CTMSP, for example, the lower the value of t, the easier it should be for CPLEX to optimally solve the problem. To better understand this relationship, the authors performed the following experiments. CPLEX was applied to each problem – concerning the CTMSP and FFMSP – for each value of $t \in \{0.05m, 0.02m, \ldots, 0.95m\}$. This was done with a time limit of 3,600 seconds per run. The corresponding optimality gaps (averaged over 100 problems) and the number of instances (out of 100) that were optimally solved are presented in Figure 5.6. The results reveal that, in the case of the CTMSP, the problem becomes difficult for approx. $t \le 0.72m$. In the case of the FFMSP, the problem becomes difficult for approx. $t \ge 0.78m$. Therefore, the following values for t were chosen for the final experimental evaluation: $t \in \{0.65m, 0.7m, 0.75m\}$ in the case of the CTMSP, and $t \in \{0.75m, 0.8m, 0.85m\}$ in the case of the FFMSP. The results obtained are reported in Table 5.5 for the CTMSP and in Table 5.6 for the FFMSP.

n	m	t	GREEDY value	GREEDY time	HEURISTIC-200 value	HEURISTIC-200 time	HEURISTIC-3600 value	HEURISTIC-3600 time	CPLEX-200 value	CPLEX-200 time	CPLEX-200 gap	CPLEX-3600 value	CPLEX-3600 time	CPLEX-3600 gap
100	300	0.65m	4.18	< 0.009	31.87	140.45	33.79	2315.36	23.39	110.15	262.64%	27.14	1509.07	210.56%
100	300	0.7m	55.94	< 0.009	72.08	125.04	74.75	1642.93	69.95	62.70	41.98%	72.14	1411.02	37.19%
100	300	0.75m	98.30	< 0.009	99.98	2.55	100.00	4.45	100.00	0.81	0.00%	100.00	1.06	0.00%
100	600	0.65m	0.70	< 0.009	29.28	130.18	31.45	2182.52	21.96	100.77	289.23%	23.16	1165.62	268.94%
100	600	0.7m	56.05	< 0.009	72.50	77.33	75.05	876.32	71.30	109.45	40.03%	73.44	1106.52	35.80%
100	600	0.75m	99.74	< 0.009	100.00	1.17	100.00	1.20	100.00	1.72	0.00%	100.00	1.97	0.00%
100	800	0.65m	0.18	< 0.009	28.13	126.89	30.35	2131.77	20.14	70.47	328.33%	25.86	1866.29	228.77%
100	800	0.7m	56.84	< 0.009	73.14	51.06	76.03	837.32	72.88	119.22	37.34%	75.23	1052.56	32.93%
100	800	0.75m	99.94	< 0.009	99.99	2.24	100.00	2.91	100.00	2.31	0.00%	100.00	2.16	0.00%
200	300	0.65m	2.16	< 0.009	32.12	146.42	36.93	2493.67	23.81	94.62	576.99%	24.30	735.91	562.71%
200	300	0.7m	65.51	< 0.009	81.25	145.30	92.82	2720.97	85.61	144.05	121.06%	92.37	1784.17	103.87%
200	300	0.75m	186.07	< 0.009	192.90	43.00	195.05	595.86	200.00	3.22	0.00%	200.00	3.05	0.00%
200	600	0.65m	0.05	< 0.009	28.46	129.11	32.54	2242.65	20.01	32.28	712.81%	23.25	1192.03	594.35%
200	600	0.7m	50.04	< 0.009	70.71	137.05	88.04	2570.76	66.95	118.40	185.15%	81.96	1794.91	132.00%
200	600	0.75m	196.29	< 0.009	196.23	44.52	198.05	647.22	200.00	4.86	0.00%	200.00	4.75	0.00%
200	800	0.65m	0.03	< 0.009	27.21	128.22	30.84	2141.78	20.13	46.58	709.14%	22.70	2238.87	615.48%
200	800	0.7m	43.27	< 0.009	67.18	137.80	86.59	2552.02	63.94	122.52	198.62%	79.93	2266.09	138.14%
200	800	0.75m	198.40	< 0.009	196.50	44.65	198.27	623.50	200.00	7.00	0.00%	200.00	9.00	0.00%

Table 5.5. Numerical results for the CTMS problem

n	m	t	GREEDY value	GREEDY time	HEURISTIC-200 value	HEURISTIC-200 time	HEURISTIC-3600 value	HEURISTIC-3600 time	CPLEX-200 value	CPLEX-200 time	CPLEX-200 gap	CPLEX-3600 value	CPLEX-3600 time	CPLEX-3600 gap
100	300	0.75m	98.40	< 0.009	100.00	0.09	100.00	0.16	100.00	0.10	0.00%	100.00	0.11	0.00%
100	300	0.8m	54.67	< 0.009	71.79	134.70	74.41	2594.31	69.87	69.91	42.69%	71.56	1069.58	38.61%
100	300	0.85m	1.71	< 0.009	28.83	118.05	30.01	1831.47	23.41	118.42	298.96%	26.37	1881.75	249.42%
100	600	0.75m	99.82	< 0.009	100.00	0.29	100.00	0.31	100.00	0.30	0.00%	100.00	0.34	0.00%
100	600	0.8m	53.52	< 0.009	71.88	113.65	74.64	1976.14	70.93	81.89	40.91%	71.97	575.00	38.64%
100	600	0.85m	0.10	< 0.009	25.93	107.92	27.34	1808.34	20.37	101.20	360.32%	24.11	2014.55	285.93%
100	800	0.75m	99.99	< 0.009	100.00	0.49	100.00	0.53	100.00	0.47	0.00%	100.00	0.56	0.00%
100	800	0.8m	53.42	< 0.009	71.88	111.76	74.79	1685.50	71.17	105.51	40.63%	72.55	514.75	37.80%
100	800	0.85m	0.04	< 0.009	25.08	105.12	26.28	1804.13	19.82	109.72	374.61%	22.46	1573.26	317.03%
200	300	0.75m	188.58	< 0.009	199.99	0.35	199.99	0.36	200.00	0.33	0.00%	200.00	0.43	0.00%
200	300	0.8m	60.63	< 0.009	78.58	124.40	91.91	2635.07	82.90	143.63	136.67%	89.56	1775.12	118.20%
200	300	0.85m	0.61	< 0.009	28.41	113.99	31.68	1869.94	20.13	71.95	813.23%	24.88	2155.67	635.34%
200	600	0.75m	196.81	< 0.009	200.00	0.56	200.00	0.60	200.00	0.57	0.00%	200.00	0.68	0.00%
200	600	0.8m	43.29	< 0.009	69.11	138.76	88.42	2459.95	62.67	116.46	213.91%	77.34	1778.80	153.80%
200	600	0.85m	0.00	< 0.009	24.93	103.93	27.82	1815.27	19.88	128.44	826.66%	21.53	1173.71	753.46%
200	800	0.75m	198.75	< 0.009	200.00	0.93	200.00	0.94	200.00	0.93	0.00%	200.00	1.11	0.00%
200	800	0.8m	36.03	< 0.009	69.45	139.97	86.77	2536.96	59.55	110.48	230.10%	73.93	2565.90	166.09%
200	800	0.85m	0.00	< 0.009	23.82	103.74	26.42	1803.11	18.67	47.26	887.78%	20.79	808.43	784.97%

Table 5.6. Results for the FFMS problem

Looking at the numerical results for the CTMSP (for the FFMSP, similar arguments can be made), the following observations can be drawn:

– both CPLEX and the ILP-based heuristic greatly outperform GREEDY;

– when the problem is rather easy – that is, for a setting of $t = 0.75\ m$ – CPLEX usually has slight advantages over the ILP-based heuristic, especially for instances with a larger number of input strings ($n = 200$);

– with growing problem difficulty, the ILP-based heuristic starts to outperform CPLEX; for a setting of $t = 0.65\ m$, the differences in the qualities of the solutions obtained between the ILP-based heuristic and CPLEX are significant.

For the FFMSP, the ILP-based heuristic was also compared with what was then the best state-of-the-art methods, i.e. GRASP+PR proposed by Ferone *et al.* [FER 13b], the ACO, and the hybrid ACO proposed by Blum and Festa [BLU 14c]. Results of this comparison are presented in Figure 5.7 for all instances where $t = 0.8\ m$ and $t = 0.85\ m$. The results show that, for $t = 0.8\ m$, HEURISTIC-3600 is generally outperformed by the other state-of-the-art methods. However, note that when the instance size (in terms of the number of input strings and their length) grows, HEURISTIC-3600 starts to produce better results than the competitors that are outperformed in the harder instances characterized by $t = 0.85\ m$.

5.6. Future work

Following Mousavi *et al.*, one line for future work involves a deeper study of the special characteristics of the objective functions of these consensus problems, whose solution has large plateaus. For problems with this type of objective function, it would be fruitful to apply results from the *fitness landscape analysis* [PIT 12] , which would greatly help in classifying problems according to their hardness for local search heuristics and meta-heuristics based on local search.

Another line for future research includes the exploration of alternative hybrid approaches obtained by embedding ILP-based method within metaheuristic frameworks.

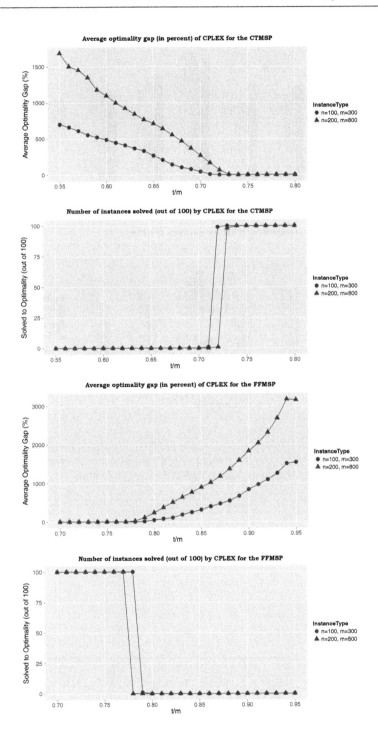

Figure 5.6. *Justification for the choice of parameter t for the CTMSP and the FFMSP*

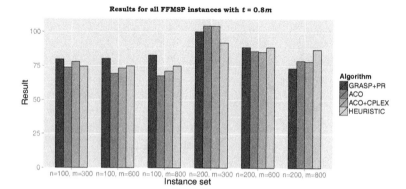

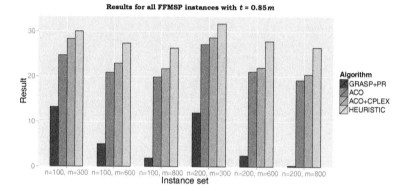

Figure 5.7. *Graphical representation of the comparison between* HEURISTIC-3600 *and the current FFMSP state-of-the-art methods (GRASP+PR, ACO, and ACO+CPLEX) for* $t = 0.8\ m$ *and* $t = 0.85\ m$

6

Alignment Problems

This chapter provides an overview of pairwise and multiple alignment problems. Solution techniques are discussed, with special emphasis on combinatorial optimization (CO), with the goal of providing conceptual insights and references to literature written by a broad community of researchers and practitioners.

6.1. Introduction

Real-world systems and phenomena are often conveniently represented by strings and sequences of symbols, as is the case of spins in magnetic unidimensional systems, or sequences of bits in the recording and transmission of digital data. Analysis of a sequence of symbols aims to extrapolate from it the information that it carries, i.e. its properties and characteristics. In the field of molecular biology, DNA and RNA strings have an immediate and intrinsic interpretation as sequences of symbols and, for example, one may be interested in determining the activity of specific subsequences. Since researchers in molecular biology claim that similar primary biological structures correspond to similar activities, techniques that compare sequences are used to obtain information about an unknown sequence from the knowledge of two or more sequences that have already been. Comparing genomic sequences drawn from individuals from different species consists of determining their similarity or difference. Such comparisons are needed to identify not only functionally relevant DNA regions, but also spot fatal mutations and evolutionary relationships. To compute the similarity between protein and amino acid sequences is, in general, a computationally intractable problem. Moreover, the concept of similarity itself does not have a single definition. Proteins and DNA segments can be considered similar in several different ways. They can have a similar structure or can have a similar primary amino acid sequence. Given two linearly-ordered sequences, one evaluates their similarity through a measure that associates a pair of sequences with a number related to the cardinality of subsets of corresponding elements/symbols (*alignment*). The correspondence must be order-preserving, i.e. if the i-th element of the first sequence s corresponds to the k-th element of the second sequence t, no element following i in s can correspond to an element preceding k in t. Furthermore, an element can be aligned with a blank or gap ('-') and two gaps cannot be aligned. Figure 6.1 shows a possible alignment of two sequences.

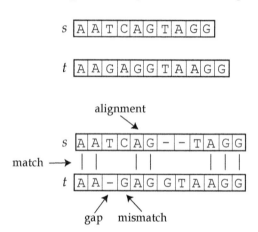

Figure 6.1. *An example of alignment of two sequences*

6.1.1. *Organization of this chapter*

The remainder of this chapter is organized as follows. Sections 6.2 and 6.3 are devoted to the pairwise and multiple alignment problem, respectively. These problems are mathematically formulated, their properties are described, and the most popular techniques to solve them are surveyed. Future directions are discussed in the last section.

6.2. The pairwise alignment problem

The simplest, computationally-tractable family of alignment problems concern the pairwise alignment of two sequences, s and t, considering only contiguous substrings with no internal deletions and/or insertions. The more general problem has been solved with methods developed to measure the minimum number of "events" needed to transform one string into another.

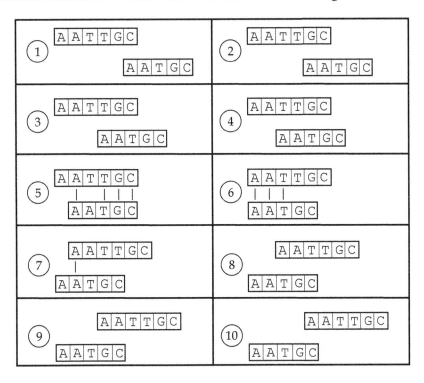

Figure 6.2. *All possible alignments of two sequences without gaps*

A naïve algorithm that computes all possible alignments of two sequences without the insertion of gaps simply slides one sequence along the other, and for each configuration it counts the number of letters that are exactly paired. Figure 6.2 shows the ten different possible alignments without gaps of two sequences with a length of 5 and 6 characters, respectively. With exactly four pairings, the alignment shown in number 5 is the best. Note that the concept of *best alignment* is clearly related to the criterion used to assess similarity. In general, the alignment with the largest number of matches (pairings) is considered to be best. The number of different alignments between two sequences of length n and m, is $n + m - 1$, under the assumption that no gaps can be inserted. Since for each possible alignment, each letter of the first sequence must be compared with each letter of the second sequence, the total computational complexity is $O(n \times m)$.

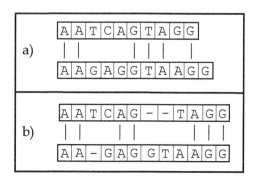

Figure 6.3. *Two possible alignments of two sequences: a) not inserting gaps with 6 pairings; b) inserting gaps with 7 pairings*

The possibility of inserting gaps strongly affects the quality of the solution obtained. See, for example, the two alignments depicted in Figure 6.3: alignment (a) does not allow the insertion of gaps and has 6 pairings while alignment (b) works with gaps and has 7 pairings. Nevertheless, the insertion of gaps influences the computational complexity of an algorithm that computes the best alignment. It is easy to understand that a naïve algorithm sliding one sequence along the other one is no longer suitable when considering gaps. This is because the number of different, gapped sequences that can be produced from an input sequence is exponential. Therefore, the design of more efficient alignment algorithms, such as the ones described in section 6.2.1, has been fundamental. Needleman and Wunsch's algorithm is among the first methods that was proposed [NEE 70]. This algorithm uses a simple iterative matrix method of calculation. Later, Sankoff [SAN 72] and Reichert *et al.* [REI 73] proposed – from a mathematical point of view – more complex methods, but unfortunately they are not able to perfectly represent real biological scenarios. In 1974, Sellers [SEL 74] proposed a true metric measure of distance between strings, later generalized by Waterman *et al.* [WAT 76] to consider deletions/insertions of arbitrary length. In 1981, Smith and Waterman [SMI 81] extended the above ideas to design a dynamic programming algorithm able to determine the pair of segments of the two strings given with maximum similarity. This algorithm is outlined in section 6.2.1.

A simple graphical representation of the alignment of two sequences, called a *dot matrix*, was introduced around 1970. Given input sequences s of length n and t of length m, a $n \cdot m$ matrix A is produced as follows. The n rows of A correspond (in the same order) to the n characters of s, and the m columns of A correspond (in the same order) to the m characters of t. The generic element a_{ij} of A – where $i = 1, \ldots, n$ and $j = 1, \ldots, m$ – refers to the pairing of letters s_i and t_j. In the simplest case, when $s_i = t_j$, a_{ij} contains a black dot; other cases it is painted white. Note that any alignment of a certain length will appear as a diagonal segment of black dots and will be visually distinguishable. Even though a dot matrix is intuitive and immediately provides useful information, it does not provide a numerical alignment value. In the end, it is only a graphical representation. Note that the concept of the dot matrix can also be applied to gapped sequences. Aligned subsequences appear, in this case, as diagonals with shifts. Figure 6.4 depicts the dot matrix representing the alignment in Figure 6.1.

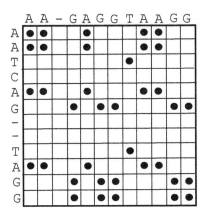

Figure 6.4. *Dot matrix representing the alignment in Figure 6.1*

In general, alignment problems can be divided into two categories: global and local. When looking for a global alignment, the problem consists of aligning two sequences over their entire length. In local alignment, one discards portions of the sequences that do not share any homology. Most alignment methods are global, leaving it up to the user to decide on the portion of sequences to be incorporated in the alignment.

Formally, the global pairwise alignment problem can be stated as follows: given symmetric costs $\gamma(a, b)$ for replacing character a with character b and costs $\gamma(a, -)$ for deleting or inserting character a, find a minimum cost set of character operations that transforms s into t. In the case of genomic strings, the costs are specified by *substitution matrices* which score the likelihood of specific letter mutations, deletions and insertions. An alignment A of two sequences s and t is a bi-dimensional array containing the gapped input sequences in rows. The total cost of A is computed by totalling the costs for the pairs of characters in corresponding positions. An optimal alignment A^* of s and t is an alignment corresponding to the minimum total cost $d_A^*(s, t)$, also called the *edit distance* of s and t. The next section is devoted to the description of the most popular exact pairwise alignment method.

6.2.1. *Smith and Waterman's algorithm*

Smith and Waterman's algorithm is a well-known dynamic programming approach capable of finding the optimal local alignment of two strings considering a predefined scoring system that includes a substitution matrix and a gap-scoring scheme. Scores consider matches, mismatches and substitutions or insertions/deletions.

Given two strings $s = s_1 s_2 \cdots s_n$ and $t = t_1 t_2 \cdots t_m$, the similarity $S(s_i, t_j)$ between sequence elements s_i and t_j is defined and deletions of length k are given a weight W_k. For each $0 \leq i \leq n$ and $0 \leq j \leq m$, let H_{ij} be the optimal objective function corresponding to the subproblem of aligning subsequences ending in s_i and in t_j, respectively. There are

$(n + 1) + (m + 1)$ elementary subproblems, whose optimal objective function value can be obtained as follows:

$$H_{i0} = 0, 0 \leq i \leq n;$$

(initial conditions)   [6.1]

$$H_{0j} = 0, 0 \leq j \leq m.$$

Then, for each $1 \leq i \leq n$ and for each $1 \leq j \leq m$, the optimal objective function value H_{ij} of the remaining $n \times m$ subproblems are recursively computed by the following *recurrence equation*:

$$H_{ij} = \max \Big\{ H_{i-1,j-1} + S(s_i, t_j), \max_{k \geq i}\{H_{i-k,j} - W_k\},$$

$$\max_{j \geq l}\{H_{i,j-l} - W_l\}, 0\Big\}.$$ [6.2]

This recurrence equation considers all the possibilities for ending the subsequences at any s_i and any t_j. The following three cases may occur:

1) case 1: s_i and t_j are associated. Then, the similarity is

$$H_{i-1,j-1} + S(s_i, t_j);$$

2) case 2: s_i is at the end of a deletion of length k. Then, the similarity is

$$H_{i-k,j} - W_k;$$

3) case 3: t_j is at the end of a deletion of length l. Then, the similarity is

$$H_{i,j-l} - W_l.$$

Moreover, in recurrence equation [6.2], a "0" is included to avoid the computation of negative similarity, indicating no similarity up to s_i and t_j. In cases where $S(s_i, t_j) \geq 0$, for all $1 \leq i \leq n$ and $1 \leq j \leq m$, "0" does not need to be included.

An algorithm based on recurrence equation [6.2] and initial conditions [6.1] can be formulated. Moreover, we can prove that its worst case computational complexity is linear in relation to the number of subproblems to be solved, i.e. $O(n \times m)$.

		C	A	G	C	C	U	C	G	C	U	U	A	G
	0-0	0-0	0-0	0-0	0-0	0-0	0-0	0-0	0-0	0-0	0-0	0-0	0-0	0-0
A	0-0	0-0	1-0	0-0	0-0	0-0	0-0	0-0	0-0	0-0	0-0	0-0	1-0	0-0
A	0-0	0-0	1-0	0-7	0-0	0-0	0-0	0-0	0-0	0-0	0-0	0-0	1-0	0-7
U	0-0	0-0	0-0	0-7	0-3	0-0	0-0	0-0	0-0	0-0	1-0	1-0	0-0	0-7
G	0-0	0-0	0-0	1-0	0-3	0-0	0-0	0-7	1-0	0-0	0-0	0-7	0-7	1-0
C	0-0	1-0	0-0	0-0	2-0	1-3	0-3	1-0	0-3	2-0	0-7	0-3	0-3	0-3
C	0-0	1-0	0-7	0-0	1-0	3-0	1-7	1-3	1-0	1-3	1-7	0-3	0-0	0-0
A	0-0	0-0	2-0	0-7	0-3	1-7	2-7	1-3	1-0	0-7	1-0	1-3	1-3	0-0
U	0-0	0-0	0-7	1-7	0-3	1-3	2-7	2-3	1-0	0-7	1-7	2-0	1-0	1-0
U	0-0	0-0	0-3	0-3	1-3	1-0	2-3	2-3	2-0	0-7	1-7	2-7	1-7	1-0
G	0-0	0-0	0-0	1-3	0-0	1-0	1-0	2-0	3-3	2-0	1-7	1-3	2-3	2-7
A	0-0	0-0	1-0	0-0	1-0	0-3	0-7	0-7	2-0	3-0	1-7	1-3	2-3	2-0
C	0-0	1-0	0-0	0-7	1-0	2-0	0-7	1-7	1-7	3-0	2-7	1-3	1-0	2-0
G	0-0	0-0	0-7	1-0	0-3	0-7	1-7	0-3	2-7	1-7	2-7	2-3	1-0	2-0
G	0-0	0-0	0-0	1-7	0-7	0-3	0-3	1-3	1-3	2-3	1-3	2-3	2-0	2-0

Figure 6.5. *Matrix H generated by the application of Smith and Waterman's algorithm to strings $s = \text{A A U G C C A U U G A C G G}$ and $t = \text{C A G C C U C G C U U A G}$*

The optimal solution computed by the dynamic programming algorithm is obtained by analyzing the matrix H. First, the maximum value in H must be located. Then, the other matrix elements leading to this maximum value are identified sequentially through a backtrack procedure ending with a "0" element in H, in this way producing the pair of subsequences and the corresponding optimal alignment. Smith and Waterman, described in their article how their algorithm applies to optimal alignment of the two sequences $s = \text{A A U G C C A U U G A C G G}$ and $t = \text{C A G C C U C G C U U A G}$. In this example, relying on an *a priori* statistical basis, the parameter values have been set as follows:

$$S(s_i, t_j) = \begin{cases} 1, & \text{if } s_i = t_j; \text{ (match)} \\ -\frac{1}{3}, & \text{if } s_i \neq t_j \text{ (mismatch).} \end{cases}$$

$$W_k \quad = 1 + \frac{1}{3} \cdot k.$$

```
- G - C - C - A - U - U - G -
- G - C - C - - - - U - C- G -
```

Figure 6.6. *The alignment obtained for
the simple example in Figure 6.5*

The resulting matrix H is reported in Figure 6.5. The matrix elements in gray cells indicate the backtrack path from the element with maximum value, i.e. the backtracking starting point. The alignment obtained is shown in Figure 6.6.

6.3. The multiple alignment problem

The problem of aligning a set $\{s_1, s_2, \ldots, s_k\}$ of k sequences is a generalization of the pairwise alignment problem and is called the *multiple alignment problem*. Contrary to the case of only two sequences, this problem is computationally intractable. One of the most important measures of multiple alignment quality considers an alignment as in matrix A with the input sequences (possibly extended by gaps) in the rows. Therefore, it is required that all extended sequences have the same length, which can be achieved by conveniently adding gaps. The *Sum-Of-Pairs* (SP) score of an alignment A, which is denoted by $SP(A)$, is computed by adding the costs of symbols matched up at the same positions across all pairs in the sequences. Formally, the SP score of an alignment A is given by:

$$SP(A) = \sum_{1 \leq i < j \leq k} d_A(s_i, s_j) = \sum_{1 \leq i < j \leq k} \sum_{l=1}^{|A|} \gamma(A[i][l], A[j][l]), \quad [6.3]$$

where $|A|$ is the alignment length, i.e. its number of columns. The goal is to find an alignment that minimizes the SP score.

The computational intractability of the multiple alignment problem was proven in 1994 by Wang and Jiang [WAN 94]. A generalization of Smith and Waterman's dynamic programming algorithm has exponential computational complexity given by $O(2^k l^k)$ and therefore it cannot be used to solve even small problems. In 2000, Kececioglu *et al.* [KEC 00] proposed an alternative and more effective method based on the *maximum weight trace problem*, which was introduced by Kececioglu [KEC 93] as a different optimization problem that generalizes the SP objective function score. A *trace* has a graph theoretic definition, but in the following we will provide a definition tailored to alignment problems. Let us suppose that k sequences have to be aligned that have $o_1, o_2, \ldots, o_k$ elements, respectively. A complete k-partite graph[1] $G = (V, E)$ can be defined, where $V = \cup_{i=1}^{k} V_i$ (for each $i = 1, 2, \ldots, k$, $V_i = \{v_{i1}, v_{i2}, \ldots, v_{io_k}\}$ is the subset of vertices of level i) and $E = \cup_{1 \leq i < j \leq k} V_i \times V_j$ is the set of edges called *lines*. A line $[i, j] \in E$ is realized by an alignment A if i and j are put in the same column of A and a trace, T, is a set of lines where there is an alignment A_T that realizes all the lines in T. Given weights w_{ij} associated with the lines $[i, j] \in E$, the maximum weight trace problem (MWT) finds a trace T^* with maximum total weight.

Recall that a cycle in a graph $G = (V, E)$ is a sequence of vertices $[v_1, v_2, \ldots, v_m]$ such that $m \geq 1$, $[v_i, v_{i+1}] \in E$ for $i = 1, \ldots, m-1$, $v_1 = v_m$ and except for the first and the last vertex there are no repeated vertices. Moreover, a directed mixed cycle is one containing both directed arcs (elements of $\overline{E}$, as defined below) and undirected edges (lines of T), in which the arcs are crossed according to their orientation, while the edges can be crossed in either direction. Let $\overline{E} = \{(v_{ih}, v_{ir}) \mid i = 1, \ldots, k, 1 \leq h < r \leq o_i\}$ be the set of directed arcs connecting each element v_{ir} ($i = 1, \ldots, k$) to the elements that are behind v_{ir} in sequence s_i. Kececioglu *et al.* [REI 97] have shown that a trace, T, must satisfy the following proposition:

PROPOSITION 6.1.– T is a trace if and only if there is no directed mixed-cycle $\mathcal{C}$ in the graph $\overline{G} = (V, T \cup \overline{E})$.

The property of trace T stated in proposition 6.1 is important since it has been used to formulate the MWT problem mathematically. In fact, by defining a Boolean variable x_{ij} for each line $[i, j] \in E$, the problem admits

---

1 A graph $G = (V, E)$ is said *complete* if E contains an edge connecting each pair of vertices in V. A k-partite graph $G = (V, E)$ is a graph whose vertex set V can be partitioned into k subsets, $V_1, V_2, \ldots, V_k$ and whose edge set $E \subseteq \cup_{1 \leq i < j \leq k} V_i \times V_j$. If a k-partite graph $G = (V, E)$ is complete, then $E = \cup_{1 \leq i < j \leq k} V_i \times V_j$.

the following 0/1 integer programming formulation:

$$\max \sum_{[i,j]\in E} w_{ij}x_{ij} \qquad [6.4]$$

subject to:

$$\sum_{[i,j]\in \mathcal{C}\cap\overline{E}} x_{ij} \leq |\mathcal{C} \cap \overline{E}| - 1 \quad \forall\, \mathcal{C} \text{ in } \overline{G} \qquad [6.5]$$

$$x_{ij} \in \{0,1\} \quad \forall[i,j] \in E \qquad [6.6]$$

Mixed-cycle inequality constraints [6.5] have been used by Kececioglu *et al.*, who in [KEC 00] proposed an branch and cut algorithm. A branch and cut solution framework belongs to the family of B&B algorithms. It combines a B&B strategy with ideas from cutting planes. The first approach to find in an optimal alignment for a set of 15 proteins of about 300 amino acids was proposed by Kececioglu *et al.* However, it has been shown experimentally that it is not suitable for aligning sequences longer than a few hundred characters. Given the high computational complexity of multiple sequence alignment problems, several polynomial time approximation and heuristic methods have been designed to deal with long sequences and proposed in the literature. In the operations research community, an approximation method finds a possibly suboptimal solution providing an approximation-guarantee on the quality of the solution found. An algorithm $\mathcal{A}lg$ for a minimization problem is said to be an approximation algorithm if the worst solution returned by $\mathcal{A}lg$ is no greater than ϵ times the best solution, for $\epsilon > 1$. In this case, ϵ is called the approximation guarantee of the proposed algorithm. Such approximation algorithms are important for intractable combinatorial optimization problems, since they are in a sense the best that can be done to guarantee the quality of the solution returned. A vast literature on approximation algorithms has been developed in the last decade and good starting points are [HOC 96] and [VAZ 01]. Nevertheless, sometimes it is preferable to approach and solve the problem heuristically, especially in the presence of large-scale problems. A heuristic approach finds a suboptimal solution whose quality can only be verified experimentally and, therefore, in general it is meaningful to apply it to optimization problems that are too complicated to be approximated. One of the most effective approximation methods for multiple alignment problems was devised by Gusfield [GUS 93] who proposed an iterative technique that progressively builds an alignment by considering one sequence at a time. It starts by building a star[2] with a node for each of the k sequences. One of these nodes is selected as the center. The procedure, uses the tree as a guide for aligning the input sequences. With s_c, $c \in \{1, \ldots, k\}$ is the sequence selected as the center of the star, Gusfield's algorithm first computes $k - 1$ pairwise alignments A_i, one for each sequence s_i, $i \neq c$, aligned with s_c such that each A_i corresponds to the edit distance between the pair (s_i, s_c). The $k - 1$ alignments can then be merged into a single alignment $A(c)$, by putting two characters aligned with the same character of s_c in the same column. Note that, in $A(c)$ each sequence s_i remains optimally aligned with s_c, i.e.

$$d_{A(c)}(s_i, s_c) = d_{A_i}(s_i, s_c), \qquad \forall \, i = 1, \ldots, k, \; i \neq c. \tag{6.7}$$

Therefore, it can be written that:

$$d_{A_i}(s_i, s_c) = d(s_i, s_c), \qquad \forall \, i = 1, \ldots, k, \; i \neq c, \tag{6.8}$$

neglecting the specific alignment the edit distance d refers to. Moreover, by assuming that the cost function γ is a metric over the alphabet Σ, the distance is a metric defined over the set of sequences and, therefore, the triangle of inequality holds, i.e.

$$d_{A(c)}(s_i, s_j) \leq d(s_i, s_c) + d(s_j, s_c), \qquad \forall \, i, j = 1, \ldots, k, \; i \neq j \neq c. \tag{6.9}$$

Let I be a generic multiple sequence alignment problem and let SP_I^* and $\hat{SP}_I$ be the optimal objective function value and the objective function value corresponding to the suboptimal solution found by Gusfield's algorithm. In [GUS 93] Gusfield proved that $\hat{SP}_I \leq (2 - \frac{2}{k})SP_I^*$, for any instance I. In 1999, Wu *et al.* [WU 99] generalized Gusfield's method to use any tree and not only stars, preserving an approximation guarantee of 2.

---

2 A tree is a connected and acyclic graph and a star is a tree with at most one node (center of the star) which is not a leaf.

Given the computational intractability of the multiple alignment problem, to obtain good suboptimal solutions within a realistic and acceptable amount of time it was also necessary to design efficient heuristics and metaheuristics to cope with the rapid increase in the availability of biological sequence data.

6.3.1. Heuristics for the multiple alignment problem

One of the first heuristic strategies for performing multiple alignment is the *progressive technique* that builds up an alignment by performing a series of pairwise alignments on successively less closely related sequences. The most popular progressive method are known as *Clustal* [HIG 88] and its weighted variant *ClustalW* [THO 94]. Efficient implementations can be accessed and used via several web portals, such as GenomeNet[3] and EMBNet[4]. ClustalW performs three main steps: 1) alignment scores are used to build a distance matrix by taking the divergence of the sequences into account; 2) from the distance matrix, a guide (phylogenetic) tree is built that has branches of different lengths proportional to the estimated divergence along each branch; 3) progressive alignment of the sequences is done by following the order of branches. Although ClustalW is among the most widely used algorithm, it suffers from its greediness and its performance depends strongly on the quality of the initial alignment. To overcome this drawback, an alternative progressive alignment method called *T-Coffee* [NOT 00] (Tree-based Consistency Objective Function for alignment Evaluation), has been designed. T-Coffee is also a greedy algorithm, but it is capable of finding more accurate solutions than *ClustalW* because it uses information from all of the sequences during each alignment step, not just those being aligned at the current stage.

Another line of research concerned with the reduction of negative effects of the shortcomings of progressive methods has led to the design of the so-called "iterative" approaches. The reason behind the choice of name lies in their characteristic of repeatedly realigning the initial sequences as well as adding new sequences to the growing multiple alignment. Progressive methods are strongly dependent on the quality of the initial alignment,

---

3 http://align.genome.jp/.
4 http://www.ch.embnet.org/software/ClustalW.html.

because those alignments are always incorporated into the final solution. Iterative methods in contrast, can return to previously calculated pairwise alignments. Although in the scientific literature, a number of iterative methods has been proposed, implemented and made available in software packages, reviews and surveys [EDG 06, HIR 95, LEC 01] do not claim that there is one that always outperforms the competitors. The software package PRRN/PRRP, based on Gotoh's algorithm [GOT 96], applies a greedy hill-climbing algorithm to optimize its multiple sequence alignment score and iteratively corrects alignment weights. CHAOS/DIALIGN is an alternative suite, based on the method proposed by Brudno *et al.* [BRU 03], that uses fast local alignments as anchor points for a slower global alignment procedure. Another iteration-based method is called MUSCLE (Multiple Sequence alignment by Log-Expectation). Proposed by Edgar in 2004 [EDG 04a, EDG 04b], it improves on progressive methods with a more accurate measure of distance.

Besides *MUSCLE*, there is *ProbCons* which is based on a technique that uses a pair-hidden Markov model and has been proposed by Wallace *et al.* in 2005 [WAL 05]. ProbCons introduces the notion of *probabilistic consistency*, a novel scoring function for multiple sequence comparisons. The use of this scoring function allows us to restrain and, therefore, cut down errors made at early stages of the alignment that not only propagate to the final alignment but also increase the likelihood of misalignment due to incorrect conservation signals.

6.3.2. *Metaheuristics for the multiple alignment problem*

One basic interesting question regarding multiple alignment problems is whether sophisticated metaheuristic techniques can solve large-scale molecular biology problems efficiently. For the general multiple alignment problem, besides a pioneering GA proposed by Notredame and Higgins [NOT 96], a Tabu search proposed by Riaz *et al.* [RIA 04], a SA proposed by Qi-wen Dong *et al.* [DON 06] and a hybrid ant colony proposed by Chen *et al.*, [CHE 06], more effort has been put into this line of research recently.

6.3.2.1. *Genetic algorithms*

A GA is a stochastic local search procedure proposed by Holland in 1975 [HOL 75] whose main characteristic is to simulate the natural evolutionary process of species. As with any heuristic and metaheuristic approach, this type of evolutionary technique is not guaranteed to find an optimal solution. Nevertheless, in many research papers and text books (see [EIB 91, GOL 89, GOL 87]) the authors define the evolutionary process as a Markov chain and find conditions implying that there is a high probability evolution is optimum (provided infinite time or space).

Competition among individuals results in the survival and reproduction of the fittest individuals. This is a natural phenomenon called *the survival of the fittest*: the genes of the fittest survive, while the genes of weaker individuals perish. The reproduction process generates diversity in the gene pool. Evolution is initiated when the genetic material (chromosomes) from two (or more) parents recombines during reproduction. The exchange of genetic material among chromosomes is called *crossover* and can generate good combinations of genes for better individuals. Another natural phenomenon called *mutation* introduces new genetic material. Repeated selection, mutation and crossover causes continuous evolution of the gene pool and the generation of individuals that survive better in a competitive environment. In complete analogy with nature, once each possible point in the search space of the problem is encoded by means of a suitable representation, a GA transforms into a population of individual solutions, each with an associated *fitness* (or objective function value), into a new generation. By applying genetic operators, such as crossover and mutation [KOZ 92, KOZ 99], a GA successively tries to produce better approximations of the solution. At each iteration, a new generation of approximations is created by the process of selection and reproduction.

In solving a given optimization problem $\mathcal{P}$, a GA passes through the following basic steps:

1) randomly create an initial population $P(0)$ of individuals, i.e. solutions for $\mathcal{P}$;

2) assign a fitness value to each individual using the fitness function;

3) iteratively perform the following substeps on the current generation of the population until the termination criterion has been satisfied:

a) select parents to mate,

b) create children from the selected parents by crossover and mutation,

c) evaluate the individual fitness of the offspring,

d) identify the best individual so far for this iteration of the GA,

e) replace worst ranked individuals with offspring.

Next, we describe how the above principles were tailored to produce a GA for the multiple alignment problem.

6.3.2.1.1. Representation and initial population

The population is represented as an array of sequences where each sequence is encoded as an array of characters over the alphabet considered. The symbol "-" refers to a gap in the alignment which represents the insertion or deletion of an amino acid residue.

6.3.2.1.2. Evaluation function

The association of each individual with a fitness value is done through the fitness function SP score, as defined in equation [6.3].

6.3.2.1.3. Parent selection

Pairs of individuals are randomly selected. Therefore, probability each individual is selected is proportional to its fitness function value: the fitter the individual, the more likely it will be chosen. Once pairs of individuals are randomly selected, clones are obtained which may then be subjected to genetic operators, such as mutation or recombination.

6.3.2.1.4. Genetic operators

Genetic operators aim to explore new regions of feasible solutions:

– *Crossover*: the crossover operator uses point-to-point crossover where the operator takes two alignment sequences from the population and randomly selects a fully matched (no gap) column. After crossover, the offspring are evaluated. The fittest offspring will survive in the next iteration.

– *Mutation*: the mutation operator picks a random amino acid from a randomly chosen row (sequence) in the alignment and checks whether one of its neighbors has a gap. If this is the case, the algorithm swaps (2-opt) the selected amino acid with a neighboring gap. If both neighbors are gaps, one of them will be picked randomly.

6.3.2.1.5. *Replacement*

This module replaces individuals that have lower fitness function values and inserts new offspring in the next population.

In 2012, Naznin *et al.* [NAZ 12] proposed GAPAM, an alternative progressive alignment method that applies a GA. One of the innovative aspects of this algorithm compared to the state-of-the-art is the generation of the initial population. The authors introduced two new mechanisms for this task: the first mechanism generates guide trees with randomly-selected sequences and the second one shuffles the sequences within these trees. The population size has been set to 100 individuals and in each generation, to generate a child population of 100 individuals, the following three genetic operators have been used:

– *Single-point crossover:* one parent is selected from the top 50% individuals and another from the bottom 50%. The single of point crossover initially randomly selects a column position. The parent with the better score is then divided vertically at that column. The second parent is also divided into two pieces in such a way that each piece has the same number of elements as the first parent. The pieces of the two parents are then exchanged and merged together to generate two new individuals and the better new individual is considered the child.

– *Multiple-point crossovers:* as in single-point crossover, one parent is selected from the top 50% of individuals and another from the bottom 50%. Unlike single-point crossover, multiple-point crossover divides each parent into three pieces that are then exchanged and merged together to generate two new individuals. The better new individual is considered the child.

To cut the first piece, the scores of the first 25% of columns for both parents are compared and the parent with the better score is divided vertically at that column, while the other parent is divided using the mechanism introduced in the single-point crossover. To create another piece and obtain three pieces for each parent, the authors applied the same idea but considered the last 25% of columns. To complete the crossover, the middle pieces are exchanged and all three pieces merged together to generate two new individuals.

– *Mutation:* one individual is randomly selected from the current generation. From the individual selected, the distance between sequences is calculated and stored in a distance table. Taking into account the distance calculated a new guide tree is constructed where the sequence numbers are shuffled to find a better guide tree and the solution is considered a mutated child.

To test the performance of their algorithm, Naznin *et al.* compared it with existing methods, such as PRRP and different versions of Clustal, as well as the other GA-based algorithm. The experimental results showed that GAPAM achieved better solutions than the others in most cases and also revealed that the overall performance of the proposed method outperformed the other methods mentioned above.

6.3.2.2. *Simulated annealing*

SA is commonly said to be the oldest among the metaheuristic frameworks and one of the first algorithms that had an explicit strategy to escape the local minima. It allows moves resulting in solutions of worse quality than the current solution (uphill moves) in order to move outside local minima (see section 1.2.5 for an introduction to SA). In 2004, Kleinjung *et al.* [KLE 04] proposed a contact-based sequence alignment method that uses the structural information from side-chain contacts and alignment scores provided by CAO (Contact Accepted mutatiOn) substitution matrices. CAO matrices describe the probability of mutation of side-chain contacts within a protein and, therefore, they combine sequence and structure information into a single score. With alignment scores provided by the CAO, we have an approximate dynamic programming algorithm for protein sequence alignment that works assuming that the distance between the residues in contact during evolution has been conserved. Since this assumption is not suitable for insertion/deletion events during evolution, Qi-wen Dong *et al.* [DON 06] designed a contact-based simulated annealing alignment method that solves the problem without any restriction. The innovative aspect of this method lies in the introduction of a new parameter called contact-penalty. This parameter was introduced to efficiently and better manage the scenario where contact in the template sequence is aligned with gaps in the query sequence. In fact, when there are gaps in the contact pair, the total score of an alignment is decreased by a fixed contact-penalty. In the contact-based sequence alignment, as proposed by Kleinjung *et al.*, there were no gaps in the contact pair due to the assumption that the distance between the residues in contact has been conserved.

6.3.2.3. *Ant colony optimization*

As outlined in more detail in section 1.2.1, ACO algorithms are metaheuristics that are inspired by the shortest path-finding behavior of natural ant colonies. In 2006, Chen *et al.* [CHE 06] designed a hybrid ACO algorithm with a divide and conquer approach for the multiple sequence alignment problem. The basic idea of this algorithm is to divide the set of sequences into several sections. The division is carried out via an ACO method by bisecting the sequences vertically and recursively. The recursive procedure ends when the length of all the sections obtained is equal to one, and hence the result of alignment is obtained. During the division phase, the proposed ant colony algorithm bisects the sequence set iteratively at approximately optimum cut-off points. Each ant searches for a set of cutting points by starting from the midpoint of a sequence and moving along the other sequences to choose the matching characters.

Let $\{s_0, \ldots, s_{N-1}\}$ be the input set of N sequences. An artificial ant starts from a randomly-selected character around the middle position of s_0. Let $s_0[m_0]$ be such character, where $m_0 \in [mid_0 - \delta, mid_0 + \delta]$, $mid_0 = \left\lceil \frac{|s_0|}{2} \right\rceil$ and δ is the scope of the ants search in s_0. The ant selects one character from or inserts a gap into the middle part of sequences $s_1, \ldots, s_{N-1}$ matching $s_0[0]$. Furthermore, from the remaining sequences s_i, $i = 1, \ldots, N-1$, the ant selects a character $s_i[j]$ with a probability determined by the matching score with $s_0[m_0]$, the deviation of its location from the middle position of s_i which is given by $mid_i = \left\lceil \frac{|s_i|}{2} \right\rceil$ and pheromone on the logical edge between $s_i[j]$ and $s_0[m_0]$. The ant might select an empty character corresponding to the insertion of a gap into the sequence in the alignment. The other ants select their path in the same manner, but start from different sequences. In general, the i-th ant starts from s_i and successively goes through sequences $s_{i+1}, \ldots, s_{n-1}$. Once is s_{n-1}, reached it continues going through $s_0, \ldots, s_{i-1}$

to complete the path. At the end of each iteration, the algorithm calculates the fitness of the solutions constructed and updates the pheromone on the logical edges accordingly.

In 2008, Lee *et al.* [LEE 08] presented a hybrid ACO algorithm to enhance the performance of a GA. In the proposed algorithm (GA-ACO), the GA is applied to provide the diversity of alignments, while ACO is performed to improve the solution generated by the GA. The initial population is randomly generated. The innovative aspect of the GA component of this hybrid approach lies in the introduction of three new crossover operators: the *singlepoint* operator, the *recombinematchcolumn* operator and the *uniformexchangeblock* operator. By exchanging information in parent alignments, *singlepoint* produces two offspring. Parent 1 is cut at randomly chosen positions and parent 2 is cut at the same ordered base position for each sequence. The remaining parts of both parents are exchanged to keep the original sequence base order, if there is a single cutting point in both parent alignments. Extra spaces may be inserted into the junction points. The *recombinematchcolumn* operator generates an offspring with match columns by swapping blocks and inserting spaces into the junction points, while *uniformexchangeblock* maps the match columns that are consistent in parent alignments. Match columns are consistent if they contain the same ordered base. Two consistent match columns are randomly selected as the two cutting points and then blocks can be directly swapped between two consistent match columns. The ACO component is embedded into GA as local search to improve poorly aligned regions.

6.3.2.4. *Particle swarm optimization and Hidden Markov Models*

A Hidden Markov Model (HMM) consists of a set of q states $(S_1, \ldots, S_q)$. In the case of multiple sequence alignment, in [SUN 14], Sun *et al.* divided them into three groups: match (M), insert (I) and delete (D). As in any HMM: 1) two special states are defined: the begin state and the end state; 2) states are connected to each other by transition probabilities. Match and insert states emit an observable symbol (i.e. a character from the alphabet Σ) with a given probability, while the delete states do not emit observable symbols and are, therefore, called silent states. From the initial state and until the end state is not reached, the HMM generates sequences, i.e. strings of observable symbols, by making non-deterministic walks that randomly go from one state to another according to the transition probabilities. In the case of multiple sequence alignment, the sequence of observable symbols is given in the form of an unaligned sequence and the target is to find a path generating the best alignment. For a given sequence s and a HMM, a *learning phase* must be performed whose objective is to estimate the parameters (transition and emission probabilities). Typically, this learning task is performed by either the Baum-Welch technique, which is based on statistical re-estimation formulas, or by random search methods such as SA. In [SUN 14], Sun *et al.* proposed a population-based optimization (PSO) technique inspired by the collective behavior of social organisms [ENG 05, KEN 04, CLE 06, KEN 95, JOR 15]. In a (PSO) with L particles, each particle i, $i = 1, \ldots, L$, represents a potential solution to the problem to be solved in a D-dimensional space. At any iteration k of the PSO, three D-dimensional vectors are associated with each particle: its current position $X_{i,k}$, its velocity $V_{i,k}$ and its best position $P_{i,k}$, i.e. the position with the best objective function value or fitness value so far. A global best position vector G_k is also kept, which is defined as the position of the best particle from among all the particles in the population. For HMM learning in multiple sequence alignment, the position of a particle is composed by the parameters of the HMM, i.e. each component of the position vector is a parameter of the HMM; each component of the velocity vector represents the variation of the corresponding parameter during HMM training.

Recently, Lalwani *et al.* [LAL 15] proposed a two-level particle swarm optimization approach. At the first level, the particle swam optimization maximizes the matched columns, while in the second one it maximizes pairwise similarities to the best solutions found in the first level.

6.3.2.5. *Tabu search*

A Tabu search (TS) approach usually starts from an initial solution that plays the role of the current solution. Then, the algorithm explores the neighborhood of the current solution by generating some moves iteratively. As in the case of SA, the fundamental idea of a TS is to allow moves resulting in uphill moves in order to escape from local minima. Furthermore, it explicitly uses the history of the search, both to escape from local minima and to implement an explorative strategy. To avoid local optima and cycles, it uses a short-term memory, i.e. a *Tabu list*, that keeps track of the most recently visited solutions and forbids moves toward them. The length l of the Tabu list, called the *Tabu tenure*, controls the memory of the search process. With small Tabu tenures the search will concentrate on small areas of the search space. A large Tabu tenure forces the search process to explore larger regions, because it forbids a higher number of solutions to be revisited. The Tabu tenure can be varied during the search, leading to more robust algorithms. An example can be found in [TAI 91], where the Tabu tenure is periodically reinitialized at random from an interval $[l_{\min}, l_{\max}]$.

The TS proposed by Riaz *et al.* in 2004 [RIA 04] has two phases. During the first phase, the search process leads iteratively to the point where the solution stabilizes, i.e. there is no improvement in the quality of solution for a specified number of iterations. Then, the second phase starts by performing intensification and diversification strategies, realized by means of elite solutions, which are the best from each iteration. The idea behind the idea of interrelating intensification and diversification strategies with elite solutions is that the neighborhoods of elite solutions likely contain attractive regions and exploring them more exhaustively may lead to better solutions than those previously encountered. Therefore, during both intensification and diversification phases, the algorithm explores the neighborhood of elite solutions. The algorithm stops when intensification and diversification strategies fail to identify new attractive regions and the best solution found is returned as the output.

As an initial solution, Riaz *et al.* used both an unaligned initial solution, obtained by inserting a fixed number of gaps into sequences at regular intervals and an aligned initial solution, obtained by applying a simple progressive alignment algorithm. The objective function used to measure the overall alignment quality and to evaluate candidate moves in the local search is the objective function used in T-Coffee [NOT 00]. The algorithm performs two kinds of move: single sequence moves and block moves. With single sequence moves, a patch of gap(s) of arbitrary length is moved in a randomly selected sequence while the remaining sequences in the alignment remain isolated. Block moves relocate a rectangle of gaps involving more than one sequence from one position to another in the alignment. Experimentally it has been observed that block moves are better for improving the current alignment since they involve a larger number of sequences compared with single sequence moves. Intensification strategies are based on modifying the rules that encourage the combinations of moves and solution features that have historically been good [GLO 97], while diversification strategies encourage the search process to examine unvisited regions and generate solutions that are significantly different from those already visited.

In 2015, Mehenni [MEH 15] designed an improved TS that benefits from a set of operations on the guide tree of the initial solution in order to search the neighborhood of the current solution. The guide tree carries information about the relationships between the sequences and is usually calculated on the basis of the distance matrix that is generated from the pairwise scores. The initial solution of Mehenni's TS is represented by a tree generated by clustering the nearby sequences in a stepwise manner. At each step of sequence clustering, the sum of branch lengths is minimized by selecting the two nearest sequences/nodes and joining them. Next, the distance between the new node and the remaining ones is recalculated and this process is iterated until all sequences are joined to the root of the guide tree. Finally, the solution is obtained from the tree as follows: the pair of sequences on the lowest level are aligned, then, the entire branch containing these two sequences is aligned starting from the lowest level and progressing upward to sequences on higher levels. The SP score is used as an objective function. The innovative aspect of this metaheuristic approach lies in the local search phase, where the neighborhood of the current solution may be generated by applying one of the following four moves:

1) *swapping move*: the order of the sequences is swapped (i.e. leaves of the guide tree);

2) *node insertion move*: a certain number of nodes are inserted into the current guide tree. A node insertion can cause a sequence node to move to another location in the guide tree, therefore changing its topology. The newly obtained guide tree can be considered a neighbor of the original;

3) *branch insertion move*: a whole sub-tree (or branch) of the guide tree can be moved to another location. The topology of the resulting guide tree will change and this new tree is considered a neighbor of the current guide tree;

4) *distance variation move*: N different guide trees are produced by introducing some randomness (or noise) into the clustering algorithm used to generate the initial solution.

The TS variant that uses the branch insertion neighborhood generally outperformed the competitor strategies. No comparison is reported with other state-of-the-art algorithms.

6.3.2.6. *Musical composition*

In 2015, Mora-Gutiérrez *et al.* [MOR 15] designed two algorithms based on the method of musical composition (MMC) [MOR 12, MOR 14a]. A MMC is inspired by creativity involved in the musical composition process. The model design takes into account that musical composition can be viewed as an algorithm that is developed within a creative system, where a composer learns from his own experience and from other composers. Interactions between composers then causes the establishment of a social network. In other words, a MMC is grounded on an agent-based model of a specific social network, which is made up of a set of V nodes or agents (i.e. composers) and a set of edges E representing relationships between composers. Each composer is equipped with prior knowledge and a set of mechanisms and policies for interacting with other composers. The composers can communicate and exchange information with each other. The prior knowledge consists of a set of solutions, called *tunes*. The initial social network with $|V|$ composers and a set E of links is randomly generated. For each composer $i \in V$, a set of solutions (artworks) is randomly generated. Each set generated, called a *scoring matrix*, represents the prior knowledge of composer i. Then, the algorithm proceeds in iterations, until a stopping criterion is satisfied. At each iteration, composers exchange information: composer i will exchange information with composer j, $i \neq j$, if $(i, j) \in E$ and the worst solution in the prior knowledge of composer j is better than the worst solution in the prior knowledge of composer i. If this is the case, then a new solution for composer i is generated. To evaluate the overall alignment quality, Mora-Gutiérrez *et al.* used two different objective functions: (1) the Euclidean distance; and (2) a multiple linear regression. The first relates the *T-Coffee* function, the SP-score function and the gap penalty function, while the second combines the *T-Coffee* function, the SP-score, the gap penalty function, the number of sequences aligned, the average length of the sequences aligned, their variation in length and Euclidean distance. Based on the experimental results, the MMC uses multiple linear regression as the objective function has been shown to have better behavior, since for 25% of the instances in the literature, it found the best alignment with respect to data.

6.4. Conclusion and future work

Sequence alignment problems are relevant to several heterogeneous scientific fields, especially in computational biology and bioinformatics, where it is fundamental to efficiently discovering the structural homologies of protein/DNA sequences and determining the functions of protein/DNA sequences to predict patients' diseases by comparing the DNA of patients in disease discovery among others.

While the simplest alignment problem involving the alignment of two sequences (pairwise alignment) is optimally solvable in polynomial time and has been widely studied in the literature, multiple sequence alignment is a computationally intractable optimization problem and biology, computer science and operations research communities have given it less attention. An interesting, and indeed fruitful, line for future research on the multiple alignment problem includes the exploration of alternative and more sophisticated approximation and/or metaheuristic solution approaches.

7

Conclusions

Here, we will provide references and short descriptions of optimization problems from the bio-informatics field that not have been dealt with in detail so far. In particular, these include DNA sequencing problems and founder sequence reconstruction.

7.1. DNA sequencing

DNA sequencing is the process of determining the precise order of the nucleotides in a DNA molecule. The knowledge of the precise composition of DNA sequences has become very important in numerous application fields such as medical diagnosis, biotechnology, forensic biology, virology and biological systematics. Computational methods such as metaheuristics have played an important role in DNA sequencing technology. The first basic DNA sequencing technologies were developed in the 1970s (see [JAY 74]). An example of a basic DNA sequencing technology is *shotgun sequencing* [STA 79]. Small genomes (4,000 to 7,000 base pairs) had already been sequenced by means of shotgun sequencing in 1997 [STA 79]. The first of the *next-generation* sequencing technologies, known as *massively parallel signature sequencing*, was developed in the 1990s [BRE 00]. Another example is *DNA sequencing by hybridization* [BAI 88, LYS 87, DRM 89]. In the following section, we will provide several examples in which metaheuristics play an important role.

7.1.1. *DNA fragment assembly*

The so-called *DNA fragment assembly* problem is a computational problem that is a major component of DNA sequencing, often on the basis of shotgun sequencing. In shotgun sequencing, first, many copies of the DNA strands that are to be sequenced – i.e. the target sequence – are produced. These DNA strands are then cut into pieces at random sites in order to obtain fragments that are short enough (up to approx. 1,000 base pairs) to sequence directly. The fragments then need to be assembled into the most plausible DNA sequence. Moreover, in order to have a good chance assembling a DNA sequence close to the target sequence, a coverage of at least 10 is required, which means that each base from a specific position of the target sequence should appear in at least 10 DNA fragments. A variety of approaches have been applied for the assembly of the DNA fragments. One of the most popular is the overlap-layout-consensus (OLC) approach. Large eukaryotic genomes[1] have been successfully sequenced with the OLC approach (see [ADA 00]).

The first step of the OLC approach consists of calculating the *overlaps* between the suffix and the prefix of any two fragments. In order to do so, note that both orientations of each DNA fragment must be considered. This is because it is not clear from which of the two DNA strands forming the double helix (see Chapter 1), the fragment was obtained. The overlap scores are, generally, obtained by applying a semi-global alignment algorithm such as the Smith-Waterman algorithm [SMI 81] (see also section 6.2).

The most challenging part of the OLC approach is the *layout phase* in which one or more contigs (sequences of DNA fragments whose respective overlaps are greater than a pre-defined threshold) are produced. This is where metaheuristics often come into play. Even without considering noise such as reading errors, etc., this problem has been shown to be NP-hard in [PEV 00]. Finally, the last phase of the OLC approach is the *consensus phase* in which the most likely contig is determined based on the layout phase. For an overview of the existing heuristic and metaheuristic approaches for the layout phase see Table 7.1.

---

1 A *eukaryote* is any organism whose cells contain a nucleus and other organelles enclosed within membranes.

Type of algorithm	Publication
Genetic algorithm	Parsons and Johnson [PAR 95a], 1995
Genetic algorithm	Parsons *et al.* [PAR 95b], 1995
Genetic algorithm	Fang *et al.* [FAN 05], 2005
Genetic algorithm	Kikuchi and Chakraborty [KIK 06], 2006
Ant colony optimization	Zhao *et al.* [ZHA 08], 2008
Genetic algorithm	Nebro *et al.* [NEB 08], 2008
Genetic algorithm	Hughes *et al.* [HUG 14], 2014
Local search	Ben Ali *et al.* [BEN 15], 2015
Hybrid particle swarm optimization	Huang *et al.* [HUA 15], 2015
Hybrid gravitation search	Huang *et al.* [HUA 16], 2016

Table 7.1. *Heuristic and metaheuristic approaches for the layout phase in DNA fragment assembly*

7.1.2. DNA sequencing by hybridization

DNA sequencing by hybridization works roughly as follows. The first phase of the method consists of a chemical experiment which requires a so-called DNA array. A DNA array is a two-dimensional grid whose cells typically contain all possible DNA strands – called probes – of a certain length l. For example, consider a DNA array of all possible probes of length $l = 3$ (see [IDU 95]):

AAA AAC AAG AAT CAA CAC CAG CAT
ACA ACC ACG ACT CCA CCC CCG CCT
AGA AGC AGG AGT CGA CGC CGG CGT
ATA ATC ATG ATT CTA CTC CTG CTT
GAA GAC GAG GAT TAA TAC TAG TAT
GCA GCC GCG GCT TCA TCC TCG TCT
GGA GGC GGG GGT TGA TGC TGG TGT
GTA GTC GTG GTT TTA TTC TTG TTT

The chemical experiment is started after the generation of the DNA array. In order to do so, the DNA array is brought together with many copies of the DNA target sequence that is to be sequenced. The target sequence possibly reacts to a probe on the DNA array, if and only if the probe is a subsequence of the target sequence. This reaction is also called hybridization. After the experiment, the DNA array allows us to identify the probes that reacted with target sequences. The set(s) of probes involved in some reaction is called the *spectrum.* However, it has to be taken into account that two types of errors may occur during the hybridization experiment:

1) *negative errors:* some probes do not form part of the spectrum even though they are part of the target sequence. Note that a particular type of negative error is caused by the multiple existence of a probe in the target sequence. Such a probe will appear at most once in the spectrum;

2) *positive errors:* a probe of the spectrum that does not appear in the target sequence is called a positive error.

After the chemical experiment, the second phase of DNA sequencing by hybridization consists of the reconstruction of the target sequence from the spectrum by means of computational optimization methods. If we assume that the obtained spectrum is free of errors, the original sequence can be reconstructed in polynomial time with an algorithm proposed by Pevzner in [PEV 89]. However, as this is not usually the case, a perfect reconstruction is not always possible. Therefore, DNA sequencing by hybridization is, generally, expressed by means of optimization problems with optimal solutions that can be shown to have a high probability of resembling the target sequence. In the following section, we present the one proposed by Baewicz *et al.* in [BŁA 99], which was shown to be NP-hard.

Henceforth, let the target sequence be denoted by s_t. The length – i.e. the number of nucleotide bases – of s_t is denoted by n, i.e. $s_t \in \{A,C,G,T\}^n$. Furthermore, the spectrum – as obtained by the hybridization experiment – is denoted by $S = \{1, \ldots, m\}$. More specifically, each $i \in S$ is an oligonucleotide (a short DNA strand) of length l, that is, $i \in \{A,C,G,T\}^l$. Let $G = (V, A)$ be the completely connected directed graph defined by $V = S$ (see [IDU 95]). To each link $a_{ij} \in A$ is assigned a weight o_{ij}, which is defined as the length of the longest DNA strand, that is a suffix of i and a prefix of j (i.e. the overlap). Each directed, node-disjoint path $p = (i_1, \ldots, i_k)$ in G is considered a valid solution to the problem. The number of vertices (i.e. oligonucleotides) on a path p is called the length of the path, denoted by $\text{len}(p)$. In the following, we denote by $p[r]$ the rth vertex on a given path p (starting from position 1). In contrast to the length, the cost of a path p is defined as follows:

$$c(p) \leftarrow \text{len}(p) \cdot l - \sum_{r=1}^{\text{len}(p)-1} o_{p[r]\,p[r+1]} \qquad [7.1]$$

The first term sums up the length of the oligonucleotides on the path and the second term (which is subtracted from the first one) sums up the overlaps between the neighboring oligonucleotides on p. In fact, $c(p)$ is equivalent to the length of the DNA sequence that is obtained by the sequence of oligonucleotides in p. The problem of DNA sequencing by hybridization consists of finding a solution (or path), p^*, in G with $\text{len}(p^*) \geq \text{len}(p)$, for all possible solutions p that fulfill $c(p) \leq n$.

Consider, for example, the target sequence $s_t = $ ACTGACTC. Assuming $l = 3$, the ideal spectrum is {ACT, CTG, TGA, GAC, ACT, CTC}. However, let us assume that the hybridization experiment results in the following faulty spectrum $S = $ {ACT, TGA, GAC, CTC, TAA}. This spectrum has two negative errors, because ACT should appear twice, but can – due to the characteristics of the hybridization experiment – only appear once, and CTG does not appear at all in S. Moreover, S has one positive error, because it includes oligonucleotide TAA, which does not appear in the target sequence. An optimal solution in this example is $p^* = $ (ACT, TGA, GAC, CTC) with $\text{len}(p^*) = 4$ and $c(p^*) = 8$. The DNA sequence that is retrieved from this path is equal to the target sequence (see Figure 7.1).

7.1.2.1. *Existing heuristics and metaheuristics*

The first approach to solve the SBH problem was a branch and bound method proposed in [BŁA 99]. However, this approach becomes unpractical when problem size gets bigger. The algorithm was capable of solving only one out of 40 problem instances with target sequences of length 209 within one hour to optimality. Another argument against this branch and bound algorithm is the fact that an optimal solution to the SBH problem does not necessarily provide a DNA sequence that is equal to the target sequence. This implies that the importance of finding *optimal* solutions is not the same as for other optimization problems. Therefore, the research community has focused on heuristics and metaheuristics for tackling the SBH problem. Most of the existing approaches are either constructive heuristics or metaheuristics such as evolutionary algorithms, Tabu search, GRASP and ant colony optimization. For an overview on the existing approaches to the SBH problem, see Table 7.2.

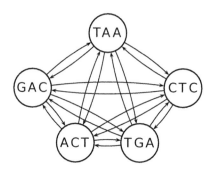

(a) Completely connected directed graph G.

A C⌈T⌉
 ⌈T⌉G⌈A⌉
 ⌊G⌋⌊A⌋⌈C⌉
    ⌊C⌋T C

─────────────────

A C T G A C T C

(b) DNA sequence retrieval from a solution.

Figure 7.1. a) *The completely connected directed graph G with the spectrum $S = \{ACT, TGA, GAC, CTC, TAA\}$ as vertex set. The edge weights (i.e. overlaps) are not indicated for readability reasons. For example, the weight on the edge from TGA to GAC is 2, because GA is the longest DNA strand that is a suffix of TGA and a prefix of GAC. An optimal solution is $p^* = (ACT, TGA, GAC, CTC)$. b) How to retrieve the DNA sequence that is encoded by p^*. Note that $c(p^*) = 8$, which is equal to the length of the encoded DNA sequence*

7.2. Founder sequence reconstruction

Given a sample of sequences from a population of individuals, a possible goal of valuable research is to study the evolutionary history of the population. For example, an important application is the discovery of the genetic basis of multi-factorial diseases. If the population under study has evolved from a relatively small number of founder ancestors, the evolutionary history can be studied by trying to reconstruct the sample sequences as fragments from the set of founder sequences. The genetic material of the population's individuals is the result of recombination and mutation of their founders. Many findings from biological studies support the validity of this model, such as, for example, the fact that the "*Ferroplasma* type II genome seems to be a composite from three ancestral strains that have undergone homologous recombination to form a large population of mosaic genomes" [THY 04].

Type of algorithm	Publication
Constructive heuristic	Baewicz *et al.* [BŁA 99], 1999
Constructive heuristic	Baewicz *et al.* [BŁA 02a], 2002
Evolutionary algorithm	Baewicz *et al.* [BŁA 02b, BŁA 05], 2002
Evolutionary algorithm	Endo [END 04], 2004
Evolutionary algorithm	Brizuela *et al.* [BRI 04a], 2004
Evolutionary algorithm	Bui and Youssef [BUI 04], 2004
Tabu search	Baewicz *et al.* [BŁA 00], 2000
Tabu search / scatter search hybrid	Baewicz *et al.* [BŁA 04, BŁA 05], 2004
GRASP-like multi-start technique	Fernandes and Ribeiro [FER 05], 2005
Ant colony optimization	Blum *et al.* [BLU 08], 2008
Constructive heuristic	Chen and Hu [CHE 11a], 2011
Hyper-heuristics	Baewicz *et al.* [BŁA 11], 2013

Table 7.2. *Heuristic and metaheuristic approaches to the SBH problem*

The main problem is that the number of founder sequences as well as the founder sequences themselves are generally unknown. Nevertheless, given a specific evolutionary model, it is possible to phrase a combinatorial optimization problem whose solutions are biologically plausible founder sequences. This problem is usually called the *founder sequence reconstruction problem* (FSRP). From an optimization perspective, the FSRP problem is a hard combinatorial optimization problem and it is of interest *per se* as it constitutes a challenge for current optimization techniques.

7.2.1. *The FSRP problem*

The FSRP problem can technically be defined as follows: take a set of n *recombinants* $C = \{C_1, \ldots, C_n\}$. Each recombinant C_i is a string of length

m over a given alphabet Σ, i.e. $C_i = c_{i1}c_{i2} \ldots c_{im}$ with $c_{ij} \in \Sigma$. Most of the literature consider typical biological applications where the recombinants are haplotyped sequences. Hence, $\Sigma = \{0, 1\}$. The symbols 0 and 1 encode the two most common alleles of each haplotype site.

A *candidate solution* consists of a set of k_f *founders* $\mathcal{F} = \{F_1, \ldots, F_{k_f}\}$. Each founder F_i is a string of length m over the alphabet Σ: $F_i = f_{i1}f_{i2} \ldots f_{im}$ with $f_{ij} \in \Sigma \; \forall j$. A candidate solution $\mathcal{F}$ is *valid* if it is possible to reconstruct the set of recombinants C from $\mathcal{F}$. This is the case when each $C_i \in C$ can be decomposed into a sequence of $p_i \leq m$ fragments (that is, strings) $Fr_{i1}Fr_{i2} \ldots Fr_{ip_i}$, such that each fragment Fr_{ij} appears at the same position in at least one of the founders. Therefore, a decomposition with respect to a valid solution is said to be *reduced* if two consecutive fragments do not appear in the same founder. Moreover, a decomposition is said to be *minimal* if $\sum_{i=1}^m p_i - m$ is minimal. In [WU 08] it was shown that for each valid solution $\mathcal{F}$ it is possible to derive a minimal decomposition in $O(n \; m \; k_f)$ time. Henceforth, this number is called the objective function value of $\mathcal{F}$ and is denoted by $f(\mathcal{F})$. In biological terms, $f(\mathcal{F})$ is called the number of *breakpoints* of C with respect to $\mathcal{F}$.

The optimization goal considered by the FSRP problem is the following one. Given a fixed k_f, that is, a fixed number of founders, find a valid solution $\mathcal{F}^*$ that minimizes the number of breakpoints. As an example, see Figure 7.2. The FSRP was first proposed by Ukkonen [UKK 02] and the problem is proved to be $\mathcal{NP}$-complete [RAS 07] for $k_f > 2$.

7.2.2. *Existing heuristics and metaheuristics*

This section provides an overview of existing algorithmic approaches for the FSRP. One of the first algorithms proposed for the FSRP was a dynamic programming algorithm [UKK 02]. However, this method is not efficient when the number of founders and the number or length of recombinants is high. Another dynamic programming algorithm was introduced in [RAS 07]. In [LYN 05] a branch and bound algorithm has been proposed which works independently of the lower bound method used. Although promising, this method has been evaluated only on a limited test set composed of rather small instances.

01001000		a a| b| a a| c c c
00111000		a| c c c c c c c
10011100		b b b b| a a| c c
10111010	01101110 (a)	c c c c c c| a a
01101110	10010011 (b)	a a a a a a a a
10110011	10111000 (c)	c c c c| b b b b

(a) Set of recombinants. (b) Set of founders $\mathcal{F}$. (c) Corresponding decomposition.

Figure 7.2. *a) A set of six recombinants in matrix form. Assuming that the number of founders (k_f) is fixed to three, b) shows a valid solution, that is, a matrix of three founders. Denoting the first founder by a, the second founder by b, and the third one by c, c) shows a decomposition of the recombinant matrix into fragments taken from the founders. Note that breakpoints are marked by vertical lines. This is a decomposition with 8 breakpoints, which is the minimum value for this instance*

Wu and Gusfield proposed a constructive tree-search solver, called RECBLOCK, which uses bounding information [WU 08]. RECBLOCK can be run as an exact or an approximate heuristic-solver. Although the results of RECBLOCK are very good for instances with a rather small number of founders, the computation time of RECBLOCK scales exponentially with the number of founders and makes its application infeasible for large instances. This was the motivation for developing metaheuristic approaches [BLU 03], the first of which was a Tabu search method, equipped with an effective constructive procedure [ROL 09]. An IG algorithm that achieves state-of-the-art results for large instances or in the case of many founders was presented in [BEN 10]. Furthermore, a parthenogenetic algorithm was proposed in [WU 13]. Finally, the current state-of-the-art method – which is a large neighborhood search technique based on RECBLOCK – was introduced in [ROL 12].

The FSRP is widely studied and is related to a number of different problems. In [EL 04] the authors focus on a much simpler and more tractable reconstruction problem: given a founder set and a recombinant, they want to find a minimal decomposition for the recombinant.

A similar problem, called *Haplotype Coloring*, has been introduced in [SCH 02] by Schwartz *et al.* Given a recombinant matrix, a partition of contiguous sites, called blocks, is identified according to a particular rule and each recombinant is subdivided accordingly into haplotype substrings. The objective is to assign, for each block, a different color to the distinct haplotype substrings in a block, such that the total number of color switches between two contiguous haplotype substrings in the same recombinant is minimal. This problem can be encoded into an instance of the weighted bipartite matching problem. The haplotype coloring can be solved to optimality by a $O(m\,n^2\log n)$ algorithm.

The FSRP formulation presented so far is based on the genetic assumption that, during the genetic evolution of the initial population of founders, mutation events are unlikely to occur. Rastas and Ukkonen generalized the FSRP by introducing a different objective function that takes into account point mutation [RAS 07], namely $k + c \cdot k'$ where $c > 0$ is a constant. This new objective function is the sum of two contributions: k denotes the sum of the number of breakpoints across all recombinant sequences (i.e. the objective function we introduced in section 7.2.1) while k' is the total number of point mutations. Note that if c is large, the resulting problem is equivalent to the FSRP definition as presented in section 7.2.1 because an optimal solution will not contain any mutation.

Zhang *et al.* [ZHA 09] present a problem that is closely related to the FSRP, called the *minimum mosaic problem*. This problem aims at finding a minimum mosaic, i.e. a block partitioning of a recombinant set such that each block is *compatible* according to the four gamete test [HUD 85] and the number of blocks is minimized. In a different way to the FSRP, this problem does not rely on the existence of a founder set. The obtained mosaic structure provides a good estimation of the minimum number of recombination events (and their location) required to generate the existing haplotypes in the population, that is, a lower bound for the FSRP. The authors provide an algorithm capable of handling large datasets.

7.3. Final remarks

In conclusion, we believe that heuristics and metaheuristics play – and will continue to play – a role of increasing importance in solving string problems from the field of bioinformatics. Just as in the case of other combinatorial optimization problems that are not related to bioinformatics, it is possible to identify a clear trend towards the application of hybrid metaheuristics, i.e.

algorithmic approaches that result from combinations of metaheuristics with other techniques for optimization such as, for example, mathematical programming techniques. The current state-of-the-art algorithms for the most strings with few bad columns problem (see Chapter 4) and for longest common subsequence problems (see Chapter 3), just to name two examples, confirm this trend.

Bibliography

[ACH 09] ACHTERBERG T., "SCIP: solving constraint integer programs", *Mathematical Programming Computation*, vol. 1, no. 1, pp. 1–41, 2009.

[ADA 00] ADAMS M.D., CELNIKER S.E., HOLT R.A. *et al.*, "The genome sequence of *Drosophila* melanogaster", *Science*, vol. 287, no. 5461, pp. 2185–2195, 2000.

[ADI 08] ADI S.S., BRAGA M.D.V., FERNANDES C.G. *et al.*, "Repetition-free longest common subsequence", *Electronic Notes in Discrete Mathematics*, vol. 30, pp. 243–248, 2008.

[ADI 10] ADI S.S., BRAGA M.D.V., FERNANDES C.G. *et al.*, "Repetition-free longest common subsquence", *Discrete Applied Mathematics*, vol. 158, pp. 1315–1324, 2010.

[AHO 83] AHO A., HOPCROFT J., ULLMAN J., *Data Structures and Algorithms*, Addison-Wesley, Reading, MA, 1983.

[AIE 02] AIEX R.M., RESENDE M.G.C., RIBEIRO C.C., "Probability distribution of solution time in grasp: an experimental investigation", *Journal of Heuristics*, vol. 8, pp. 343–373, 2002.

[AKE 09] AKEB H., HIFI M., MHALLAH R., "A beam search algorithm for the circular packing problem", *Computers & Operations Research*, vol. 36, no. 5, pp. 1513–1528, 2009.

[BÄC 97] BÄCK T., FOGEL D.B., MICHALEWICZ Z., *Handbook of Evolutionary Computation*, Oxford University Press, 1997.

[BAI 88] BAINS W., SMITH G.C., "A novel method for nucleid acid sequence determination", *Journal of Theoretical Biology*, vol. 135, pp. 303–307, 1988.

[BEN 10] BENEDETTINI S., BLUM C., ROLI A., "A randomized iterated greedy algorithm for the founder sequence reconstruction problem", in BLUM C., BATTITI R. (eds), *Proceedings of LION 4 – Fourth Learning and Intelligent Optimization Conference*, Lecture Notes in Computer Science, vol. 6073, Springer-Verlag, Berlin, 2010.

[BEN 15] BEN ALI A., LUQUE G., ALBA E. *et al.*, "An improved problem aware local search algorithm for the DNA fragment assembly problem", *Soft Computing*, 2015.

[BER 98] BERGROTH L., HAKONEN H., RAITA T., "New approximation algorithms for longest common subsequences", *Proceedings of String Processing and Information Retrieval: A South American Symposium*, pp. 32–40, 1998.

[BER 00] BERGROTH L., HAKONEN H., RAITA T., "A survey of longest common subsequence algorithms", *Proceedings of SPIRE 2000 – 7th International Symposium on String Processing and Information Retrieval*, pp. 39–48, 2000.

[BŁA 99] BŁAŻEWICZ J., FORMANOWICZ P., KASPRZAK M. *et al.*, "DNA sequencing with positive and negative errors", *Journal of Computational Biology*, vol. 6, pp. 113–123, 1999.

[BŁA 00] BŁAŻEWICZ J., FORMANOWICZ P., KASPRZAK M. *et al.*, "Tabu search for DNA sequencing with false negatives and false positives", *European Journal of Operational Research*, vol. 125, pp. 257–265, 2000.

[BŁA 02a] BŁAŻEWICZ J., FORMANOWICZ P., GUINAND F. *et al.*, "A heuristic managing errors for DNA sequencing", *Bioinformatics*, vol. 18, no. 5, pp. 652–660, 2002.

[BŁA 02b] BŁAŻEWICZ J., KASPRZAK M., KUROCZYCKI W., "Hybrid genetic algorithm for DNA sequencing with errors", *Journal of Heuristics*, vol. 8, pp. 495–502, 2002.

[BŁA 04] BŁAŻEWICZ J., GLOVER F., KASPRZAK M., "DNA sequencing—Tabu and scatter search combined", *INFORMS Journal on Computing*, vol. 16, no. 3, pp. 232–240, 2004.

[BŁA 05] BŁAŻEWICZ J., GLOVER F., KASPRZAK M., "Evolutionary approaches to DNA sequencing with errors", *Annals of Operations Research*, vol. 138, pp. 67–78, 2005.

[BŁA 11] BŁAŻEWICZ J., BURKE E.K., KENDALL G. *et al.*, "A hyper-heuristic approach to sequencing by hybridization of DNA sequences", *Annals of Operations Research*, vol. 207, no. 1, pp. 27–41, 2011.

[BLU 03] BLUM C., ROLI A., "Metaheuristics in combinatorial optimization: overview and conceptual comparison", *ACM Computing Surveys*, vol. 35, no. 3, pp. 268–308, 2003.

[BLU 04] BLUM C., DORIGO M., "The hyper-cube framework for ant colony optimization", *IEEE Transactions on Man, Systems and Cybernetics – Part B*, vol. 34, no. 2, pp. 1161–1172, 2004.

[BLU 05] BLUM C., "Beam-ACO—Hybridizing ant colony optimization with beam search: an application to open shop scheduling", *Computers & Operations Research*, vol. 32, no. 6, pp. 1565–1591, 2005.

[BLU 08] BLUM C., YÁBAR VALLÈS M., BLESA M.J., "An ant colony optimization algorithm for DNA sequencing by hybridization", *Computers & Operations Research*, vol. 35, no. 11, pp. 3620–3635, 2008.

[BLU 09] BLUM C., BLESA M.J., LÓPEZ-IBÁNEZ M., "Beam search for the longest common subsequence problem", *Computers & Operations Research*, vol. 36, no. 12, pp. 3178–3186, 2009.

[BLU 10] BLUM C., "Beam-ACO for the longest common subsequence problem", *Proceedings of CEC 2010 – Congress on Evolutionary Computation*, vol. 2, Piscataway, NJ, pp. 1–8, 2010.

[BLU 13] BLUM C., "Construct, merge, solve & adapt: application to unbalanced minimum common string partition", in BLESA M.J., BLUM C., CANGELOSI A. *et al.* (eds), *Proceedings of HM 2016 Eighth International Workshop on Hybrid Metaheuristics*, vol. 9668, Springer-Verlag, 2013.

[BLU 14a] BLUM C., LOZANO J.A., PINACHO DAVIDSON P., "Iterative probabilistic tree search for the minimum common string partition problem", in BLESA M.J., BLUM C., VOSS S. (eds), *Proceedings of HM 2010 4–9th International Workshop on Hybrid Metaheuristics*, vol. 8457, Springer, 2014.

[BLU 14b] BLUM C., BLESA M.J., CALVO B., "Beam-ACO for the repetition-free longest common subsequence problem", in LEGRAND P., CORSINI M.-M., HAO J.-K. *et al.* (eds), *Proceedings of EA 2013 – 11th Conference on Artificial Evolution*, vol. 8752, Springer-Verlag, Berlin, 2014.

[BLU 14c] BLUM C., FESTA P., "A hybrid ant colony optimization algorithm for the far from most string problem", *Proceedings of EvoCOP 2014 – 14th European Conference on Evolutionary Computation in Combinatorial Optimisation*, vol. 8600, Springer-Verlag, 2014.

[BLU 15a] BLUM C., CALVO B., "A matheuristic for the minimum weight rooted arborescence problem", *Journal of Heuristics*, vol. 21, no. 4, pp. 479–499, 2015.

[BLU 15b] BLUM C., LOZANO J.A., PINACHO DAVIDSON P., "Mathematical programming strategies for solving the minimum common string partition problem", *European Journal of Operational Research*, vol. 242, no. 3, pp. 769–777, 2015.

[BLU 16a] BLUM C., BLESA M.J., "Construct, merge, solve & adapt: application to the repetition-free longest common subsequence problem", in CHICANO F., HU B. (eds), *Proceedings of EvoCOP 2016 – 16th European Conference on Evolutionary Computation in Combinatorial Optimization*, vol. 9595, Springer-Verlag, Berlin, 2016.

[BLU 16b] BLUM C., PINACHO P., LÓPEZ-IBÁNEZ M., LOZANO J.A., "Construct, merge, solve & adapt: a new general algorithm for combinatorial optimization", *Computers & Operations Research*, vol. 68, pp. 75–88, 2016.

[BLU 16c] BLUM C., FESTA P., "Selected string problems", in RESENDE M.G.C., MARTÌ R., PARDALOS P.M. (eds), *Handbook of Heuristics*, Springer-Verlag, 2016.

[BLU 16d] BLUM C., RAIDL G.R., "Computational performance evaluation of two integer linear programming models for the minimum common string partition problem", *Optimization Letters*, vol. 10, no. 1, pp. 189–205, 2016.

[BLU 16e] BLUM C., RAIDL G.R., *Hybrid Metaheuristics – Powerful Tools for Optimization*, Springer, 2016.

[BON 01] BONIZZONI P., DELLA VEDOVA G., MAURI G., "Experimenting an approximation algorithm for the LCS", *Discrete Applied Mathematics*, vol. 110, no. 1, pp. 13–24, 2001.

[BON 07] BONIZZONI P., DELLA VEDOVA G., DONDI R. *et al.*, "Exemplar longest common subsequence", *IEEE/ACM Transactions on Computational Biology and Bioinformatics*, vol. 4, no. 4, pp. 535–543, 2007.

[BON 10] BONIZZONI P., DELLA VEDOVA G., DONDI R. *et al.*, "Variants of constrained longest common subsequence", *Information Processing Letters*, vol. 110, no. 20, pp. 877–881, 2010.

[BOU 13] BOUCHER C., LANDAU G.M., LEVY A. *et al.*, "On approximating string selection problems with outliers", *Theoretical Computer Science*, vol. 498, pp. 107–114, 2013.

[BRE 00] BRENNER S., JOHNSON M., BRIDGHAM J. *et al.*, "Gene expression analysis by massively parallel signature sequencing (MPSS) on microbead arrays", *Nature Biotechnology*, vol. 18, no. 6, pp. 630–634, 2000.

[BRI 04a] BRIZUELA C.A., GONZ ÁLEZ L.C., ROMERO H.J., "An improved genetic algorithm for the sequencing by hybridization problem", in RAIDL G.R., CAGNONI S. *et al.* (eds), *Proceedings of the EvoWorkshops – Applications of Evolutionary Computing: EvoBIO, EvoCOMNET, EvoHOT, EvoIASP, EvoMUSART and EvoSTOC*, vol. 3005, Springer-Verlag, Berlin, 2004.

[BRI 04b] BRISK P., KAPLAN A., SARRAFZADEH M., "Area-efficient instruction set synthesis for reconfigurable system-on-chip design", *Proceedings of the 41st Design Automation Conference*, pp. 395–400, 2004.

[BRU 03] BRUDNO M., CHAPMAN M., GÖTTGENS B. *et al.*, "Fast and sensitive multiple alignment of large genomic sequences", *BMC Bioinformatics*, vol. 4, no. 66, pp. 1–11, 2003.

[BUI 04] BUI T.N., YOUSSEF W.A., "An enhanced genetic algorithm for DNA sequencing by hybridization with positive and negative errors", in DEB K., POLI R. *et al.* (eds), *Proceedings of GECCO 2004 – Genetic and Evolutionary Computation Conference*, vol. 3103, Springer-Verlag, Berlin, 2004.

[BUL 13] BULTEAU L., FERTIN G., KOMUSIEWICZ C. *et al.*, "A fixed-parameter algorithm for minimum common string partition with few duplications", in DARLING A., STOYE J. (eds), *Proceedings of WABI 2013 – Algorithms in Bioinformatics*, vol. 8126, Springer, Berlin, 2013.

[CAN 01] CANUTO S.A., RESENDE M.G.C., RIBEIRO C.C., "Local search with perturbations for the prize-collecting Steiner tree problem in graphs", *Networks*, vol. 38, pp. 50–58, 2001.

[CAS 13] CASTELLI M., BERETTA S., VANNESCHI L., "A hybrid genetic algorithm for the repetition free longest common subsequence problem", *Operations Research Letters*, vol. 41, no. 6, pp. 644–649, 2013.

[CER 85] CERNY V., "A thermodynamical approach to the travelling salesman problem: an efficient simulation algorithm", *Journal of Optimization Theory and Applications*, vol. 45, pp. 41–51, 1985.

[CHE 05] CHEN X., ZHENG J., FU Z. *et al.*, "Computing the assignment of orthologous genes via genome rearrangement", *Proceedings of the Asia Pacific Bioinformatics Conference*, pp. 363–378, 2005.

[CHE 06]   CHEN Y., PAN Y., CHEN J. *et al.*, "Multiple sequence alignment by ant colony optimization and divide-and-conquer", *Proceedings of ICCS 2006 – 6th International Conference on Computational Science*, pp. 646–653, 2006.

[CHE 11a]   CHEN Y., HU J., "Accurate reconstruction for dna sequencing by hybridization based on a constructive heuristic", *IEEE/ACM Transactions on Computational Biology and Bioinformatics*, vol. 8, no. 4, pp. 1134–1140, 2011.

[CHE 11b]   CHEN Y.-C., CHAO K.-M., "On the generalized constrained longest common subsequence problems", *Journal of Combinatorial Optimization*, vol. 21, no. 3, pp. 383–392, 2011.

[CHI 94]   CHIN F., POON C.K., "Performance analysis of some simple heuristics for computing longest common subsequences", *Algorithmica*, vol. 12, nos 4–5, pp. 293–311, 1994.

[CHI 04]   CHIN F.Y.L., DESANTIS A., FERRARA A.L. *et al.*, "A simple algorithm for the constrained sequence problems", *Information Processing Letters*, vol. 90, no. 4, pp. 175–179, 2004.

[CHR 04]   CHROBAK M., KOLMAN P., SGALL J., "The greedy algorithm for the minimum common string partition problem", in JANSEN K., KHANNA S., ROLIM J.D.P. *et al.* (eds), *Proceedings of APPROX 2004 – 7th International Workshop on Approximation Algorithms for Combinatorial Optimization Problems*, vol. 3122, Springer, 2004.

[CLE 06]   CLERC M. (ed), *Particle Swarm Optimization*, ISTE, London, 2006.

[COR 07]   CORMODE G., MUTHUKRISHNAN S., "The string edit distance matching problem with moves", *ACM Transactions on Algorithms*, vol. 3, no. 2, pp. 1–19, 2007.

[CRO 12]   CROCE F.D., SALASSA F., "Improved LP-based algorithms for the closest string problem", *Computers & Operations Research*, vol. 39, pp. 746–749, 2012.

[CRO 14]   CROCE F.D., GARRAFFA M., "The selective fixing algorithm for the closest string problem", *Computers & Operations Research*, vol. 41, pp. 24–30, 2014.

[DE 11]   DE LEONE R., FESTA P., MARCHITTO E., "Solving a bus driver scheduling problem with randomized multistart heuristics", *International Transactions in Operational Research*, vol. 18, no. 6, pp. 707–727, 2011.

[DON 06]   DONG Q.-W., LIN L., WANG X.-L. *et al.*, "Contact-based simulated annealing protein sequence alignment method", *Proceedings of IEEE-EMBS 2005 – 27th Annual International Conference of the Engineering in Medicine and Biology Society*, pp. 2798–2801, 2006.

[DOR 97]   DORIGO M., GAMBARDELLA L.M., "Ant colony system: a cooperative learning approach to the traveling salesman problem", *IEEE Transactions on Evolutionary Computation*, vol. 1, no. 1, pp. 53–66, 1997.

[DOR 04]   DORIGO M., STÜTZLE T., *Ant Colony Optimization*, MIT Press, Cambridge, MA, 2004.

[DOR 10] DORIGO M., STÜTZLE T., "Ant colony optimization: overview and recent advances", in GENDREAU M., POTVIN J.Y. (eds), *Handbook of Metaheuristics*, 2nd ed., Springer, 2010.

[DRM 89] DRMANAC R., LABAT I., BRUKNER R. *et al.*, "Sequencing of megabase plus DNA by hybridization: theory of the method", *Genomics*, vol. 4, pp. 114–128, 1989.

[EAS 07] EASTON T., SINGIREDDY A., "A spezialized branching and fathoming technique for the longest common subsequence problem", *International Journal of Operations Research*, vol. 4, no. 2, pp. 98–104, 2007.

[EAS 08] EASTON T., SINGIREDDY A., "A large neighborhood search heuristic for the longest common subsequence problem", *Journal of Heuristics*, vol. 14, no. 3, pp. 271–283, 2008.

[EDG 04a] EDGAR R.C., "MUSCLE: multiple sequence alignment with high accuracy and high throughput", *Nucleic Acids Research*, vol. 32, no. 5, pp. 1792–1797, 2004.

[EDG 04b] EDGAR R.C., "MUSCLE: a multiple sequence alignment method with reduced time and space complexity", *BMC Bioinformatics*, vol. 5, no. 1, pp. 1–19, 2004.

[EDG 06] EDGAR R.C., BATZOGLOU S., "Multiple sequence alignment", *Current Opinion in Structural Biology*, vol. 16, no. 3, pp. 368–373, 2006.

[EIB 91] EIBEN A.E., AARTS E.H.L., VAN HEE K.M., "Global convergence of genetic algorithms: a Markov chain analysis", *Proceedings of PPSN 1991 – 1st Workshop on Parallel Problem Solving from Nature*, vol. 496, Springer, pp. 3–12, 1991.

[EL 04] EL-MABROUK N., LABUDA D., "Haplotypes histories as pathways of recombinations", *Bioinformatics*, vol. 20, no. 12, pp. 1836–1841, 2004.

[END 04] ENDO T.A., "Probabilistic nucleotide assembling method for sequencing by hybridization", *Bioinformatics*, vol. 20, no. 14, pp. 2181–2188, 2004.

[ENG 05] ENGELBRECHT A.P., *Fundamentals of Computational Swarm Intelligence*, John Wiley and Sons, 2005.

[ERE 05] EREL E., SABUNCUOGLU I., SEKERCI H., "Stochastic assembly line balancing using beam search", *International Journal of Production Research*, vol. 43, no. 7, pp. 1411–1426, 2005.

[FAN 05] FANG S.-C., WANG Y., ZHONG J., "A genetic algorithm approach to solving DNA fragment assembly problem", *Journal of Computational and Theoretical Nanoscience*, vol. 2, no. 4, pp. 499–505, 2005.

[FAR 05] FARIA JR H., BINATO S., RESENDE M.G.C. *et al.*, "Transmission network design by a greedy randomized adaptive path relinking approach", *IEEE Transactions on Power Systems*, vol. 20, no. 1, pp. 43–49, 2005.

[FEL 68] FELLER W., *An Introduction to Probability Theory and its Applications*, 3rd ed., John Wiley and Sons, 1968.

[FEO 89] FEO T.A., RESENDE M.G.C., "A probabilistic heuristic for a computationally difficult set covering problem", *Operations Research Letters*, vol. 8, pp. 67–71, 1989.

[FEO 95] FEO T.A., RESENDE M.G.C., "Greedy randomized adaptive search procedures", *Journal of Global Optimization*, vol. 6, pp. 109–133, 1995.

[FER 05] FERNANDES E.R., RIBEIRO C.C., "Using an adaptive memory strategy to improve a multistart heuristic for sequencing by hybridization", in NIKOLETSEAS S.E. (ed), *Proceedings of WEA 2005 – 4th International Workshop on Experimental and Efficient Algorithms*, Springer-Verlag, Berlin, 2005.

[FER 13a] FERDOUS S.M., SOHEL RAHMAN M., "Solving the minimum common string partition problem with the help of ants", in TAN Y., SHI Y., MO H. (eds), *Proceedings of ICSI 2013 – 4th International Conference on Advances in Swarm Intelligence*, Springer, pp. 306–313, 2013.

[FER 13b] FERONE D., FESTA P., RESENDE M.G.C., "Hybrid metaheuristics for the far from most string problem", *Proceedings of HM 2013 – 8th International Workshop on Hybrid Metaheuristics*, vol. 7919, Springer, 2013.

[FER 14] FERDOUS S.M., SOHEL RAHMAN M., "A MAX-MIN ant colony system for minimum common string partition problem", *CoRR*, abs/1401.4539, available at: http://arxiv.org/abs/1401.4539, 2014.

[FER 15] FERDOUS S.M., SOHEL RAHMAN M., "An integer programming formulation of the minimum common string partition problem", *Plos ONE*, vol. 10, no. 7, p. e0130266, 2015.

[FER 16] FERONE D., FESTA P., RESENDE M.G.C., "Hybridizations of grasp with path-relinking for the far from most string problem", *International Transactions in Operational Research*, vol. 23, no. 3, pp. 481–506, 2016.

[FES 02a] FESTA P., PARDALOS P.M., RESENDE M.G.C. *et al.*, "Randomized heuristics for the MAX-CUT problem", *Optimization Methods and Software*, vol. 7, pp. 1033–1058, 2002.

[FES 02b] FESTA P., RESENDE M.G.C., "GRASP: an annotated bibliography", in RIBEIRO C.C., HANSEN P. (eds), *Essays and Surveys on Metaheuristics*, Kluwer Academic Publishers, 2002.

[FES 06] FESTA P., PARDALOS P.M., PITSOULIS L.S. *et al.*, "GRASP with path-relinking for the weighted MAXSAT problem", *ACM Journal of Experimental Algorithmics*, vol. 11, pp. 1–16, 2006.

[FES 07] FESTA P., "On some optimization problems in molecular biology", *Mathematical Bioscience*, vol. 207, no. 2, pp. 219–234, 2007.

[FES 09a] FESTA P., RESENDE M.G.C., "An annotated bibliography of GRASP – Part I: algorithms", *International Transactions in Operational Research*, vol. 16, no. 1, pp. 1–24, 2009.

[FES 09b] FESTA P., RESENDE M.G.C., "An annotated bibliography of GRASP – Part II: applications", *International Transactions in Operational Research*, vol. 16, no. 2, pp. 131–172, 2009.

[FES 13] FESTA P., RESENDE M.G.C., "Hybridizations of GRASP with path-relinking", *Studies in Computational Intelligence*, vol. 434, pp. 135–155, 2013.

[FOG 62] FOGEL L.J., "Toward inductive inference automata", *Communications of the ACM*, vol. 5, no. 6, pp. 319–319, 1962.

[FOG 66] FOGEL L.J., OWENS A.J., WALSH M.J., *Artificial Intelligence through Simulated Evolution*, Wiley, 1966.

[FRA 95] FRASER C.B., Subsequences and supersequences of strings, PhD Thesis, University of Glasgow, 1995.

[FRA 97] FRANCES M., LITMAN A., "On covering problems of codes", *Theory of Computing Systems*, vol. 30, no. 2, pp. 113–119, 1997.

[GAR 79] GAREY M.R., JOHNSON D.S., *Computers and Intractability: A Guide to the Theory of NP-Completeness*, W.H. Freeman, New York, 1979.

[GEN 10a] GENDREAU M., POTVIN J.-Y. (eds), *Handbook of Metaheuristics*, 2nd ed., Springer, 2010.

[GEN 10b] GENDREAU M., POTVIN J.-Y., "Tabu search", in *Handbook of Metaheuristics*, Springer, 2010.

[GHI 05] GHIRARDI M., POTTS C.N., "Makespan minimization for scheduling unrelated parallel machines: a recovering beam search approach", *European Journal of Operational Research*, vol. 165, no. 2, pp. 457–467, 2005.

[GLO 96] GLOVER F., "Tabu search and adaptive memory programming – advances, applications and challenges", in BARR R.S., HELGASON R.V., KENNINGTON J.L. (eds), *Interfaces in Computer Science and Operations Research*, Kluwer, 1996.

[GLO 97] GLOVER F., LAGUNA M., *Tabu Search*, Kluwer Academic Publishers, 1997.

[GLO 00a] GLOVER F., "Multi-start and strategic oscillation methods – principles to exploit adaptive memory", LAGUNA M., GONZÁLES-VELARDE J.L. (eds), *Computing Tools for Modeling, Optimization and Simulation: Interfaces in Computer Science and Operations Research*, Kluwer, 2000.

[GLO 00b] GLOVER F., LAGUNA M., MARTÍ R., "Fundamentals of scatter search and path relinking", *Control and Cybernetics*, vol. 39, no. 3, pp. 653–684, 2000.

[GOL 87] GOLDBERG D.E., SEGREST P., "Finite Markov chain analysis of genetic algorithms", in *Proceedings of the Second International Conference on Genetic Algorithms*, 1987.

[GOL 89] GOLDBERG D.E., *Genetic Algorithms in Search, Optimization, and Learning*, Addison-Wesley, Reading, MA, 1989.

[GOL 05] GOLDSTEIN A., KOLMAN P., ZHENG J., "Minimum common string partition problem: hardness and approximations", in FLEISCHER R., TRIPPEN G. (eds), *Proceedings of ISAAC 2004 – 15th International Symposium on Algorithms and Computation*, Springer, 2005.

[GOL 11] GOLDSTEIN I., LEWENSTEIN M., "Quick greedy computation for minimum common string partitions", in GIANCARLO R., MANZINI G. (eds), *Proceedings of CPM 2011 – 22nd Annual Symposium on Combinatorial Pattern Matching*, Springer, 2011.

[GOM 58] GOMORY R.E., "Outline of an algorithm for integer solutions to linear programs", *Bulletin of the American Mathematical Society*, vol. 64, pp. 275–278, 1958.

[GOT 96] GOTOH O., "Significant improvement in accuracy of multiple protein sequence alignments by iterative refinement as assessed by reference to structural alignments", *Journal of Molecular Biology*, vol. 264, no. 4, pp. 823–838, 1996.

[GOT 08] GOTTHILF Z., HERMELIN D., LEWENSTEIN M., "Constrained LCS: hardness and approximation", in FERRAGINA P., LANDAU G.M. (eds), *Proceedings of CPM 2008 – 19th Annual Symposium on Combinatorial Pattern Matching*, Springer, Berlin, 2008.

[GRA 02] GRAMM J., HÜFFNER F., NIEDERMEIER R. *et al.*, "Closest strings, primer design, and motif search", *Proceedings of RECOMB 2002 – Sixth Annual International Conference on Computational Molecular Biology*, pp. 74–75, 2002.

[GRA 03a] GRAMM J., Fixed-parameter algorithms for the consensus analysis of genomic data, PhD Thesis, University of Tübingen, Germany, 2003.

[GRA 03b] GRAMM J., NIEDERMEIER R., ROSSMANITH P., "Fixed-parameter algorithms for closest string and related problems", *Algorithmica*, vol. 37, pp. 25–42, 2003.

[GUE 95] GUENOCHE A., VITTE P., "Longest common subsequence with many strings: exact and approximate methods", *Technique et science informatiques*, vol. 14, no. 7, pp. 897–915, 1995, In French.

[GUE 04] GUENOCHE A., "Supersequence of masks for oligo-chips", *Journal of Bioinformatics and Computational Biology*, vol. 2, no. 3, pp. 459–469, 2004.

[GUR 15] GUROBI OPTIMIZATION INC., Gurobi Optimizer Reference Manual, available at: https://www. gurobi.com/documentation/6.5/refman/refman.html, 2015.

[GUS 93] GUSFIELD D., "Efficient methods for multiple sequence alignment with guaranteed error bounds", *Bulletin of Mathematical Biology*, vol. 55, pp. 141–154, 1993.

[GUS 97] GUSFIELD D., *Algorithms on Strings, Trees, and Sequences*, Cambridge University Press, 1997.

[HAN 10] HANSEN P., MLADENOVIĆ N., BRIMBERG J. *et al.*, "Variable neighborhood search", *Handbook of Metaheuristics*, Springer, pp. 61–86, 2010.

[HE 07] HE D., "A novel greedy algorithm for the minimum common string partition problem", in MANDOIU I., ZELIKOVSKY A. (eds), *Proceedings of ISBRA 2007 – Third International Symposium on Bioinformatics Research and Applications*, Springer, 2007.

[HER 00] HERTZ A., KOBLER D., "A framework for the description of evolutionary algorithms", *European Journal of Operational Research*, vol. 126, pp. 1–12, 2000.

[HIG 88] HIGGINS D.G., SHARP P.M., "Clustal: a package for performing multiple sequence alignment on a microcomputer", *Gene*, vol. 73, pp. 237–244, 1988.

[HIR 95] HIROSAWA M., TOTOKI Y., HOSHIDA M. *et al.*, "Comprehensive study on iterative algorithms of multiple sequence alignment", *Computer Applications in the Biosciences*, vol. 11, no. 1, pp. 13–18, 1995.

[HOC 96] HOCHBAUM D. ed., *Approximation Algorithms for NP-hard Problems*, PWS Publishing, 1996.

[HOL 75] HOLLAND J.H., *Adaptation in Natural and Artificial Systems*, University of Michigan Press, Ann Arbor, MI, 1975.

[HOO 15] HOOS H.H., STÜTZLE T., "Stochastic local search algorithms: an overview", in *Springer Handbook of Computational Intelligence*, Springer, 2015.

[HSU 84] HSU W.J., DU M.W., "Computing a longest common subsequence for a set of strings", *BIT Numerical Mathematics*, vol. 24, no. 1, pp. 45–59, 1984.

[HUA 04] HUANG K., YANG C., TSENG K., "Fast algorithms for finding the common subsequences of multiple sequences", in *Proceedings of the International Computer Symposium*, IEEE Press, 2004.

[HUA 15] HUANG K.-W., CHEN J.-L., YANG C.-S. *et al.*, "A memetic particle swarm optimization algorithm for solving the DNA fragment assembly problem", *Neural Computing and Applications*, vol. 26, no. 3, pp. 495–506, 2015.

[HUA 16] HUANG K.-W., CHEN J.-L., YANG C.-S. *et al.*, "A memetic gravitation search algorithm for solving DNA fragment assembly problems", *Journal of Intelligent & Fuzzy Systems*, vol. 30, no. 4, pp. 2245–2255, 2016.

[HUD 85] HUDSON R.R., KAPLAN N.L., "Statistical properties of the number of recombination events in the history of a sample of DNA sequences", *Genetics*, vol. 111, pp. 147–164, 1985.

[HUG 14] HUGHES J., HOUGHTEN S., MALLEN-FULLERTON G.M. *et al.*, "Recentering and restarting genetic algorithm variations for DNA fragment assembly", in *Proceedings of the 2014 IEEE Conference on Computational Intelligence in Bioinformatics and Computational Biolog*, IEEE Press, 2014.

[IBM 16] IBM CORPORATION., User's Manual for CPLEX, available at: http://www.ibm.com/support/knowledgecenter/en/SSSA5P_12.6.3/ilog.odms.studio.help/Optimization_Studio/topics/PLUGINS_ROOT/ilog.odms.studio.help/pdf/usrcplex.pdf, 2016.

[IDU 95] IDURY R.M., WATERMAN M.S., "A new algorithm for DNA sequence assembly", *Journal of Computational Biology*, vol. 2, no. 2, pp. 291–306, 1995.

[JAY 74] JAY E., BAMBARA R., PADMANABHAN R. *et al.*, "DNA sequence analysis: a general, simple and rapid method for sequencing large oligodeoxyribonucleotide fragments by mapping", *Nucleic Acids Research*, vol. 1, no. 3, pp. 331–354, 1974.

[JIA 95] JIANG T., LI M., "On the approximation of shortest common supersequences and longest common subsequences", *SIAM Journal on Computing*, vol. 24, no. 5, pp. 1122–1139, 1995.

[JIA 02] JIANG T., LIN G., MA B. *et al.*, "A general edit distance between RNA structures", *Journal of Computational Biology*, vol. 9, no. 2, pp. 371–388, 2002.

[JOR 15] JORDEHI A.R., JASNI J., "Particle swarm optimisation for discrete optimisation problems: a review", *Artificial Intelligence Review*, vol. 43, no. 2, pp. 243–258, 2015.

[KAP 06] KAPLAN H., SHAFRIR N., "The greedy algorithm for edit distance with moves", *Information Processing Letters*, vol. 97, no. 1, pp. 23–27, 2006.

[KAR 07] KARABOGA D., BASTURK B., "A powerful and efficient algorithm for numerical function optimization: artificial bee colony (ABC) algorithm", *Journal of Global Optimization*, vol. 39, no. 3, pp. 459–471, 2007.

[KAR 08] KARABOGA D., BASTURK B., "On the performance of artificial bee colony (ABC) algorithm", *Applied Soft Computing*, vol. 8, no. 1, pp. 687–697, 2008.

[KEC 93] KECECIOGLU J., "The maximum weight trace problem in multiple sequence alignment", in *Proceedings of CPM 1993 – Annual Symposium on Combinatorial Pattern matching*, Springer, 1993.

[KEC 00] KECECIOGLU J., LENHOF H.-P., MEHLHORN K. *et al.*, "A polyhedral approach to sequence alignment problems", *Discrete Applied Mathematics*, vol. 104, pp. 143–186, 2000.

[KEN 95] KENNEDY J., EBERHART R.C., "Particle swarm optimization", *Proceedings of the 1995 IEEE International Conference on Neural Networks*, Piscataway, NJ, pp. 1942–1948, 1995.

[KEN 04] KENNEDY J., EBERHART R.C., SHI Y., *Swarm Intelligence*, Morgan Kaufmann Publishers, San Francisco, CA, 2004.

[KIK 06] KIKUCHI S., CHAKRABORTY G., "Heuristically tuned GA to solve genome fragment assembly problem", *Proceedings of CEC 2006 – IEEE Congress on Evolutionary Computation*, IEEE Press, pp. 1491–1498, 2006.

[KIR 83] KIRKPATRICK S., GELLAT C., VECCHI M., "Optimization by simulated annealing", *Science*, vol. 220, pp. 671–680, 1983.

[KLE 04] KLEINJUNG J., ROMEIN J., LIN K. *et al.*, "Contact-based sequence alignment", *Nucleic Acids Research*, vol. 32, pp. 2464–2473, 2004.

[KOL 05] KOLMAN P., "Approximating reversal distance for strings with bounded number of duplicates", in JEDRZEJOWICZ J., SZEPIETOWSKI A. (eds), *Proceedings of MFCS 2005 – 30th International Symposium on Mathematical Foundations of Computer Science*, Springer, 2005.

[KOL 07] KOLMAN P., WALEŃ T., "Reversal distance for strings with duplicates: linear time approximation using hitting set", in ERLEBACH T., KAKLAMANIS C. (eds), *Proceedings of WAOA 2007 – 4th International Workshop on Approximation and Online Algorithms*, Springer, 2007.

[KOZ 92] KOZA J.R., *Genetic Programming: On the Programming of Computers by Means of Natural Selection*, MIT Press, Cambridge, MA, 1992.

[KOZ 99] KOZA J.R., BENNETT III F.H., ANDRE D. *et al.*, *Genetic Programming III, Darwinian Invention and Problem Solving*, Morgan Kaufmann Publishers, 1999.

[LAG 99] LAGUNA M., MARTÍ R., "GRASP and path relinking for 2-layer straight line crossing minimization", *INFORMS Journal on Computing*, vol. 11, pp. 44–52, 1999.

[LAL 15] LALWANI S., KUMAR R., GUPTA N., "A novel two-level particle swarm optimization approach for efficient multiple sequence alignment", *Memetic Computing*, vol. 7, pp. 119–133, 2015.

[LAM 12] LAM A.Y.S., LI V.O.K., "Chemical reaction optimization: a tutorial", *Memetic Computing*, vol. 4, no. 1, pp. 3–17, 2012.

[LAN 99] LANCTOT J.K., LI M., MA B. *et al.*, "Distinguishing string selection problems", *Proceedings of SODA 1999 – Tenth Annual ACM-SIAM Symposium on Discrete Algorithms*, 1999.

[LAN 01] LANDAU G.M., SCHMIDT J.P., SOKOL D., "An algorithm for approximate tandem repeat", *Journal of Computational Biology*, vol. 8, no. 1, pp. 1–18, 2001.

[LAN 03] LANCTOT J.K., LI M., MA B. *et al.*, "Distinguishing string selection problems", *Information and Computation*, vol. 185, no. 1, pp. 41–55, 2003.

[LAN 04] LANCTOT J.K., Some string problems in computational biology, PhD Thesis, 2004.

[LEC 01] LECOMPTE O., THOMPSON J.D., PLEWNIAK F. *et al.*, "Multiple alignment of complete sequences (MACS) in the post-genomic era", *Gene*, vol. 30, nos 1–2, pp. 17–30, 2001.

[LEE 08] LEE Z.-J., SU S.-F., CHUANG C.-C. *et al.*, "Genetic algorithm with ant colony optimization (GA-ACO) for multiple sequence alignment", *Applied Soft Computing*, vol. 8, pp. 55–78, 2008.

[LI 99] LI M., MA B., WANG L., "Finding similar regions in many strings", *Proceedings of STOC 1999 – Thirty-first annual ACM symposium on Theory of computing*, ACM, pp. 473–482, 1999.

[LIU 05] LIU X., HE H., O.SÝKORA., "Parallel genetic algorithm and parallel simulated annealing algorithm for the closest string problem", in LI X., WANG S., DONG Z.Y. (eds), *Proceedings of ADMA 2005 – First International Conference on Advanced Data Mining and Applications*, Springer, pp. 591–597, 2005.

[LIU 11] LIU X., LIU S., HAO Z. *et al.*, "Exact algorithm and heuristic for the closest string problem", *Computers & Operations Research*, vol. 38, no. 11, pp. 1513–1520, 2011.

[LIZ 15] LIZÁRRAGA E., BLESA M.J., BLUM C. *et al.*, "On solving the most strings with few bad columns problem: an ILP model and heuristics", in *Proceedings of INISTA 2015 – International Symposium on Innovations in Intelligent SysTems and Applications*, IEEE Press, pp. 1–8, 2015.

[LIZ 16] LIZÁRRAGA E., BLESA M.J., BLUM C. *et al.*, "Large neighborhood search for the most strings with few bad columns problem", *Soft Computing*, 2016.

[LÓP 11] LÓPEZ-IBÁNEZ M., DUBOIS-LACOSTE J., STÜTZLE T. *et al.*, The irace package, iterated race for automatic algorithm configuration, Technical Report TR/IRIDIA/2011-004, IRIDIA, Université libre de Bruxelles, Belgium, 2011.

[LOU 10] LOUREN ÇO H.R., MARTIN O.C., STÜTZLE T., "Iterated local search: framework and applications", in *Handbook of Metaheuristics*, Springer, 2010.

[LOZ 10] LOZANO M., BLUM C., "A hybrid metaheuristic for the longest common subsequence problem", in BLESA M.J., BLUM C., RAIDL G. *et al.* (eds), *Proceedings of HM 2010 – Proceedings of the 7th International Workshop on Hybrid Metaheuristics*, Springer, Berlin, 2010.

[LU 78] LU S.Y., FU K.S., "A sentence-to-sentence clustering procedure for pattern analysis", *IEEE Transactions on Systems, Man and Cybernetics*, vol. 8, no. 5, pp. 381–389, 1978.

[LYN 05] LYNGSØR.B., SONG Y.S., "Minimum recombination histories by branch and bound", in CASADIO R., MYERS G. (eds), *Proceedings of WABI 2005 – Workshop on Algorithms in Bioinformatics*, Springer Verlag, Berlin, 2005.

[LYS 87] LYSOV Y.P., FLORENTIEV V.L., KHORLIN A.A. *et al.*, "Determination of the nucleotide sequence of DNA using hybridization with oligonucleotides: a new method", *Doklady Akademii nauk SSSR*, vol. 303, no. 6, pp. 1508–1511, 1987.

[MA 08] MA B., SUN X., "More efficient algorithms for closest string and substring problems", in VINGRON M., WONG L. (eds), *Proceedings of RECOMB 2008 – 12th Annual International Conference on Research in Computational Molecular Biology*, Springer, 2008.

[MA 09] MA B., SUN X., "More efficient algorithms for closest string and substring problems", *SIAM Journal on Computing*, vol. 39, no. 4, pp. 1432–1443, 2009.

[MAC 90] MACARIO A.J.L., CONWAY DE MACARIO E., (eds), *Gene Probes for Bacteria*, San Diego Academic Press, 1990.

[MAI 78] MAIER D., "The complexity of some problems on subsequences and supersequences", *Journal of the ACM*, vol. 25, pp. 322–336, 1978.

[MEH 15] MEHENNI T., "Multiple guide trees in a tabu search algorithm for the multiple sequence alignment problem", in AMINE A. *et al.* (eds), *Proceedings of the 5th IFIP TC 5 International Conference (CIIA 2015)*, Springer, 2015.

[MEN 05] MENESES C.N., OLIVEIRA C.A.S., PARDALOS P.M., "Optimization techniques for string selection and comparison problems in genomics", *IEEE Engineering in Medicine and Biology Magazine*, vol. 24, no. 3, pp. 81–87, 2005.

[MET 53] METROPOLIS N., ROSENBLUTH A., ROSENBLUTH M. *et al.*, "Equation of state calculations by fast computing machines", *Journal of Chemical Physics*, vol. 21, pp. 1087–1092, 1953.

[MOR 12] MORA-GUTIÉRREZ R.A., RAMÍREZ-RODRÍGUEZ J., RINCÓN-GARCÌA E.A. *et al.*, "An optimization algorithm inspired by social creativity systems", *Computing*, vol. 94, no. 11, pp. 887–914, 2012.

[MOR 14a] MORA-GUTIÉRREZ R.A., RAMÍREZ-RODRÍGUEZ J., RINCÓN-GARCÌA E.A., "An optimization algorithm inspired by musical composition", *Artificial Intelligence Review*, vol. 41, no. 3, pp. 301–315, 2014.

[MOR 14b] MORÁN-MIRABAL L.F., GONZÁLEZ-VELARDE J.L., RESENDE M.G.C., "Randomized heuristics for the family traveling salesperson problem", *International Transactions in Operational Research*, vol. 21, no. 1, pp. 41–57, 2014.

[MOR 15] MORA-GUTIÉRREZ R.A., LÁRRAGA-RAMÍREZ M.E., RINCÓN-GARCÌA E.A. *et al.*, "Adaptation of the method of musical composition for solving the multiple sequence alignment problem", *Computing*, vol. 97, pp. 813–842, 2015.

[MOU 12a] MOUSAVI S.R., BABAIE M., MONTAZERIAN M., "An improved heuristic for the far from most strings problem", *Journal of Heuristics*, vol. 18, pp. 239–262, 2012.

[MOU 12b] MOUSAVI S.R., TABATABA F., "An improved algorithm for the longest common subsequence problem", *Computers & Operations Research*, vol. 39, no. 3, pp. 512–520, 2012.

[NAZ 12] NAZNIN F., SARKER R., ESSAM D., "Progressive alignment method using genetic algorithm for multiple sequence alignment", *IEEE Transactions on Evolutionary Computation*, vol. 16, no. 5, pp. 615–631, 2012.

[NEB 08] NEBRO A.J., LUQUE G., LUNA F. *et al.*, "DNA fragment assembly using a grid-based genetic algorithm", *Computers & Operations Research*, vol. 35, no. 9, pp. 2776–2790, 2008.

[NEE 70] NEEDLEMAN S.B., WUNSCH C.D., "A general method applicable to the search for similarities in the amino acid sequence of two proteins", *Journal of Molecular Biology*, vol. 48, pp. 443–453, 1970.

[NEM 88] NEMHAUSER G.L., WOLSEY L.A., *Integer and Combinatorial Optimization*, John Wiley and Sons, 1988.

[NIK 10] NIKOLAEV A.G., JACOBSON S.H., "Simulated annealing", in *Handbook of Metaheuristics*, Springer, 2010.

[NOT 96] NOTREDAME C., HIGGINS D.G., "SAGA: sequence alignment by genetic algorithm", *Nucleic Acids Research*, vol. 24, no. 8, pp. 1515–1524, 1996.

[NOT 00] NOTREDAME C., HIGGINS D.G., HERINGA J., "T-Coffee: a novel method for fast and accurate multiple sequence alignment", *Journal of Molecular Biology*, vol. 302, pp. 205–217, 2000.

[OW 88] OW P.S., MORTON T.E., "Filtered beam search in scheduling", *International Journal of Production Research*, vol. 26, pp. 297–307, 1988.

[PAP 82] PAPADIMITRIOU C.H., STEIGLITZ K., *Combinatorial Optimization – Algorithms and Complexity*, Dover Publications, NY, 1982.

[PAP 13] PAPPALARDO E., PARDALOS P.M., STRACQUADANIO G., *Optimization Approaches for Solving String Selection Problems*, Springer, NY, 2013.

[PAR 95a] PARSONS R.J., JOHNSON M.E., "DNA sequence assembly and genetic algorithms – new results and puzzling insights", *Proceedings ISMB – Third International Conference on Intelligent Systems for Molecular Biology*, pp. 277–84, 1995.

[PAR 95b] PARSONS R.J., FORREST S., BURKS C., "Genetic algorithms, operators, and DNA fragment assembly", *Machine Learning*, vol. 21, no. 1–2, pp. 11–33, 1995.

[PAR 04] PARDALOS P.M., OLIVEIRA C.A.S., LU Z. *et al.*, "Optimal solutions for the closest string problem via integer programming", *INFORMS Journal on Computing*, vol. 16, pp. 419–429, 2004.

[PEV 89] PEVZNER P.A., "1-tuple DNA sequencing: Computer analysis", *Journal of Biomulecular Structure and Dynamics*, vol. 7, pp. 63–73, 1989.

[PEV 00] PEVZNER P., *Computational Molecular Biology: An Algorithmic Approach*, MIT Press, 2000.

[PIS 10] PISINGER D., ROPKE S., "Large neighborhood search", in GENDREAU M., POTVIN J.-Y. (eds), *Handbook of Metaheuristics*, Springer, 2010.

[PIT 12] PITZER E., AFFENZELLER M., *Recent Advances in Intelligent Engineering Systems*, Springer, 2012.

[RAJ 01a] RAJASEKARAN S., NICK H., PARDALOS P.M. *et al.*, "Efficient algorithms for local alignment search", *Journal of Combinatorial Optimization*, vol. 5, no. 1, pp. 117–124, 2001.

[RAJ 01b] RAJASEKARAN S., HU Y., LUO J. *et al.*, "Efficient algorithms for similarity search", *Journal of Combinatorial Optimization*, vol. 5, no. 1, pp. 125–132, 2001.

[RAS 07] RASTAS P., UKKONEN E., "Haplotype inference via hierarchical genotype parsing", in GIANCARLO R., HANNENHALLI S. (eds), *Proceedings of WABI2007 – 7th Workshop on Algorithms in Bioinformatics*, Springer, 2007.

[REC 73] RECHENBERG I., *Evolutionsstrategie: Optimierung technischer Systeme nach Prinzipien der biologischen Evolution*, Frommann-Holzboog, 1973.

[REI 73] REICHERT T.A., COHEN D.N., WONG A.K.C., "An application of information theory to genetic mutations and the matching of polypeptide sequences", *Journal of Theoretical Biology*, vol. 42, no. 2, pp. 245–261, 1973.

[REI 97] REINELT K., LENHOF H.-P., MUTZEL P. *et al.*, "A branch-and-cut algorithm for multiple sequence alignment", in *Proceedings of RECOMB 1997 – Annual International Conference of Computational Molecular Biology*, ACM, pp. 241–249, 1997.

[RES 04] RESENDE M.G.C., WERNECK R.F., "A hybrid heuristic for the p-median problem", *Journal of Heuristics*, vol. 10, pp. 59–88, 2004.

[RES 10a] RESENDE M.G.C., RIBEIRO C.C., "Greedy randomized adaptive search procedures: Advances, hybridizations, and applications", in *Handbook of Metaheuristics*, Springer, 2010.

[RES 10b] RESENDE M.G.C., MARTÍ R., GALLEGO M. *et al.*, "GRASP and path relinking for the max-min diversity problem", *Computers & Operations Research*, vol. 37, pp. 498–508, 2010.

[RIA 04] RIAZ T., WANG Y., LI K.-B., "Multiple sequence alignment using tabu search", in AMINE A. *et al.* (eds), *Proceedings of APBC 2004 – Second conference on Asia-Pacific Bioinformatics*, vol. 29, Australian Computer Society, pp. 223–232, 2004.

[RIB 07] RIBEIRO C.C., ROSSETI I., "Efficient parallel cooperative implementations of GRASP heuristics", *Parallel Computing*, vol. 33, pp. 21–35, 2007.

[RIB 12] RIBEIRO C.C., RESENDE M.G.C., "Path-relinking intensification methods for stochastic local search algorithms", *Journal of Heuristics*, vol. 18, pp. 193–214, 2012.

[ROL 09] ROLI A., BLUM C., "Tabu search for the founder sequence reconstruction problem: a preliminary study", in OMATU S., ROCHA M.P., BRAVO J. *et al.* (eds), *Proceedings of IWPACBB 2009 – 3rd International Workshop on Practical Applications of Computational Biology and Bioinformatics*, vol. 5518, Springer Verlag, Berlin, 2009.

[ROL 12] ROLI A., BENEDETTINI S., STÜTZLE T. *et al.*, "Large neighbourhood search algorithms for the founder sequence reconstruction problem", *Computers & Operations Research*, vol. 39, no. 2, pp. 213–224, 2012.

[ROM 92] ROMAN S., *Coding and Information Theory*, Springer-Verlag, 1992.

[RUB 77] RUBIN S.M., REDDY R., "The locus model of search and its use in image interpretation", REDDY R. (ed), in *Proceedings of IJCAI 1977 – 5th International Joint Conference on Artificial Intelligence*, vol. 2, William Kaufmann, pp. 590–595, 1977.

[SAB 99] SABUNCUOGLU I., BAYIZ M., "Job shop scheduling with beam search", *European Journal of Operational Research*, vol. 118, no. 2, pp. 390–412, 1999.

[SAN 72] SANKOFF D., "Matching sequences under deletion-insertion constraints", *Proceedings of the National Academy of Sciences of the United States of America*, vol. 69, no. 1, pp. 4–6, 1972.

[SAN 83] SANKOFF D., KRUSKAL J.B., *Time Warps, String Edits, and Macromolecules: The Theory and Practice of Sequence Comparison*, Addison-Wesley, Reading, UK, 1983.

[SCH 02] SCHWARTZ R., CLARK A., ISTRAIL S., "Methods for inferring block-wise ancestral history from haploid sequences", *Proceedings of WABI 2002 – Workshop on Algorithms in Bioinformatics*, Springer Verlag, Berlin, 2002.

[SEL 74] SELLERS P.H., "On the theory and computation of evolutionary distances", *SIAM Journal of Applied Mathematics*, vol. 26, no. 4, pp. 787–793, 1974.

[SEL 88] SELLIS T., "Multiple query optimization", *ACM Transactions on Database Systems*, vol. 13, no. 1, pp. 23–52, 1988.

[SHA 02] SHAPIRA D., STORER J.A., "Edit distance with move operations", in APOSTOLICO A., TAKEDA M. (eds), *Proceedings of CPM 2002 – 13th Annual Symposium on Combinatorial Pattern Matching*, Lecture Notes in Computer Science, vol. 2373, Springer, pp. 85–98, 2002.

[SHY 09] SHYU S.J., TSAI C.-Y., "Finding the longest common subsequence for multiple biological sequences by ant colony optimization", *Computers & Operations Research*, vol. 36, no. 1, pp. 73–91, 2009.

[SIM 99] SIM J.S., PARK K., "The consensus string problem for a metric is NP-complete", *Proceedings of AWOCA 1999 – Annual Australiasian Workshop on Combinatorial Algorithms*, pp. 107–113, 1999.

[SIM 03] SIM J.S., PARK K., "The consensus string problem for a metric is NP-complete", *Journal of Discrete Algorithms*, vol. 1, no. 1, pp. 111–117, 2003.

[SIN 07] SINGIREDDY A., Solving the longest common subsequence problem in bioinformatics, Thesis, Kansas State University, 2007.

[SMI 81] SMITH T., WATERMAN M., "Identification of common molecular subsequences", *Journal of Molecular Biology*, vol. 147, no. 1, pp. 195–197, 1981.

[STA 79] STADEN R., "A strategy of DNA sequencing employing computer programs", *Nucleic Acids Research*, vol. 6, no. 7, pp. 2601–2610, 1979.

[STO 88] STORER J., *Data Compression: Methods and Theory*, Computer Science Press, MD, 1988.

[STÜ 00] STÜTZLE T., HOOS H.H., "MAX-MIN ant system", *Future Generation Computer Systems*, vol. 16, no. 8, pp. 889–914, 2000.

[SUN 14] SUN J., PALADE V., WU X. *et al.*, "Multiple sequence alignment with hidden markov models learned by random drift particle swarm optimization", *IEEE/ACM Transactions on Computational Biology and Bioinformatics*, vol. 11, no. 1, pp. 243–257, 2014.

[TAI 91] TAILLARD É.D., "Robust Taboo Search for the Quadratic Assignment Problem", *Parallel Computing*, vol. 17, pp. 443–455, 1991.

[TAN 12] TANAKA S., "A heuristic algorithm based on lagrangian relaxation for the closest string problem", *Computers & Operations Research*, vol. 39, pp. 709–717, 2012.

[THO 94] THOMPSON J.D., HIGGINS D.G., GIBSON T.J., "CLUSTAL W: improving the sensitivity of progressive multiple sequence alignment through sequence weighting, positions-specific gap penalties and weight matrix choice", *Nucleic Acids Research*, vol. 22, no. 8, pp. 4673–4680, 1994.

[THY 04] THYSON G.W., CHAPMAN J., HUGENHOLTZ P. *et al.*, "Community structure and metabolism through reconstruction of microbial genomes from the environment", *Nature*, vol. 428, no. 6978, pp. 37–43, 2004.

[TSA 03] TSAI Y.-T., "The constrained longest common subsequence problem", *Information Processing Letters*, vol. 88, no. 4, pp. 173–176, 2003.

[UKK 02] UKKONEN E., "Finding founder sequences from a set of recombinants", in GUIGÓ R., GUSFIELD D. (eds), *Proceedings of the 2nd Workshop on Algorithms in Bioinformatics – WABI 2002*, Springer Verlag, Berlin, Germany, pp. 277–286, 2002.

[VAZ 01] VAZIRANI V., *Approximation Algorithms*, Springer-Verlag, 2001.

[VOß 05] VOSS S., FINK A., DUIN C., "Looking ahead with the pilot method", *Annals of Operations Research*, vol. 136, no. 1, pp. 285–302, 2005.

[WAL 05] WALLACE I.M., O'SULLIVAN O., HIGGINS D.G., "Evaluation of iterative alignment algorithms for multiple alignment", *Bioinformatics*, vol. 21, no. 8, pp. 1408–1414, 2005.

[WAN 94] WANG L., JIANG T., "On the complexity of multiple sequence alignment", *Journal of Computational Biology*, vol. 1, pp. 337–348, 1994.

[WAN 07] WANG F., LIM A., "A stochastic beam search for the berth allocation problem", *Decision Support Systems*, vol. 42, no. 4, pp. 2186–2196, 2007.

[WAN 09] WANG L., ZHU B., "Efficient algorithms for the closest string and distinguishing string selection problems", in DENG X., HOPCROFT J.E., XUE J. (eds), *Proceedings of FAW 2009 – Third International Workshop on Frontiers in Algorithmics*, Springer, pp. 261–270, 2009.

[WAT 76] WATERMAN M.S., SMITH T.F., BEYER W.A., "Some biological sequence metrics", *Advances in Mathematics*, vol. 20, no. 3, pp. 367–387, 1976.

[WIL 11] WILLIAMSON D.P., SHMOYS D.B., *The Design of Approximation Algorithms*, Cambridge University Press, 2011.

[WU 99] WU B.Y., LANCIA G., BAFNA V. *et al.*, "A polynomial-time approximation scheme for minimum routing cost spanning trees", *SIAM Journal on Computing*, vol. 29, no. 3, pp. 761–778, 1999.

[WU 08] WU Y., GUSFIELD D., "Improved algorithms for inferring the minimum mosaic of a set of recombinants", *Proceedings of CPM 2007 – Proceedings of the 18th Annual Symposium on Combinatorial Pattern Matching*, Springer Verlag, Berlin, 2008.

[WU 13] WU J., WANG H., "A parthenogenetic algorithm for the founder sequence reconstruction problem", *Journal of Computers*, vol. 8, no. 11, pp. 2934–2941, 2013.

[ZHA 08] ZHAO Y., MA P., LAN J. *et al.*, "An improved ant colony algorithm for DNA sequence alignment", *Proceedings of ISISE 2008 – International Symposium on Information Science and Engineering*, IEEE Press, 2008.

[ZHA 09] ZHANG Q., WANG W., MCMILLAN L. *et al.*, "Inferring genome-wide mosaic structure", *Bioinformatics*, pp. 150–161, 2009.

[ZHU 15] ZHU D., WU Y., WANG X., "A dynamic programming algorithm for a generalized LCS problem with multiple subsequence inclusion constraints", in HSU C.-H., XIA F., LIU X. *et al.* (eds), *Proceedings of IOV 2015 – Second International Conference on Internet of Vehicles - Safe and Intelligent Mobility*, Springer, 2015.

[ZÖR 11] ZÖRNIG P., "Improved optimization modelling for the closest string and related problems", *Applied Mathematical Modelling*, vol. 35, no. 12, pp. 5609–5617, 2011.

[ZÖR 15] ZÖRNIG P., "Reduced-size integer linear programming models for string selection problems: application to the farthest string problem", *Journal of Computational Biology*, vol. 22, no. 8, pp. 729–742, 2015.

Index

Other titles from

in

Computer Engineering

2016

DEROUSSI Laurent
Metaheuristics for Logistics (Metaheuristics Set – Volume 4)

LABADIE Nacima, PRINS Christian, PRODHON Caroline
*Metaheuristics for Vehicle Routing Problems
(Metaheuristics Set – Volume 3)*

LEROY Laure
Eyestrain Reduction in Stereoscopy

MAGOULÈS Frédéric, ZHAO Hai-Xiang
Data Mining and Machine Learning in Building Energy Analysis

2015

BARBIER Franck, RECOUSSINE Jean-Luc
*COBOL Software Modernization: From Principles to Implementation with
the BLU AGE® Method*

CHEN Ken
*Performance Evaluation by Simulation and Analysis with Applications to
Computer Networks*

PASCHOS Vangelis Th
Combinatorial Optimization – 3-volume series, 2ⁿᵈ Edition
Concepts of Combinatorial Optimization – Volume 1, 2ⁿᵈ Edition
Problems and New Approaches – Volume 2, 2ⁿᵈ Edition
Applications of Combinatorial Optimization – Volume 3, 2ⁿᵈ Edition

QUESNEL Flavien
Scheduling of Large-scale Virtualized Infrastructures: Toward Cooperative Management

RIGO Michel
Formal Languages, Automata and Numeration Systems 1: Introduction to Combinatorics on Words
Formal Languages, Automata and Numeration Systems 2: Applications to Recognizability and Decidability

SAINT-DIZIER Patrick
Musical Rhetoric: Foundations and Annotation Schemes

TOUATI Sid, DE DINECHIN Benoit
Advanced Backend Optimization

2013

ANDRÉ Etienne, SOULAT Romain
The Inverse Method: Parametric Verification of Real-time Embedded Systems

BOULANGER Jean-Louis
Safety Management for Software-based Equipment

DELAHAYE Daniel, PUECHMOREL Stéphane
Modeling and Optimization of Air Traffic

FRANCOPOULO Gil
LMF — Lexical Markup Framework

GHÉDIRA Khaled
Constraint Satisfaction Problems

ROCHANGE Christine, UHRIG Sascha, SAINRAT Pascal
Time-Predictable Architectures

WAHBI Mohamed
Algorithms and Ordering Heuristics for Distributed Constraint Satisfaction Problems

ZELM Martin *et al.*
Enterprise Interoperability

2012

ARBOLEDA Hugo, ROYER Jean-Claude
Model-Driven and Software Product Line Engineering

BLANCHET Gérard, DUPOUY Bertrand
Computer Architecture

BOULANGER Jean-Louis
Industrial Use of Formal Methods: Formal Verification

BOULANGER Jean-Louis
Formal Method: Industrial Use from Model to the Code

CALVARY Gaëlle, DELOT Thierry, SÈDES Florence, TIGLI Jean-Yves
Computer Science and Ambient Intelligence

MAHOUT Vincent
Assembly Language Programming: ARM Cortex-M3 2.0: Organization, Innovation and Territory

MARLET Renaud
Program Specialization

SOTO Maria, SEVAUX Marc, ROSSI André, LAURENT Johann
Memory Allocation Problems in Embedded Systems: Optimization Methods

2011

BICHOT Charles-Edmond, SIARRY Patrick
Graph Partitioning

BOULANGER Jean-Louis
Static Analysis of Software: The Abstract Interpretation

CAFERRA Ricardo
Logic for Computer Science and Artificial Intelligence

HOMES Bernard
Fundamentals of Software Testing

KORDON Fabrice, HADDAD Serge, PAUTET Laurent, PETRUCCI Laure
Distributed Systems: Design and Algorithms

KORDON Fabrice, HADDAD Serge, PAUTET Laurent, PETRUCCI Laure
Models and Analysis in Distributed Systems

LORCA Xavier
Tree-based Graph Partitioning Constraint

TRUCHET Charlotte, ASSAYAG Gerard
Constraint Programming in Music

VICAT-BLANC PRIMET Pascale *et al.*
Computing Networks: From Cluster to Cloud Computing

2010

AUDIBERT Pierre
Mathematics for Informatics and Computer Science

BABAU Jean-Philippe *et al.*
Model Driven Engineering for Distributed Real-Time Embedded Systems 2009

BOULANGER Jean-Louis
Safety of Computer Architectures

MONMARCHE Nicolas *et al.*
Artificial Ants

PANETTO Hervé, BOUDJLIDA Nacer
Interoperability for Enterprise Software and Applications 2010

PASCHOS Vangelis Th
Combinatorial Optimization and Theoretical Computer Science: Interfaces and Perspectives

WALDNER Jean-Baptiste
Nanocomputers and Swarm Intelligence

2007

BENHAMOU Frédéric, JUSSIEN Narendra, O'SULLIVAN Barry
Trends in Constraint Programming

JUSSIEN Narendra
A to Z of Sudoku

2006

BABAU Jean-Philippe *et al.*
From MDD Concepts to Experiments and Illustrations – DRES 2006

HABRIAS Henri, FRAPPIER Marc
Software Specification Methods

MURAT Cecile, PASCHOS Vangelis Th
Probabilistic Combinatorial Optimization on Graphs

PANETTO Hervé, BOUDJLIDA Nacer
Interoperability for Enterprise Software and Applications 2006 / IFAC-IFIP I-ESA'2006

2005

GÉRARD Sébastien *et al.*
Model Driven Engineering for Distributed Real Time Embedded Systems

PANETTO Hervé
Interoperability of Enterprise Software and Applications 2005

CPSIA information can be obtained at www.ICGtesting.com
Printed in the USA
BVOW06*0932040816

457871BV00002B/2/P